DIZZY

THE JASON GILLESPIE STORY

DIZZY

THE JASON GILLESPIE STORY

AS TOLD TO LAWRIE COLLIVER

HarperSports
An imprint of HarperCollins*Publishers*

Harper*Sports*
An imprint of HarperCollins*Publishers*

First published in Australia in 2007
by HarperCollins*Publishers* Australia Pty Limited
ABN 36 009 913 517
www.harpercollins.com.au

HarperCollins*Publishers*
25 Ryde Road, Pymble, Sydney, NSW 2073, Australia
31 View Road, Glenfield, Auckland 10, New Zealand
77–85 Fulham Palace Road, London, W6 8JB, United Kingdom
2 Bloor Street East, 20th floor, Toronto, Ontario M4W 1A8, Canada
10 East 53rd Street, New York NY 10022, USA

National Library of Australia Cataloguing-in-Publication data:

Colliver, Lawrie.
Dizzy: the Jason Gillespie story as told to Lawrie Colliver.
ISBN: 978 0 7322 8525 8 (pbk.).
1. Gillespie, Jason. 2. Cricket players, Aboriginal Australian – Biography. 3. Cricket players – Australia – Biography. 4. Cricket. I. Title.
796.358092

Cover design by Michael Donohue
Cover images courtesy of Getty Images
Photographs on page 8 (top) of picture section 1, and page 5 (top) of picture section 2, courtesy of Hamish Blair, Getty Images
Internal design by Kirby Jones
Typeset in 11.5/16pt Minion by Kirby Jones
Printed and bound in Australia by Griffin Press
79gsm Bulky Paperback used by HarperCollins*Publishers* is a natural, recyclable product made from wood grown in a combination of sustainable plantation and regrowth forests. It also contains up to a 20% portion of recycled fibre. The manufacturing processes conform to the environmental regulations in Tasmania, the place of manufacture.

5 4 3 2 1 07 08 09 10

To my beautiful wife, Anna.
Without your love and support,
we wouldn't be where we are today.

Contents

Foreword

For my wife, Pauline, and me, Jason is like a son, having lived with us for a time during the early stages of his cricket career in 1995. As coach of South Australia from 1993–94 to 1995–96, one of my first encounters with Jason was in late 1993 when he was first picked for the South Australian Second Eleven.

He had been plucked from a handful of games in Grade cricket and the initial thought of many in the training squad was, 'Jason who?' At first he didn't catch the eye of too many people. Thankfully it didn't take long before he backed up the early faith put in him and made the most of his opportunities, cracking it into the Australian squad for the World Cup in early 1996 and making his Test debut against the West Indies later that year.

In his early games, South Australian Cricket Medico Clive Matthews and I often called him 'The Road Runner'. He would bound in off a long run, with steely eye, gnashing teeth and long hair trailing at the back of his head; it was an inspiring sight.

In those fledgling days of his First Class career, Jason trained in the gym with left-arm quick Mark Harrity, working ever so purposefully increasing his strength, never missing a session or taking any shortcuts. Jason and Mark were an inspiration and their training culture was an example to their South Australian teammates. A stint at the Cricket Academy under the watchful eye of Richard Done saw further improvement and as time wore on, Jason grew stronger and matured, developing the extra pace needed to be a success as a strike bowler at First Class level.

As you will read in the pages that follow, it hasn't always come easily for Jason. He has had his share of bad luck, but I think he has proved that he is a true professional, having never shirked an issue, and always been thoroughly dedicated to Australia, South Australia and his Grade club Adelaide, which he loves dearly. In the early days, he was shy in the media, but like the other obstacles he has faced, he overcame that and is now an accomplished performer in front of the microphones and cameras.

One of the special memories I have of Jason's career came when I moved to Port Elizabeth to coach Eastern Province in South Africa. The Australians were there having won the first Test of the vital three-match 1997 series. South Africa headed into the third day of that second Test in an almost unbeatable position, 184 runs ahead with 10 second innings wickets in hand. On that third morning, an inspired spell from Jason broke open the home side's top order, the remaining wickets falling for just a further 85 runs. In a tight finish, Australia got home by two wickets with Jason, playing just his fourth Test, at the crease at the end. He had to play out five balls of an over, supporting Ian Healy, who hit the winning runs shortly after, in one of the tensest Test matches played in recent times. Following on from that series, he went on to have a major impact in the Ashes series that year in England, culminating in a haul of 7/37 which earned him the Man of the Match at Headingley.

Jason currently stands as the fifth-highest wicket taker for Australia in Tests and is certainly the best fast bowler South Australia has produced. He may well go down in the record books as the last person to make 200 in a Test match and not get selected again. I hope not. It seems in many ways that he is a scapegoat for Australia losing the Ashes in 2005, a tag he doesn't deserve.

I feel that Jason will adapt to life after cricket fairly easily. He is a dedicated husband to his lovely-natured wife, Anna, and a devoted father to his beautiful daughter, Sapphire, and recently arrived son, Jackson. They will keep him well occupied and no matter what else he takes on in the future, be it cricket or business related, I am sure he will be successful. As a man, Jason has always been well liked by his teammates and has been a favourite of cricket fans worldwide for the way he conducts himself.

The Jason Gillespie story has been an interesting one. I hope you enjoy it.

Jeff 'Bomber' Hammond
August 2007

Born sporty

Apparently there was no cricket ball curled up in my hand when I came into the world on 19 April 1975. Hard to imagine because I've spent so much of my life in and around cricket since then. I was the first-born child of Vicki and Neil Gillespie. Two-and-a-half years later they welcomed my brother Rob, and in 1987 Luke's birth completed the trifecta. We were just like any other young family; Dad was the one who worked and Mum did a great job bringing us boys up and didn't go out to work. It was a busy time growing up as apart from school we all had our own interests.

My first memory is of the excitement when Mum and Dad bought a block of land in Bangor, southwest of Sydney. While the house was being built, we rented for a year in Dharruk, out in the western part of Sydney towards Penrith. The school I went to was just down the end of the street and I used to ride there on my bike.

As a kid, I was sports mad from the word go. From about the age of four I played soccer and got straight into it. My first team was called the Emerton Rovers; two women coached us. When we moved to Bangor, I played for a team called the Menai Hawks.

Drawn to cricket

I DIDN'T PLAY CRICKET UNTIL WE MOVED TO BANGOR. THERE was no school cricket so I ended up playing for the Illawong Cricket Club. Mum and Dad both had a strong involvement, running me around to practice and games. Plus I played in the front yard and on the road in front of the house with the rubbish bin as the wicket, as kids do.

Thanks to Father Christmas one year, I received my first decent cricket bat, a Stuart Surridge 'Oval Supercover'. We had muck-around bats at home and there was also a Symonds 'Super Tusker' in the team kit at Illawong Cricket Club. I opened the batting there so I had first choice of bats and would always pick that bat because it was a corker to use.

Dad liked to watch the cricket and reckons I was mesmerised by Dennis Lillee. When I started playing at Illawong Cricket Club, I used to bowl off a long run and try and mimic him. I won the Junior Cricketer of the Year at Illawong in 1985 at the age of 10, which gave me a big boost. At that stage I was like most young cricketers in that I did a bit of bowling and batting and really didn't know what I was best at.

My first ever proper holiday away with the family was on the south coast of New South Wales and we were staying in this house that was right on the beach. I must have been about eight. I remember not wanting to go down to the beach because the cricket was on the television. I was glued to the box watching these one-day internationals, and Australia was playing. I had to watch every ball. Unless it was a drinks break in the game, I wouldn't even leave the TV to go to the toilet. Thirty seconds between overs didn't give me enough time and I didn't want to risk missing a ball, so if I had to do anything I'd wait until that two or three minutes off for drinks then I'd grab something to eat or race to the toilet.

Nothing has really changed since. I was a massive cricket 'nuffy' (autograph collector) back then, and although I've discontinued that hobby, when I'm watching a game, I never like to miss a ball.

In the garage under our house in Sydney, I painted a set of stumps in green paint on the brown wall and I used to bowl at them for hours on end. It was about a half pitch, and I'd throw a tennis ball against the wall, then hit it. That was something I did until the age of about 15, even after we moved to Adelaide. Although I wasn't supposed to, I used to play inside as well and was often in trouble for smashing a ball and knocking over a photo on the mantelpiece.

Mum is a pretty quiet sort of person, but she is also a very committed person and would insist that if we started a season playing a sport, we had to finish it, we couldn't pull out of things midway. Both Mum and Dad encouraged me and my brothers, Rob and Luke, to play sport rather than sit around and bum around the house.

Whereas Rob and Luke liked playing sport up to a point, I was absolutely obsessed with sport. They used to join in sometimes with the backyard sporting activities, but you could tell their heart wasn't always in it.

Rob had a go at cricket and played some baseball and soccer when we were kids. We used to kick the soccer ball around together sometimes, but he was more into making and building things than playing sport. He's a very good artist.

Luke is about 10 years younger than me. His great love is animals; maybe he'll end up being a vet one day. He never really took cricket on. Although he bowled a few leggies, basically he wasn't interested. For a while Luke played tennis and was winning against lads of the same age who'd been playing much longer than he had. After a match he used to come home and complain of tiredness. He had a coach who was pushing him quite hard because he could see he had some natural ability. At the start of high school, Luke was diagnosed with chronic fatigue syndrome, which lasted for five or six years. Now that's behind him and he's aiming at becoming a personal trainer.

In the genes

My mum, Vicki, was talented at sport. At school, she was a good runner; she used to run in bare feet. Her mother, Kaliope Angelina, was from the Greek island of Kithera, and her father, Robert, has an Irish background. Mum has five sisters. She's little, just over 1.60 metres tall, because as a child she had Craniopharyngioma, which is a tumour near the pituitary gland that affects your physical development. It caused Mum to go blind, too. Luckily, when she was about 14, she had an operation that fixed the problem although she was still left with sight in only one eye. Within six months of that surgery, she was just like any other teenage girl. But before that she used to get teased a lot and became quite self-conscious. She left school very young and went to work at a department store in Sydney called Wynn's.

There's been sporting influence from Dad's side, too. Dad used to play cricket and ran in a few half-marathons as well. He still likes to keep fit and does plenty of exercising and running. He was very good at golf as a young fellow, but doesn't quite get enough time to play these days.

Dad's father was John Anderson Morris Gillespie, who was of Anglo Saxon Heritage. His mum was Valda Hazel Devine, whose father, Jack Albert, was from the Kamilaroi Aboriginal tribe. The Kamilaroi clan came from near Moree in northern New South Wales.

When Dad first set eyes on Mum, he was 22 and she was 18. His brother, Ian, had actually been in Mum's class at school. Not that

that gave Dad a head-start because she couldn't stand Ian. In class, he used to poke Mum with his pencil, and she hated that. Anyway, at that time Dad was working as a bank officer with the Rural Bank, which later became the State Bank of New South Wales. He spotted Mum one day when he was out buying lunch, and he asked his friend, 'Who is that good-looking girl over there?' Sharon, his sister, also happened to work at Wynn's department store, and through her, Dad asked Mum out on a date.

The story goes that Mum knocked Dad back half a dozen times and it was only because her mother and older sister, Neeva, talked her into it that she decided to go out with him. Apparently Dad looked more like 32 than 22, for some reason.

For their first outing, Dad borrowed Ian's car — a purple Ford Escort panel van. There's a touch of irony that Mum went on her first date with my father in the car of the boy who'd teased her at school. At my parents' wedding, Mum went up to Uncle Ian and said to him, 'I bet you didn't think I'd end up being your sister-in-law!'

Dad worked pretty much nine till five, so he made time to be involved with me and my brothers when we were growing up. The three of us often had varying interests. I was right into my cricket, so Dad and I would go off to the nets and play for half an hour. Then he would go and see what Rob and Luke were doing, to be fair in allocating his time. Dad is also a determined sort of man. He worked really hard and did extra study to achieve high goals — he studied for his CPA at night school while still holding down a full-time job. Then, when we lived at Dharruk, Dad bought himself a 125cc motorbike to travel to his second job. At nights he used to teach accounting and economics at a technical college to make a bit of extra money for the family. He was, and still is, an awesome role model and has a great 'can do' attitude. He always made time for us no matter how tired he was. He also thinks he's pretty funny — he's the only one! Perhaps that's where my determination and prankster sense of humour come from. I hope I can live up to his example with my own kids.

In between school and sport, I was quite lucky that chores around the house never really existed. Mum and Dad would try to impose the idea of chores but after one or two nights that would fall by the wayside. I absolutely hated doing dishes or tidying up when I could be outside playing cricket or kicking the soccer ball or footy about.

The funny thing is, while I used to kick a footy around a lot as a kid, I never played an organised game in my life. When I was 12, I played in a game with Dad's workmates, but had no real idea what I was doing out there.

Swimming is one sport I never took to. Early on, I did swimming classes at Sutherland Pool in Sydney, basic learn-to-swim stuff. At nine or 10, I got a certificate for swimming 4 metres freestyle and for 20 metres back sculling, which was a massive effort for me because I was a little bit scared of the water at that stage. Like all kids I didn't mind having a dip but was never keen on organised swimming. Now that I have a pool at home, I do laps as a warm-up to get the body loose and get me going in the morning, but that's about it.

I don't remember a lot of my early primary school days but do recall enjoying being there. I did okay at my school work. Martin School was where I was first enrolled and I spent a year there. In Year 2, at Menai Primary School, we did this fantastic class project. Each pupil wrote a letter, attached it to a helium balloon then let it go, hoping someone would find it and write back. My reply came back from someone only 300 metres away. One of my classmates received a reply from someone who was about 10 kilometres or so away.

By Year 3, almost everything in my life was based around sport, even though I did quite well at school. Like my mother, I was a reasonable runner and used to finish in the top two or three in the races at our school athletics carnival.

When I was eight or nine, I managed to contract Guillain-Barré syndrome, a potentially life-threatening disorder in which the body's immune system attacks part of the nervous system. I noticed I was having trouble walking and kept falling down. Soon after being admitted to St George Hospital, I became paralysed from the waist down. It was a very stressful time, particularly for Mum and Dad. They were worried that I might need some sort of blood transfusion; AIDS had been around for a while, and they were paranoid about blood transfusions. Fortunately, that never eventuated. With treatment, I was fine in about a week, but it was scary, to say the least.

Growing up a South Australian

We moved to Adelaide when I was 10, and I continued being right into sport. I did Years 6 and 7 at Flagstaff Hill Primary School, where I made some lifelong friends. My first memory of Jono Grant is of him making fishing flies in class. I had no idea about fishing so I asked him what it was all about. We just clicked. Like me, he played cricket at school and was into other sports, too. Later, he and I had a $1000 bet that I would play for Australia. He hasn't paid out yet and I don't think he ever will; I'm not holding that against him. Jono and I were in the same class in Year 7 at Flagstaff Hill, and because he was going to Cabra Dominican College for high school, as was another friend, Darren Starr, I decided to go there too. I wasn't Catholic, I just wanted to go to there because that's where my mates from primary school were going. At Cabra, I met Paul Bernhardt, and the four of us have been best mates ever since.

We had some great times, playing sport at recess and lunchtimes, living and breathing sport. The four of us all loved our tennis, cricket and footy, and played basketball together right through high school. At the time I thought I was okay, but in reality I was a pretty ordinary basketballer. Jono and Paul had a lot more talent than me around the hoops. Mr Jarrad, the basketball coach, was a very positive sort of person and someone I looked up to. He also taught me Physical Education.

In Year 8 I played a few cricket games for Cabra College but when I discovered that Cabra weren't serious about the sport, I lost interest in playing for the school and concentrated on playing at Adelaide Cricket Club. Basketball was the main sport I played at school. I tried squash for a year or two and while I enjoyed it, I didn't love it as much as cricket.

At school, I practised cricket quite hard at lunchtimes and sometimes after school, but I had a few injuries in my back in the early days. At the end of Year 9, I was one of the shortest students in my class. By the start of Year 10 I was the tallest. During the holidays I'd sky-rocketed 15 centimetres. Unfortunately, back trouble was the legacy of that growth spurt.

Outside of school, it wasn't all sport. At the ten pin bowling alley on Cross Road, just along from Cabra College, they had an arcade game called Wonder Boy, which we played quite often. As an adult, I have tried to relive my childhood by buying a Wonder Boy machine, which I've had for years now.

I can't say I was picked on or bullied at school, but I wasn't over-popular, either. Although I liked girls, I was a bit too shy and embarrassed to get too close. Cabra was a co-ed school, and I could hold good conversations with girls in my class but that was about it. At high school I was really timid. Occasionally a girl might call in at home and that would freak me out. I had no idea how to handle it if I liked a girl or if a girl liked me.

My spare time used to involve going to the basketball court to shoot a few hoops, kicking a footy around on my own or playing cricket by myself or with some mates, if they were around. Our house backed onto Flagstaff Hill Golf Club and sometimes I would sneak onto the course, play a few holes and have a bit of a putt on the greens. I don't think anyone from the club minded too much. I've never been much of a golfer. I think it's because I was self-taught and haven't improved — but I still enjoy a round, even though I don't hit the ball too well.

Sport was everything to me. I scraped through in Year 10 and by Years 11 and 12, lessons were almost filling in time between my next training session, be it basketball or cricket. My real ambition was to be a professional cricketer. Not that I wanted to abandon my studies. I thought I might want to be a Phys. Ed. teacher or a policeman, things that would work in with my cricket. While my mates all took the challenging courses — Maths I and II, Physics and Chemistry — I chose subjects that interested me — Business Maths, Biological Science and Physical Education. Luckily for me, in Years 11 and 12, Mrs Wheaton was my Maths teacher. She was very experienced and explained stuff clearly. Under her influence, I worked hard and did pretty well.

In Adelaide, if you wanted to get into university, in Year 12 you had to take five PES, or Public Examined Subjects. The trouble was I couldn't find more than three PES subjects that I liked. I ended up repeating Year 12 and took Media Studies, which I thought was relevant to what I wanted to do down the track. As it has turned out, that was one of the most useful subjects I did at school. Although I qualified to go to university, in the end I chose not to go as I didn't want it to interfere with potential opportunities to play cricket.

My friends all did well. Paul played State League basketball in Perth and has built a career in the mining industry, Darren became a town planner, and Jono is a finance manager.

All four of us keep in touch. Paul's sister, Michelle, married Darren Starr, and we are a pretty close group. Each year we have a Boxing Day Test pub crawl in the Eastern Suburbs of Adelaide. In 2006, Paul made the effort to come over for it from Perth, where he's lived since he was 19. He and I catch up whenever I'm playing in Perth.

Simon Burke, another former schoolmate from Cabra, introduced us to Mark Barrington, who became good mates with all of us. We used to call him Dancing Baz because he loved strutting his stuff and bopping away. One night, we were at a nightclub in Adelaide called Joplins. Mark was wearing a blue chambray shirt and a tie with fish on it. After a few drinks, he started to tear up the dance floor. To egg him on, we were buying girls drinks on the proviso they would go up to Baz and tell him he was the best dancer they'd ever seen. After a while his head was starting to swell, and he was sweating up a storm in this blue shirt he was wearing. Soon the security staff noticed him, but they were unimpressed. They came over and told us that no sane person could dance like that and he had to go. Baz was the first and only person I've ever known to be kicked out of a club for bad dancing.

When we were in our early twenties, Jono and his then girlfriend Lisa — they're married now — were over at my place one day and we decided we'd make some home-brewed beer, which we duly did. Jono's middle name is Reuben, which explains the name, Ruebenbrew, and we even came up with a logo. Then we found an old fridge, which we gutted. We put our beer keg inside, and ran the tap outside of the fridge. Ruebenbrew took down a few people over the next few years.

Jono's parents, Julie and Terry, were a tremendous support when I bought a house at Flagstaff Hill in 1998. Julie helped me plan out the garden, which was a bit of a mess when I first moved in. After training, I used to drop in to their deli and pick up some lunch and a paper. They were kind enough to have me around for dinner every second night because I was hopeless as a cook. Tuesday night at the Grants' place was card night, and Jono's grandfather would chug around in his old Toyota Corolla car and join us for a game. He was the tightest man alive, often fighting for a five or ten cent bet. When he was driving downhill in his car he would often turn off the engine and freewheel to save petrol! He was a lovely man and passed away only a few years ago.

Steadily improving as a cricketer

SOMETIMES I WONDER WHETHER THE ENVIRONMENT AND opportunities to play cricket would have come my way had my family stayed in Sydney. We arrived in Adelaide in 1985, halfway through the season, and Dad started playing at Pembroke Old Scholars. Although I wasn't playing, Dad used to bring me along to the games to get me involved and keep me interested. Before the season was out I got a game and batted in the order ahead of Dad, which I think he found slightly embarrassing.

At the start of the following season, Dad was resolute about organising a District cricket club for me, not realising that where you lived determined where you were supposed to play. He rang the South Australia Cricket Association and was put on to Sturt District Cricket Club, which was the club closest to us. Whoever it was Dad spoke to said, 'We don't care how good your lad is, we've got players as good if not better and we don't want him.' That seemed uppity. When Dad got in touch with the Adelaide Cricket Club, the response couldn't have been more welcoming. The junior organiser told him that while they had quite a few kids, they'd love to see me and would try to find a game for me somewhere. So that's how I ended up playing with the mighty Buffalos. I started with Adelaide Cricket Club in Year 6, was soon playing in the State Bank Shield competition, and I've been with the club ever since. I was very proud when they made me a Life Member.

My first game with adults was when Dad was playing for Pembroke Old Scholars. I just filled in for them. I was playing State Bank Shield in the mornings and the odd game with the Under-14s in the afternoon for Adelaide. If I didn't play Under-14s, I'd fill in with Dad's team. I'd bat right down the order and managed to get the odd 10 or 20 here and there. I think the old blokes were taking it easy on me when they bowled but I remember playing a few games and enjoying it.

In the 1991–92 season, at the age of 16, I had my first year playing senior cricket for the Adelaide Cricket Club. I played D grade and some E grade but only as a batsman. I'd hurt my back, so I couldn't bowl. Gradually it came right. My first big haul was in D grade, when I took 8/38 from 34 overs straight at Jack Fox Oval. My good mate Paul Amato, 'Tommy' as he is known, has a 'claim to fame' from that same game. In the scorebook it is recorded that one of the batsmen was dismissed stumped — Amato bowled Gillespie. He is pretty pumped about that and it tends to come out whenever we have a few beers.

Once my back improved and I picked up a few wickets in the Ds, I went up a grade. A huge bonus awaited me because the C-grade skipper was a fantastic guy named Shane Bernhardt. Shane had been my State Bank Shield coach when I first came to Adelaide as a kid. When I was 12 or 13, he also worked with me one-on-one, coaching me in my batting. Later on, we would work together again when he coached Adelaide to an A-grade premiership. Since then, he's gone on to become the Grade cricket coordinator for the South Australian Cricket Association. Shane was a major influence early on in my cricket, and I have the highest respect for him.

Shane's support was vital during this transition to senior cricket. I was a fairly shy teenager and at that level, the game was starting to get serious. In those first few games in the C-grade team, I wasn't setting the world on fire. The first week I tried playing in the C-grade side, I got 1/40 in eight overs, bowling quite quick against West Torrens at Kings Reserve West.

Then, one night at training late in the 1992–93 season, something happened. I'd been telling my teammates that I'd be playing for South Australia by the time I was 19 and that by the age of 21, I'd play for Australia. As you'd expect, they were having a good laugh about my statements. My mate Paul Amato, in particular, was taking the piss out of me, calling me 'The Lion of Adelaide', and going on about how I was big-noting myself. That fired me up. Until then, I'd been bowling medium pace in the nets, but then I decided to mark out a long run and try and bowl as fast as I could. Determined to show them they were wrong to underestimate me, I marked out my run and tried to bowl flat out. I was getting them through okay and showed a bit of pace for a 17-year-old bowler.

Our club coach, Steve Trenorden, noticed what was happening and asked, 'Who's that?' He must have liked what he saw because for the last game of the season he decided to give me a run with his A-grade team. By then the As were out of the race for the finals, and there had been a few injuries late in the season. Steve must have thought, 'Let's give this young tearaway a go.'

Dad wasn't at all keen on me making my A-grade debut with Adelaide. As an E-grade captain, he was part of the club's selection committee. Dad felt it was too early even for me to play B grade, let alone A grade. Steve Trenorden told Dad that I was more than ready, was one of the quickest bowlers in the club and should go up. It turned out that Dad was the only one who didn't want me to play up. It was decided I'd have a go with the B-grade team.

Anyway, on the Friday night before my planned debut in B grade, there was another injury in the A-grade side, so I was contacted and told that I was selected for A grade.

Dad wasn't too thrilled but he and Mum were there supporting me the next day. I took the new ball and got a wicket in my first over. It was a guy called Marcus Arula, caught behind by Warren 'Bugsy' Smith. When Dad had to leave to captain his E-grade side, he said to Mum, 'He's proven me wrong. I know nothing about cricket.' My figures were 2/70 from 22 overs against Woodville, so I did reasonably well in my first game.

In a way, that training session when I copped a sledging from the lads because of my cocky predictions was a turning point in my cricket career. I remember thinking, 'Stuff you blokes, I need to do something about this.' After I got home from training, I changed my gear and went out for a run. 'It starts now,' I thought. 'I've got to get fit.' From that moment I started doing push-ups and sit-ups in front of the TV to get stronger. I started putting pressure on myself to dig deeper and to really achieve.

At the end of 1992–93 season, Dad was offered a job in Canberra and accepted it. Mum and my brothers joined Dad in Canberra, but I decided to stay in Adelaide as I was doing Year 13 at Cabra College and I felt for a couple of reasons it would be best if I stayed put. First, I didn't want to interrupt my schooling, and second, and more importantly, the ACT didn't have a First Class cricket team and at that time it was becoming a real goal for me.

I lived with an Adelaide Cricket Club teammate, Dave Castello, and his grandmother, Beryl, who looked after me too well. We were in the self-contained unit on the side of the house, all under the one roof but we had our own door, which was handy. Beryl was an immense support to me and looked after us, doing all the cooking and cleaning. She was the kindest lady to us both and was like a grandmother to me. Living in Adelaide, she was tremendous support as my paternal grandmother died fairly early in my life and my maternal grandmother lived in Newcastle. To have that love and support from Beryl was pretty special.

Dave and I were good mates and became close friends, and are very close to this day. Dave now lives in Albury, New South Wales, with his wife, Angela, and is a bit of a legend at North Albury Cricket Club where he is a swashbuckling left-handed batsman and tries to bowl right arm medium pace, without too much luck.

Without that sort of support from Beryl and Dave, I am not sure I would have been able to get through that final year of schooling and my involvement with cricket.

SOMETIMES I HAVE TO PINCH MYSELF WHEN I LOOK BACK AND see how it has all panned out. I did make my State debut at 19 and my Test debut at 21. The reason I felt I could achieve those goals was because I was absolutely prepared to do the work needed and the belief I had in myself to achieve those goals was there. Being 'loud and proud' isn't everybody's way, but sometimes it pays to think big.

A big first year as a First Class cricketer

IT CAME AS A BOLT FROM THE BLUE WHEN I WAS PICKED TO PLAY for South Australia for the first time. I'll never forget the shock. I was at the Caltex petrol station at O'Halloran Hill, and the bloke behind the counter had the radio on. The announcer was reading out the side for the forthcoming one-day game against the touring Zimbabweans; I caught the words 'Jason Gillespie' and 'debut for South Australia'. I wasn't sure I'd heard right.

Admittedly I'd had a strong start to the season with Adelaide CC, but even though I was bowling well I wasn't getting many wickets in club cricket. When I arrived at training the news was confirmed. It was quite a bizarre feeling to know I was going to debut for SA!

It was a proud moment when I walked out onto Adelaide Oval on 27 November 1994 with the likes of Darren Lehmann and Greg Blewett. The Zimbabweans won the toss and batted but only made

186 and we beat them by seven wickets. I took 4 for 30 that day, which was a respectable start to my First Class cricketing career.

Bomber offers a steadying hand

ONCE I MADE THE STATE SIDE, FOR THE REST OF THE 1994–95 season I spent every Tuesday and Thursday night training at the South Australia Cricket Association nets under the watchful eye of coach Jeff 'Bomber' Hammond. The Adelaide Oval has superb facilities, and I wanted to get used to bowling on that wicket. I meant no disrespect to the guys at Adelaide CC I'd bowled to, but I was sure I'd progress and learn more quickly if I bowled against the likes of Jamie Siddons, Darren Lehmann, James Brayshaw and Paul Nobes, who were all established State batsmen. These guys rotated out of the net I bowled in, so by sending the ball down to them flat out for two hours a night, I improved my bowling and became a better cricketer.

As time passed, I noticed I wasn't getting hit around too much. I'm sure that period of training at State level was my greatest education in bowling.

Bomber made sure everyone at the SACA was heading in the right direction. Whether it was the players, the ground staff, the catering department — whatever — he saw to it that we were all going forward.

He took me under his wing and worked with me, and the other quicks, tinkering here and there as he saw fit. If anyone was falling away in their action, he'd spot it in a flash. Bomber kept reminding us to keep it as simple as possible. He told me to stay nice and tall and to have a good follow-through. They're basic skills, and I still use them today. Bomber was always big on swinging your arms as you run in to bowl and on having a 'pumping action' to get momentum at the crease.

Off the field Bomber's support continued; he helped me handle the early days of touring. As well as being a strong leader, he was fun. He used to wear a black 'bomber' jacket that looked a lot like the one 'The Fonz' wore on the TV show 'Happy Days'. Peter McIntyre started calling him The Fonz, and the name caught on.

One night we were heading off for a team dinner and somehow Jeff fell into a fountain. I'm not sure how he managed that feat. He was saturated except for two vital things: his pack of cigarettes in one hand and the team's supply of Cabcharge vouchers in the other. It was hilarious — he was as wet as an otter's pocket but somehow managed to keep his smokes and the vouchers dry.

Bomber made a point of looking after the fast bowlers. Mark Harrity, Shane George and I would go around to his place for dinner. Pauline, Bomber's wife, would cook up a storm and make us feel welcome. Before dinner we'd sit outside on the patio, where Bomber would have a cigarette and we'd have a beer, and we'd chat about bowling and cricket in general. That made a difference to me. I'll always appreciate how the Hammonds went to so much extra effort.

A SUPPORTIVE ATTITUDE PERMEATED ALL LEVELS OF THE SOUTH Australian Cricket Association. Barry Gibbs, the SACA's CEO, was a real players' man, too, and ensured the players had the resources they needed to get the results.

When I first started playing for South Australia, Mark Harrity was probably the guy I got to know first. We were both fast bowlers and both beginning our careers. Paul Nobes was a club teammate from Adelaide, so he was supportive, as was Darren Lehmann, who went out of his way to make me feel welcome.

Becoming involved with Jackie

MY FIRST LONG-TERM RELATIONSHIP STARTED AROUND THE TIME of my first-grade debut. I was working at Pedro's Dial-a-Pizza, and manager Mick Leonard's girlfriend, Leanne, thought I'd get on well with her friend, Jackie, who was a lovely girl. Leanne suggested I come to a 21st birthday party and meet her. That night Jackie and I chatted away, and things started well. In the beginning there were long phone conversations late at night, because I was down at Flagstaff Hill and she was about an hour away at Tranmere. I was working nights at Pedro's, then going home and talking on the phone with Jackie at one in the morning.

At that time, I was sharing a house with Mark 'Baz' Barrington and Simon Burke. One night, the lads decided to canoe across the Happy Valley Reservoir. The canoe capsized about halfway across, so the lads had to swim their way to safety. Baz had some coins in his pocket and walked a couple of kilometres to the nearest phone box to call me to get me to come and pick them up. That was in the days before mobile phones, and because I was talking to Jackie on the landline, Baz couldn't get through. He kept trying for about an hour but the line was constantly engaged, so he decided to walk home. When he eventually banged on the door, he found me still on the phone.

Baz and I drove my Holden Gemini down to where the canoe was capsized. We grabbed some rope, retrieved the boat, plonked it on the roof of the Gemini and drove back to our house at three in the morning. The lads were laughing their heads off. To this day I have no idea why they took the canoe out, but picturing them trying to paddle across the reservoir cracks me up.

Jackie and I were getting on quite well, and things progressed quickly. She had a two-and-a-half year old daughter named Star, and was renting a place at Tranmere when her lease ran out. Even though we were in the early stages of our relationship, I told her she should move in with me. At that stage, Mum and Dad were still living in Canberra and I was living in our family home at Flagstaff Hill, with my mate Baz. With hindsight, perhaps I didn't really think the idea through.

Jackie and Star moved in and not long after Jackie became pregnant with our daughter, Sapphire. I suppose I was a bit naive about contraceptives: I was young and not privy to the ways of the world. Although I'd been out with a few girls, I wasn't careful enough about taking the right precautions.

Everything was happening all at once. I was starting to make my way as a First Class cricketer, a role that demanded time and commitment, and I had a girlfriend who needed me around as she prepared to have a child. Things crept up on me. Our relationship wasn't the usual courtship in which you get to know each other and go on dates. All of a sudden we were living together, Jackie was pregnant, and I went from being a Club cricketer to being a Second Eleven player to being a First Class cricketer all in the space of a season.

A dramatic end to 1994–95

I played the last three Sheffield Shield matches with South Australia in 1994–95, including the Final. Years later, I found out from the then Redbacks coach, Bomber Hammond, how narrowly I made it into the Final. Things might have been different if I hadn't taken two wickets in the second innings of the final preliminary match against New South Wales in Sydney. I ended up with 2/30 off 15 overs, so the selectors felt I was worthy of a spot in the Final.

The Sheffield Shield Final against Queensland went right down to the wire. From the end of 1994 to the beginning of 1995, the famous home of Brisbane cricket at Woolloongabba had been renovated. The renovations were a way off from being completed, but it was still very exciting to be playing in a Final on such a famous ground. Queensland, who hadn't won a Shield since the competition started in 1892–93, were hosting the Final for the first time and were favourites to finally break their drought. Each day of the match, the Gabba was packed and the locals were hopeful of seeing Queensland finally win the Shield.

I copped my fair share of flak from the Gabba fans. Mostly I'd hear, 'Gillespie, get a haircut.' I didn't have the ponytail going at that stage, but my hair was quite long.

As it turned out, Queensland gave us a hiding. I was the last wicket to fall in the game, caught by Carl Rackemann off the bowling of Paul Jackson. It was significant that big Carl took the last catch because he'd bowled his heart out for Queensland for many years in the wilderness, when they played in most of the Finals, only to just miss out.

For South Australia, it was a disastrous way to end what had been a good season. We batted first, got fired out for 214 and spent the next two-and-a-half days in the field while Queensland made 664. We were staying at the Sheraton in Brisbane. By the end of the second day — Queensland was 3/409 — it had become obvious that the game wasn't going our way, so most of us met up in the bar downstairs and turned it into a bit of a nightclub. Even our skipper, Jamie Siddons, who wasn't renowned for sitting around the bar, had a few beers each night.

For me, the Brisbane trip was excellent. Getting to know my teammates James Brayshaw, Peter McIntyre and Darren Webber over a few drinks each night was a real positive.

It was disappointing to lose the game. Afterwards all the lads vowed there was no way it was going to happen again and that we had to make 1995–96 our year. That thrashing by Queensland hardened us up for the season ahead.

Becoming a father

SAPPHIRE WAS BORN ON 2 MARCH 1995 AT FLINDERS HOSPITAL in the south of Adelaide. If she hadn't arrived two weeks early, her birth might have coincided with my Sheffield Shield debut — not that that would have stopped me from being at the birth. It was really overwhelming but a very special time. Sapphire was Mum and Dad's first grandchild and they were over the moon.

A year with the Cricket Academy

There was no fanfare when I was selected to join the 1995 intake at the Commonwealth Bank Cricket Academy; I was simply asked, and I accepted straight away. We were to start training from 9 April, and I looked on it as a brilliant opportunity. I looked forward to learning from Rod Marsh.

The majority of the other Academy members stayed at Del Monte, in Henley. Players based in South Australia had the option of commuting from home or living at Del Monte. As the father of a newborn, there was no way I could live there so I had to commute. Things worked out reasonably well.

Jackie, Star, Sapphire and I continued living in my mum and dad's house at Flagstaff Hill while Mum and Dad were still in Canberra. Baz had moved to a place of his own. I was earning only a small training allowance, and Jackie's main income was Family Allowance. Money was tight and my parents really helped me out a lot when things were tough. It was hard work to get through, but we managed.

The Academy was fun, but at times it was hard because I was training and helping bring up a newborn baby. It wasn't quite what the average 20-year-old would normally be doing, and I hadn't realised what I'd got myself into till it was all happening. As tough as it all was, my beautiful daughter, Sapphire, made it all worthwhile.

Car hassles were a big part of my life while I was at the Cricket Academy. I had a pretty ordinary car, which kept breaking down, and I had to travel a fair distance each day. From home to Del Monte was about an hour's round trip. I had to be at Del Monte for weights training, at the Aquatic Centre in North Adelaide for swimming or at the Adelaide Oval indoor nets for cricket training. No matter where we trained, I had to drive quite a distance. Generally, I was in the car twice a day, because we had a morning session and then a four- or five-hour break, after which we did something again in the afternoon.

The times for our training sessions were pretty good: the earliest one was at 6.45 a.m. for swimming, but generally we got going about 8 a.m. to do weights and fitness. Skill sessions were mainly held in the afternoon. The guys based at Henley went to-and-fro in a Tarago 'people mover', whereas I chugged along back and forth in my shitty old car.

During the break, most of the guys went off and did some work to earn a few bucks. I headed home to help out around the house.

I HADN'T MET ROD MARSH TILL I'D JOINED THE CRICKET ACADEMY, and fortunately we got on well from the start. Rod grasped my personal situation quickly and was most understanding about it. I soaked up Rod's cricketing influence and also enjoyed learning from our bowling coach, Richard Done. Richard had played a few games with New South Wales and was great, as was Richard Chee Quee — 'Cheeks' — the Scholarship Coach in 1995. Cheeks had notched up a few games as a batsman for New South Wales and was only the second Chinese person to play First Class cricket.

The Scholarship Coach was usually someone who'd had First Class experience, and changed each year. Former South Australian wicketkeeper Tim Nielsen had the role at one point, and has since gone on to be an assistant coach to the Australian team as well as the head coach at the Commonwealth Bank Centre of Excellence (formerly Cricket Academy), in Brisbane. Cheeks helped me with my batting. Rod, Richard and Cheeks were there week in, week out, and were brilliant.

Rod also organised specialist coaches to teach us about the game. Former Australian captain Ian Chappell came over from Sydney from time to time. He did a lot of work with the batsmen, focusing on how to play hook shots and pull shots. John Inverarity, who was Western Australia captain for years and played three Tests for Australia, had special batting drills for us. Aussie fast-bowling legend Dennis Lillee came in to coach the bowlers and had a major impact on me.

Every so often, these guys spent a week at a time with us to impart their knowledge and experience. We were fortunate to have such a wealth of information to base our work on. Their enthusiasm rubbed off on everyone, and we worked hard at improving our game.

Each week, we had two or three bowling sessions at the Adelaide Oval indoor centre; once the weather improved, we headed outside. Later in the year, the Academy went on tour and played matches against the various State Second Elevens.

During that year our fitness co-ordinator was Robert Crouch. Crouchy had been running the Adelaide University gym for years and was to be a massive support to me later on, when I broke my leg in Sri Lanka in 1999. At the Academy he ran a Monday morning training session, where we would use the VersaClimber and the exercise bikes, and do circuit training and some boxing. I got along well with Crouchy and worked hard at the sessions.

Crouchy reckons that based on what he observed during those fitness sessions he was able to predict the players who'd go on and have a good career. He was pretty much on the money, and it's interesting to hear him talk about it nowadays.

Under Robert, the training was about as hard as you could get. The lads found the VersaClimber 'sprints' especially challenging. Even though we did weights at our own pace, we still found them tough because we had so much to get through.

Of all the fitness work we had to do, I found the running the hardest. When I'm actually running I'm okay, but for some reason I found I'd pull up really stiff and sore from it during the sessions. Everyone said I'd get over it and be on my way, but it didn't work out like that. Running is the only thing I've found very tough. It was much the same when we were training with the Redbacks. We had to do one-kilometre time trials and four-kilometre runs around the uni loop, and I struggled to pull up well after them. My joints would be sore for a week and my back killed me. At first I put it down to delayed muscle soreness, but if that was the case I should have moved through it eventually. Every time I did those runs, the pain lasted for a week, and really affected my training and bowling. Early on, I decided that running wasn't my first choice as a way to stay fit and that I needed to do other things to be able to train for cricket.

Running aside, during that winter, I worked hard at getting fit, and I became very strong. As a result, my bowling strength developed. Beyond doubt, the work I did at the Cricket Academy was the reason I had such a good 1995–96 season.

Inner turmoil

My personal life was under strain. Most relationships have their ups and downs but my situation with Jackie wasn't easy at all. To add to the stress, Sapphire was sick with eczema and asthma. At the time, I probably wasn't the easiest bloke to deal with, and likewise I found Jackie hard to live with. We were two people who didn't know each other that well and had landed in a situation we found tough to deal with. Certainly I wasn't mature enough to handle the situation, and I wasn't ready to cope with everything our situation entailed, but I did the best I could.

It became more and more obvious that our relationship wasn't going to be a long-term one. There was a severe clash of personalities; no way was it going to work. The main reason Jackie and I stayed together as long as we did was our daughter. I couldn't stand the idea of not being with Sapphire. It would be a while before I could make the decision to go.

Looking back on it, though, I think things worked out for the best. If you spoke to Jackie about it, I'm sure she'd agree. When you're thinking about ending a relationship, you 'umm' and 'ahh' about how and when it fell apart. You think to yourself, 'Could we have done more to make it work? Did I do the right thing? Surely I can make it work.' I entertained those thoughts. Deep down I knew it was only a matter of time before we'd part.

During that period, cricket was a total release from the pressures of my life. When I was out in the middle, I was simply being a cricketer and could concentrate on that alone. That part of my life had to go okay because if I didn't play cricket, I didn't know what the hell I was going to do. I had a daughter and a girlfriend, who also had a daughter, and I had to succeed at my cricket career.

So much hinged on me doing well with cricket. It felt like a gamble. Everything I had went into it. With this intensity, I worked on every aspect of my game; I worked hard on my fitness. It was a crucial time in my cricketing development and I just had to make a go of it. People say everyone has four or five big turning points in their life, and that period in my cricket development was one of those for me. I was lucky to have the backing of my parents. Jackie and I were paying a discounted rental rate for the house at Flagstaff Hill. Everyone at Adelaide Cricket Club was supportive. Jeff and Pauline Hammond were sensational. I felt I owed it to myself and everyone who'd supported me to make it work.

My one slight regret during my time with the Cricket Academy was that I was missing out on the fun the lads got up to on weekends. I was a young father, so I couldn't go out and have the sort of fun that young fellows take for granted. I heard the stories at Monday morning training, and thought it'd be nice to be part of the action. My responsibilities were to my baby daughter and her mother, however.

On the plus side, having to get home to help out kept me away from all the mischief and bad influences, and I was better able to get on the road to being a Test cricketer. Also, I wanted to be at home because I had a beautiful little daughter and wanted to be a part of her life as much as I could. On balance, if I had to miss out on a bit of fun, it was well worth it.

Lasting lessons from the Academy

THE ONLY MAJOR TRIP I HAD AWAY WITH THE ACADEMY WAS TO Pakistan, during September 1995, immediately before the start of the 1995–96 season. One day during the tour I was horrendously ill — as sick as I've ever been. I must have eaten something dodgy, but I wasn't throwing up or on the toilet. The bug I had left me without any energy at all. It was so bad I couldn't lift my head off the pillow, so I stayed in bed, lying there feeling as crook as a dog. Thankfully, it was only a 24-hour bug and I recovered and got back into things.

We played the first match in Lahore in extreme heat and humidity. I bowled two overs and remember thinking, *I can't bowl another ball here, I am gone.* Physically, I don't know how I kept going but I did. Somehow I got through another couple of overs in what were the worst conditions I'd ever known. Fellow paceman 'Matty' Nicholson — who played in the 1998 Boxing Day Test — was also struggling badly. It seemed insane to keep playing.

Our keeper, Peter Roach, who later played for Victoria, managed to make 136 not out in that game by sweeping the hell out of the bowlers. I reckon he must have made 100 of the 136 from the sweep because at one point they had about six blokes fielding for that shot.

BRETT LEE WAS ON THAT TRIP AS PART OF THE 1995 INTAKE. I FIRST got to know him in 1993–94, when we roomed together during the Australian Under-19s trip to India. He was only 18, so you'll have some idea of how early the Academy identified him as a fast-bowling talent.

Apart from Brett, some of the better-known guys in the 1995 intake were Corey Richards, who made quite a few runs for New South Wales; batsman Matthew Mott, who played for Queensland and Victoria; Michael Hussey, who made a brilliant start with the bat in his Test career; Clinton Perren, who's had a long and successful career making runs for Queensland; left-arm paceman Mark Harrity, who'd played for the Redbacks; and Kade Harvey, who had a good career with Western Australia. Two of the lesser-known guys were Ian Hewett, who was a left-arm paceman from Victoria, and Stephen Bell, who was a leggie from Queensland.

Overall, Peter Roach and Mike Hussey were probably the fittest blokes in the 1995 intake, and I'd class myself as being in the 'middle of the road' in the group. I've never considered myself to be the fittest person; I've always prided myself on knowing what I have to do to get strong to play. I never worried too much about winning all the 'beep tests'; I've always been a big believer in getting yourself ready for what you need to do, which in my case is to play cricket. The weights sessions were interesting, and one day I remember doing 'power cleans', in which you did a 'clean and jerk' but stopped it at the shoulders. I realised it was hurting, and because I'd suffered back trouble as a kid, it worried me that if I went much harder, I'd 'snap' and hurt myself.

My idea was to stick with light weights and work on my technique, because I found weights hard to master and was reluctant to go any heavier. Other guys were constantly going up in their weights, but I'm not sure they got fitter or played better as a result.

The other main thing I learned at the Cricket Academy was that it's important to have a strong work ethic. The trainers are there to prepare you to be a top International cricketer, not just a better

Club cricketer. They want you to go beyond the lesser ambition to become an exceptional player. They teach you how you need to train and prepare, and their help goes a long way towards sending you on your way.

I can't speak highly enough of my trainers at the Academy. They taught me so much, and I could see how they were helping develop and improve the other guys' games. I was quite sad when the Academy (now known as the Centre of Excellence) moved from Adelaide to Brisbane, but I could understand why: Brisbane's climate allows players to play and train outdoors for 12 months of the year. To be able to use the Brisbane facilities outdoors all the time was too good an opportunity to pass up.

After my time at the Cricket Academy came to a close, I was as keen as anything for the new season to come around. I'd been working hard and also training with the SACA lads once a week. They'd been putting in a lot of effort and they were highly motivated to make up for the disappointment of losing the 1994–95 Shield Final.

I was selected for the first game of the 1995–96 season, and managed to keep my spot in the team. In each game, I picked up a few wickets. Pakistan played us in a tour game, and I took four wickets in the first innings.

I suspect I started to get the attention of the National selectors when I took 6/68 against Western Australia at the WACA in early January 1996, and almost bowled our team to victory. In that game I swung the ball and was bowling a yard or two quicker than I'd bowled previously — it was an exciting time. We were winning games, so were contenders for making the Shield Final again.

Making it into the Australian team

Later that season, the World Cup was to be on in India, Pakistan and Sri Lanka, and I had no reason to think I'd be picked.

Then Craig McDermott got injured, and I was called up. I was absolutely gobsmacked by that news. I was 21, and my biggest dream was coming true.

In no time at all, I was on a plane to the subcontinent. When I arrived, I was met by our coach, Bobby Simpson. 'Simmo' made me feel welcome, as did Mark Taylor, whom I met at the hotel. Then I was introduced to all the guys, none of whom I knew at that stage, because there were no South Australians in the squad. What I found bizarre was that everyone spoke to each other on a nickname basis: Mark Taylor was 'Tubby', Steve Waugh 'Tugga', and so on. Of course, before long it would be second nature to me too, and I would be called by my nickname, Dizzy, after the jazz trumpeter Dizzy Gillespie. All the team members made me feel at ease, and early on in the trip I thought, *This is alright*. I was exactly where I wanted to be.

Even once I was in India, it was clear that our bowling line-up was well and truly settled. I didn't expect to get a game but I did plenty of bowling in the nets and kept myself fit, in case an opportunity came up. I was a young tearaway doing his best.

The fielding sessions were incredibly tough. Our coach Bob Simpson ran them and he had an uncanny knack of hitting high balls so either you could barely get to them or the ball fell narrowly out of your reach. As a result, you had to go flat out. I have a vivid image in my head of Glenn McGrath being totally buggered after doing about 16 catches in a row. I thought, *If this is International cricket, I have to work a lot harder to keep up with it.* Even though I didn't play, I went home with some invaluable knowledge from all the hard work. I'd had a good taste of International cricket, and I loved the experience.

The Sri Lankans had come a long way in the 20 years since their first World Cup in 1975. When we faced them in the Final in Karachi, Pakistan, we didn't make enough runs and we also dropped some catches. Overall, the Sri Lankans were too good.

Aravinda de Silva played a terrific knock, and they thoroughly deserved to win the trophy.

The 1995–96 Sheffield Shield Final

AFTER WE RETURNED FROM THE WORLD CUP, THE SHEFFIELD Shield season was approaching its climax and South Australia were right in the running. We had to play New South Wales in Sydney, and provided we gained first-innings points, we'd be hosting the Final. We managed to get the vital two points against a strong Blues side that contained Mark Taylor, Glenn McGrath, Michael Bevan, and Steve and Mark Waugh, all of whom had played in the World Cup. In the first innings, I managed to clean bowl Steve and that moment was a real highlight. I couldn't bowl in the second innings because I had a badly bruised toe. With the Final only a few days away, I needed it to come right quickly.

The Sheffield Shield Final of 1995–96, between South Australia and Western Australia, was played in Adelaide. It was one of the hardest-fought matches I've ever played in and certainly one of the tensest. Both teams produced some exceptional performances, and none better than the 189 not out that Adam Gilchrist made. He faced only 187 balls, and hit 15 fours and 5 sixes to all parts of the Adelaide Oval. One of his sixes was off my bowling; it pitched on off-stump and would have hit the off-bail except that Gilly smashed it effortlessly over mid-wicket. His knock was awesome. After being 7/291, Western Australia ended up with 9/520 declared and so were in a good position, given they needed to win outright to take the Shield.

Paul Nobes made a dogged century in the first innings, in what turned out to be his last game for South Australia. James Brayshaw scored 87, and we managed to make the follow-on to finish with 347. Western Australia went in again and eventually set us 343 to win in about four sessions.

Heading into the last day, we were 2/57; I'd gone in late on the fourth night, as nightwatchman. Things weren't looking too good when I got out early and then Darren Lehmann made a second-ball duck. We had about five hours to try to turn the game around but only six wickets left. Fortunately, Greg Blewett (72) and James Brayshaw (66) steadied things with a century partnership, then both were dismissed shortly before tea. That left us with two hours to go and only four wickets in hand. Jamie Siddons had been batting for ages with an injured hip and could hardly do more than defend. He ended up batting for 166 minutes and faced 134 balls for one scoring shot, a drive through the covers for a boundary.

Tim Nielsen got out soon after tea, leaving Tim 'Maysie' May, Peter 'Macca' McIntyre and Shane George. It looked like we were in trouble. Maysie hung in for an hour without scoring, but he and Jamie were dismissed. We had about 40 minutes to go, and it was down to Macca and Shane to try to pull back this last-session game. As the day progressed, the crowd swelled because people had heard about our grim efforts to try to salvage the match. Officially the size of the crowd was about 4000, but it was closer to 15,000 by the end as we fought to hang on for a draw.

Watching that last part of the game was agonising. A few guys left the rooms and went for a watch over on the eastern side of the ground. Greg Blewett went for a drive because he was too nervous for words. Towards the end, Darren Webber did a countdown of the balls remaining. Brad Hogg and Brendon Julian bowled well, and it was the most nail-biting finish ever. Against all odds, Peter McInytre and Shane George managed to hang on for the 59 balls to take the game. After Macca blocked that last ball, he ran off and was in the rooms quickly. He got up there in what seemed about 10 seconds and was hugging everyone as the emotions of our Shield success took over.

Everyone piled into the rooms: friends, wives, girlfriends and partners of everyone involved with the team. When it was time to go next door to have a beer with the West Aussies, lots of the girls wanted to come in as well because they had a crush on Brendon 'BJ' Julian. After a while, they formed themselves into a little semi-circle around him. It was funny to see all those grown women going ga-ga over big BJ.

After we left the ground, we went to celebrate at Tim May's nightclub, The Planet, which is on Pirie Street in the city. As I walked in and saw TV cameras at the entrance, it hit home that what we'd done was a big deal, given it was South Australia's first Sheffield Shield win for 14 seasons.

My celebrating was brief that day because I had a few issues at home. As much as I'd have liked to, I didn't spend a week in the pub, unlike the rest of the blokes. However, I did go in the parade down King William Street. It ended at the town hall with a mayoral reception.

It was an extraordinary way to win the Sheffield Shield. For me, it topped off an exciting first full season in First Class cricket. Since the 1995–96 season, South Australia has had plenty of talent. It's a pity we haven't been able to emulate that success.

My Test debut against the Windies

After the euphoria of the Sheffield Shield win settled, my mind turned to the forthcoming West Indies tour of Australia. We hadn't beaten the Windies in a home series since 1975–76, so the build-up to the team selection was pretty big. At the least, I figured, having been to Sri Lanka and India during the winter, I might be half a chance to make the squad for the first Test at the Gabba, scheduled for 22–26 November. What also gave me hope was that Craig McDermott was going to be out for the whole summer with a knee injury; also Damien Fleming couldn't be selected because he had a thigh strain.

About a week out from the game, the side was announced. To my relief, I had made it into the 12. I called Mum and Dad and told Jackie and they were all very pleased that I had been selected.

It looked as though it was going to be a battle between myself and Michael Kasprowicz for the third pace-bowling spot — both of us had yet to play a Test match for Australia. For the first Test, the selectors decided to go with Kasper, probably because he was a local and had slightly more First Class experience than me. To be going to the Gabba as part of the Australian team was a great honour, and I was delighted to be involved. It had always been on the cards that I would be twelfth man, so I wasn't disappointed when I was told.

The other player to debut was Matthew Elliott, known as 'Herb', who was selected at the top of the order to replace Michael Slater. Many critics put the axing of Slats down to his dismissal in the Test against India a month before, when in the second innings he was caught for a duck, aiming a big drive at a particularly wide ball from paceman David Johnson. Mohammad Azharuddin took one of the arsiest catches ever at slip, and although it wasn't the best shot, he may have been a bit unlucky to get dropped.

The pitch for the game had an even cover of grass, which could explain why Courtney Walsh sent us in to bat. Mark Taylor and Matty Elliott headed out first, and sadly for Herb, he was back with us in the rooms almost straight away, caught behind for a duck. Ricky Ponting went in at three and played a really aggressive innings; he made 88, so steered us out of some early trouble. Just after tea, Mark Waugh and Michael Bevan got out in consecutive balls, to make us 5/196, and we were suddenly in a spot of bother.

In front of his home crowd, Ian Healy took to the field and played superbly. He and Steve Waugh got us through the new ball and eventually to stumps, where we finished on 5/282, which was a pretty fair day's work. Heals batted magnificently — he batted well into day two for 161 — and thanks to his efforts with the tail, we finished on 479.

The Windies were going on smoothly at 3/249, but when Steve Waugh got Carl Hooper out for 102, the rest collapsed and they were all out for 277. In an intelligent bit of captaincy, Mark Taylor gave the ball to Ricky Ponting, and thanks to a late in-swinger, he knocked over Jimmy Adams for a duck! At the time, Jimmy was officially ranked the world's best batsman.

After we set the Windies 420 to win, we managed to knock them over for 296 an hour after tea. Sherwin Campbell played a gutsy knock of 113 before Michael Bevan trapped him lbw. It was terrific to go one up.

Without much time to think about things, we were off to Sydney for the next Test, which was to start on 29 November, giving us only a two-day break. Having not made too much of a mess of doing the drinks, I was still in the 12. Sadly, Steve Waugh was unable to play because he'd strained his groin. For me, the upside was that Greg Blewett was brought in, so two South Aussies were in the 12!

Test debut

When Paul Reiffel, who'd taken five wickets in the Gabba Test, cricked his neck on the morning of the match and couldn't play, that was my big chance. Jason Neil Gillespie was about to play for Australia. It was the highlight of my sporting career.

It should have been one of those golden days, but there was a cloud hanging over everything, and that was the unhappiness between Jackie and me. Life as the partner of a Test cricketer didn't agree with her. I often ended up feeling guilty for trying to forge a career in cricket and used to rush back to the hotel at the end of the day heavy-hearted in case I was shouted at for being late home.

Despite all the focus and energy I was pouring into my cricket career, Jackie didn't 'get' the scenario. What to me was something life-changing, for Jackie it was just a game, not a career. She couldn't appreciate what cricket meant to me and how it could 'set me up'. I found it difficult to make Jackie understand the notion of making a career out of cricket and how I wanted her and the girls to come on the journey. Part of the reason Jackie wasn't warming to the whole thing was that I was focused on cricket rather than giving her the time and attention she wanted. It was an impasse.

From a relationship point of view, the timing of my rise into the Australian team wasn't ideal, but that's how things turned out. There was a lot of yelling and screaming, which stripped some of gloss off my excitement. What helped make up for that was the presence of Star and Sapphire on the day of my Test debut.

THERE HAD BEEN A ROCK CONCERT AT THE SCG ABOUT A FORTNIGHT before the Test, but that didn't worry our captain Mark Taylor, who won the toss and decided to bat. Quickly we cruised along to 50 without loss but then fell into some trouble, being 3/73 just after lunch and later 5/131. As in Brisbane, Ian Healy had to go in to bat under pressure and again he produced an important knock to get us out of that tight spot. He and Greg Blewett steered us to stumps at 5/224, which was reasonably good, considering it was a slow and two-paced pitch. The next morning, Heals got out straight away, and when Blewy went for 58 not long after, I had to put the pads on.

In the lead-up to walking onto the field to bat — it was a strong bowling line-up — I was nervous, but once I got out there I came right. Before the game, I'd organised a thigh pad, an inner-thigh guard, an arm guard and a chest guard to be made by Steve Remfry, who for many years had made quality protective equipment — I still use the thigh guard and the inner-thigh guard today. The chest guard has been renewed, and I've done away with the arm guard.

Although I was quite nervous about facing these guys, what I discovered about my batting that day was that although the fast bowling was tough and hostile, I knew that if I worked hard and played as straight as possible, I could survive and might even get a couple of runs along the way.

Thankfully, I made 16, and with Glenn McGrath — who made 24 — then I added 43 for the last wicket, so helped us to 331, a respectable score.

For some reason I was less nervous in the rooms, getting ready to go out and field, and this mindset has stayed with me throughout my career. I suppose you get a second chance when bowling: if you bowl a bad ball, you can always just turn around and go back to your mark.

It was awesome to be in the field in my first Test match — standing at mid-on while Glenn, Kasper and Warnie were bowling was pretty darn surreal, to say the least!

When Tubby gave me the ball, I was a bit nervous but actually not as bad as I thought I might be — I used up all my nerves batting and waiting to field! Tubby was pretty helpful, and said to me, 'Do your thing; be patient; relax,' or words to that effect.

Curtly Ambrose was my first Test wicket. He and Ian Bishop were playing well, building a stubborn eighth-wicket partnership that was threatening our first-innings total. The score was 7/286, and I got one to reverse swing at Ambrose from around the wicket, which hit the off-stump from a good-length ball. It was a bit of a relief, because at that stage I thought I'd bowled well enough to earn a wicket. Not long after that, I bowled Kenny Benjamin with a slower ball off break. I was well and truly satisfied that I landed it well and got him out, but it didn't spin even though we were playing on the spin-friendly SCG!

The figures were 2/62 from 23 overs, and I thought I'd bowled reasonably well. Glenn McGrath took four wickets and we had knocked the Windies over for 304, so on the first innings, we had a lead of 27. It was a handy advantage considering the Windies had to bat last on a wearing wicket — every run counts when you play the West Indies.

In our second dig, Matthew Elliott was playing beautifully as we were trying to set up a big lead. Shortly before lunch on the fourth day, his personal score was 78 and he collided with Mark Waugh when running between the wickets. The collision caused Herb to tear the cartilage in his right knee, and sadly he had to retire hurt straight away, right on the verge of a Test ton.

When Herb got injured, we were all extremely upset for him: he'd worked hard to make the team, and to get injured in that way was unfortunate.

Tubby declared just before the close of day four, and set the West Indies 340 to win; if the Windies had got them, the score would have been the highest of the match.

The last day had a touch of controversy in it, when Ian Healy caught Brian Lara for just 1, to an amazing diving effort low to the ground. Lara didn't think the ball carried, and had words with us out on the ground. He seemed to think the ball had hit the ground before it went into Heals's gloves, and wasn't too happy to have been given out. Looking at the replays afterwards, we found it hard to tell whether the ball had bounced. Lara's anger might have stemmed from the 'stumping' incident at the Gabba four years earlier, in which Heals had fumbled a stumping chance, and in replays, it was clear that Lara had been given out incorrectly. Four years is a long time to hold a grudge, and unfortunately some bad feeling was re-ignited as a result of that incident. The fact that Courtney Walsh wouldn't comment on the incident after the match was suggestive of where the West Indians stood.

Because of Lara's wicket, the Windies were 3/35 and in all sorts of trouble. To their credit, Carl Hooper and Shivnarine 'Shiv' Chanderpaul decided to counter-attack, and I was one of the victims. Hooper got stuck into me in one over, in which he whacked three fours, and Chanderpaul gave Warnie a bit of a touch-up in the form of some elegant cuts and drives. The Windies were 3/152 just before lunch and needed another 188, so we were under the pump. They'd put on 172 at the Gabba in the previous

Test, and the way they were going after us, it looked as if they might do the same again.

In the last over before lunch, Shane Warne bowled one of the best deliveries of his career to get rid of Chanderpaul. The ball pitched just on the cut strip and turned viciously into the stumps, and Shiv backed away in attempting to cut. It was almost as good a ball as the one Warnie got Mike Gatting out with in 1993, and we were relieved to see him off after a terrific knock of 71.

The rest of the order fell away pretty quickly. The Windies got all out for 215, we won by 124 runs, and we got a vital 2–nil lead in the series!

When we'd won the Test, I got to sing the team song as a member of the 11 for the first time, and it was an awesome experience! I had to check with our physio Errol Alcott to make sure I had the right words, but I needn't have worried: it's a pretty easy song to remember!

The Redbacks against WA, Perth, 20–23 December 1996

After the win in Sydney, everyone headed off for a round of Sheffield Shield matches.

The Redbacks had a game in Perth against Western Australia, and it was in that match that I bowled one of my quickest spells ever. We made only 258 in our first innings, and after tea, Justin Langer was batting well, as he was always seeming to do against us! I bowled an over to Langer when he was on about 110 — he ended up with 274 not out — and hit him about four times. Even though I'd hit him, I couldn't get the little fella out — which goes to show how durable a player he was, even back then. They made 8 for 560 declared, so we had a bit of work to save the game. I finished with 5/64 from 30 overs — not bad going when the opposition made more than 500!

In the second innings, I went in as nightwatchman late on the third day. I ended up batting for almost five hours to help save the game. It was fantastic to be part of saving the match because it was James Brayshaw's last game for South Australia. 'Bray' has gone on to have a highly successful career in the media, so giving up playing turned out to be the right move for him.

The game finished on 23 December, so there wasn't a whole lot of time to rest up for the Boxing Day Test. Again there was a big build-up, because if we won, we'd go to an unbeatable 3–nil lead.

Third Test, at the MCG, 1996

I WAS BUZZING WITH EXCITEMENT ABOUT PLAYING MY FIRST Boxing Day Test at the MCG. Paul Reiffel came in for Michael Kasprowicz, and Steve Waugh had recovered, so came back in for the injured Matthew Elliott. In front of a crowd of more than 70,000, we were in real bother at 4/27. Curtly Ambrose took the first three, and Justin Langer was run out. Steve Waugh and Greg Blewett both played gritty hands, and Ian Healy again came to the rescue to get us to 5/195. This time, though, the tail didn't wag, and we were all out for a paltry 219 — somewhat poor considering such a massive crowd turned out to see us play.

I had a turn at the bowling crease early on the second day, and it was during my third — and last — over that I got injured. A couple of balls before I 'did' my side, I bowled a bouncer that cleared Heals and went for four byes. It was easily the quickest ball I'd ever bowled in my career. I knew I'd done something to my side early in that over. I managed to finish it, and then went over and told Tubby I was gone and needed to see our physio, Errol Alcott.

To my intense disappointment, I couldn't bowl again in the match, and to make matters worse, we lost by six wickets in just three days. Curtly Ambrose ran through us in the second innings; he took 4 for 17, finished with nine for the game and won the

Player of the Match award. In defence of our batsmen, I have to say that the pitch was difficult to bat on; however, we should have made more than 122 in our second innings.

After the game, Courtney Walsh came in, sat down next to me and asked, 'What have you done to yourself, young fella?' I told him, and he said, 'Welcome to the club; all fast bowlers do their intercostal muscle at some stage.' Courtney was a legend of the game, and I was most appreciative that he came and gave a few minutes of his time to chat to me.

From there, it was time to head back to Adelaide to recover and return to full fitness; that was the main concern. I can't say I was looking ahead to the tours of South Africa and England; it was more a case of trying to get myself fit and hope everything else would take care of itself.

The South African tour and the 1997 Ashes series

After that injury in the 1996 Boxing Day Test against the West Indies, I had no option but to rest and receive treatment for the first couple of weeks, in a bid to be fit for selection for the South African tour. Although I knew I had plenty of time to get things right, I wasn't overly confident I'd be selected, especially because I wasn't going to be playing any cricket at all between getting injured and when the team was to be named. *It stands to reason that the selectors will go for a bowler who hasn't been injured,* I told myself. Fortune smiled on me, however. I got myself fit and was selected, which was a huge relief. It was going to be a big tour, and the Ashes series was scheduled to follow virtually straight afterwards, so it was to be a full-on seven or eight months of cricket.

Playing in South Africa

THE FIRST GAME OF THE TOUR WAS AGAINST DIAMOND BILLIONAIRE Nicky Oppenheimer's Eleven at Ranjesfontein, half an hour north of Johannesburg. Oppenheimer had his own cricket ground and made his son, Jonathan, captain for the match. He batted at ten — making 14 — and didn't bowl, so it would be fair to say he got the gig as a result of nepotism!

I recall having to battle with my nerves before that match. I was young, reasonably new to the set-up and coming back from injury, so I wondered how I was going to hold up. Things worked out pretty well: I took 2/33 from 12 overs. Although my side was stiff and sore after I bowled, once I applied ice and had some treatment, I seemed to come out of it okay. Errol 'Hooter' Alcott was, as always, extremely thorough and assured me the muscles had healed. Despite his confidence, because I'd pulled up sore, I suspected I might have tweaked my side again — but as I've learned over the years, Hooter knew what he was talking about!

Matthew Elliott was also playing his first game after injuring his knee in the Sydney Test in December. He made 91 and seemed to get through things fine as well.

WE HAD ANOTHER ONE-DAYER A FEW DAYS LATER AGAINST BOLAND, in which I managed to give a reasonable account of myself, and then we were off to Cape Town for a four-dayer against Western Province. Along with the Adelaide Oval, Newlands is one of the world's most beautiful cricket grounds, and happily I did well in my first game there, picking up six wickets.

In the final four-day game leading up to the first Test at the Wanderers Stadium, we played at Durban against Natal. It was quite steamy, and I struggled in the humidity. My main memory from the game was that Paul 'Pistol' Reiffel had a back-related hamstring twinge. He wasn't that keen to play because he felt that if he had a few more days' recuperation, he'd be 100 per cent by the first Test. I believe that the selectors were pressuring him to play in order to prove his fitness, so he played perhaps against his own better judgement. I know that Pistol was more than a little annoyed when, after a couple of overs, he did his hamstring again and was set back another week or so and out of contention for the Test match.

I bowled quite quickly in the game and took six wickets. That performance probably explains why I got the nod for the Wanderers Test.

First Test against South Africa, Wanderers Stadium, Johannesburg, 28 February–4 March 1997

As the day of the Test drew near, doubts surfaced about the batting form of our skipper, Mark Taylor. When the team was announced, Michael 'Bevo' Bevan was named to bat at number seven and to play as the second spinner to Shane Warne. Glenn McGrath and I were to be the quicks, and were to have some support from Greg 'Blewy' Blewett and Steve Waugh. Because Bevo was in the side, there were murmurings (not only in the media, but in general discussions amongst cricket fans) that we'd played the extra batsman to compensate for the fact that Tubby was a bit out of form.

South Africa won the toss and decided to bat, but they were in trouble early at 3/25 thanks to some inspired bowling by Glenn McGrath, who took all three wickets. After lunch, I managed to pick up my first recognised batsman in Test cricket, when I had Jonty Rhodes caught behind for 22. I was pretty excited, and the boys reckon I looked like the devil, celebrating the wicket! We managed to reduce South Africa to 8/193, before Dave Richardson played a great knock of 72, helping them to 302 all out. I also picked up Allan Donald. I had him caught behind to finish with two wickets — although Glenn finished with the honours, taking 4 for 77 from 26 overs.

On the second day, Tubby's poor run of form continued: he played on to Shaun Pollock for 16. Matty Elliott played well on his return to the side, making 85, but after a couple of late wickets, we were on 4/191 when play ended early because of bad light.

The third day was going to be vital, and assisted by an inspiring stand by Steve Waugh and Greg Blewett, we put the match out of reach of the South Africans. Waugh and Blewett batted for the whole of day three, a ploy that is effective for a bowler on the same team because you can put your feet up, rest for the second innings and enjoy some great cricket. It was a superb partnership, and we were put in an unbeatable position.

DURING THE TEST, MY DAUGHTER SAPPHIRE HAD HER SECOND birthday. Jackie and I had parted by then so I hadn't been living in the same house as Jackie, Star and Sapphire since the new year. Because I was away, I missed out on being there for her important day. I put a big banner out in front of the rooms to wish her a happy birthday, hoping the TV cameras would show it. They did, but unfortunately she didn't see it — it might have been a bit much to expect from a two-year-old!

MIDWAY THROUGH THE FOURTH DAY, WE DECLARED ON EIGHT for 628, a lead of 326. Blewy finished with 214, and Steve made 160; their partnership for the fifth wicket resulted in 385. When South Africa went in to bat a second time, they seemed resigned to the fact they were beaten. Warne and Bevan ran through them: they each took four wickets and bowled the opposition out for 130 — it was a massive innings and a 196-run win for us.

Although I didn't get any wickets in the second innings, my body was feeling good and my action was going well. With the next Test to be played in Port Elizabeth, I knew I'd be catching up with former Redbacks coach Jeff Hammond, who was there coaching Eastern Province. I was pretty keen to catch up with him and do a bit of work before the Test.

In between Johannesburg and Port Elizabeth, we had a three-day game against Border in East London. I managed to pick up 7 for 34 in the first innings and two in the second, and felt that the ball came out well. I got a heap of nicks. The game was great. We won it by an innings inside two days, and could have an extra day off ahead of the second Test. The only problem I had was a badly infected big toe, which for a fast bowler is extremely painful, so I was glad to take the wickets, get off the ground and rest. I was certainly feeling confident about Port Elizabeth, hoping we could match our performance in Johannesburg and go 2–nil up.

Second Test, Port Elizabeth, 14–17 March 1997

There was a great deal of controversy as we headed into the second Test. The groundsman had prepared a 'greentop' in an attempt to nullify our spin duo of Warne and Bevan. Another ploy was that hessian wasn't used underneath the plastic cover to absorb any sweating that would occur overnight. As a consequence, any moisture that evaporated would go straight back into the surface, making it moist, which favoured the seam bowlers.

There were also a couple of issues with our own team. Before the game, when Tubby announced we were going in with only two quicks, the look on some of the players' faces was quite interesting. Given the state of the pitch, most looked rather surprised, and I know Pistol was in a state of disbelief. It was becoming more and more obvious what was going on: there was an extra batter in the 11 to compensate for our out-of-form skipper. I suppose the selectors also had to weigh up the fact that Michael Bevan, who was coming in at seven and bowling his 'chinamen', was doing a fantastic job, which was creating a headache at the selection table.

This, then, was the team that was selected. Greg Blewett was our first change bowler on probably the greenest wicket any of us had played on in a while. With all due respect to my mate Blewy, I believe that a third frontline seamer would have been ideal on that wicket.

THE SECOND TEST, AT PORT ELIZABETH, WAS AN ACTION-PACKED match from the start. I managed to have an easy rhythm straight away, and knocked over Gary Kirsten and Jacques Kallis for ducks in my opening spell. Glenn McGrath was also making the most of the conditions, and South Africa was 4/22 in the opening hour of play. In my next spell, I managed to get Darryl Cullinan, Herschelle Gibbs and Shaun Pollock — first ball — to secure my first five-wicket haul in Test cricket. Thanks to Pollock's wicket, we reduced the opposition to 7/95 and were put right in the box seat. From there, things went slightly pear-shaped as Dave Richardson again took on our bowlers. He and Brian McMillan fought hard to add 85 for the eighth wicket and helped their side to a total of 209, which was a pretty fair score given the nature of the pitch. We had to survive 13 overs that night and unfortunately lost Matty Hayden for a duck and finished the day at 1 for 10.

Day two wasn't one of our best, because by the end of it, we looked to be gone for all money. We were bowled out for just 108 — a shocker of a score even taking into account that the wicket was still playing tricks. South Africa had a strong pace attack, and despite losing Shaun Pollock because of a hamstring strain, they knocked us over to gain a first-innings lead of 101, a massive advantage under the circumstances. In the remaining time, Kirsten and Bacher added an unbeaten 83 for the first wicket, so by the close, South Africa were 184 ahead and had all second-innings wickets in hand — not a good position for us after two days of such a vital Test match.

Before we took to the field for the start of day three, Tubby said he wanted to start with the 'South Australian connection', by which he meant that Greg Blewett and I would open the bowling. Fortunately, we came out and bowled quite well, which set the tone for the remainder of the day. I managed to dismiss Kirsten, Bacher and Cullinan fairly quickly, and thanks to a fantastic direct-hit run-out by Blewy, we had Jacques Kallis out as well, so reduced South Africa from 0/83 to 4/100.

Suddenly, we were right back in the match, and thanks to Warne and Bevan, rolled the opposition's middle and lower order, and bowled them out for 168. It was an amazing effort to get us into the match. Now we faced a target of 270, whereas at the start of the day it looked as if we'd be chasing as many as 400 in the fourth innings.

In the run chase, we lost Mark Taylor and Matty Hayden quickly, and ended up at 2/30. Then in strode Mark Waugh to play one of the best knocks I've ever had the privilege to watch. On a pitch that was still difficult to bat on, Mark made a brilliant 116, which were worth watching because they were against an attack that included Allan Donald. In that match, Mark was our only batsman to pass 50; Junior made batting look incredibly easy whereas everyone else had struggled on that wicket.

Unfortunately, he couldn't quite see us to victory because he was bowled by Kallis when we still needed 12 runs to win, with four wickets in hand. Michael Bevan was dismissed without adding another run, and suddenly I had to put the pads on. I didn't have to wait long to bat because Shane Warne was unluckily given out lbw by Venkat. Warnie seemed to be struck outside the line, and to make matters worse, according to replays, it was also a no-ball.

Anyway, we still needed five runs to win and had only two wickets left. Ian Healy was up the other end and Glenn McGrath was left to bat, so I had to somehow make sure I survived the last five balls of the Kallis over. Although I was a bundle of nerves, I kept telling myself I had to watch the ball closely. The key was to get through and hopefully have Heals wrap it up at the other end.

Thankfully, the first ball was a bit of a 'sighter', which I could let go outside off-stump. The second was near enough to a half volley, which I pushed towards mid-off. The third was full again and skidded through slightly. I played back and managed to keep it out, but had I missed it, I would have been plumb lbw. The next ball was full again and angled in. Luck was on my side and I got forward and managed to keep it out, even though I played it a shade late. The last was a relief: just wide enough of the off-stump to be left alone.

Now it was Heals's turn. After he'd defended the first two deliveries safely, he eased the third off his pads and it sailed away for six. He hardly seemed to hit the ball, and the six couldn't have come at a better time — it was a minor miracle!

We'd squeaked in for a sensational 'come from behind' win, which put us 2–nil up with one to play.

The celebrations in the rooms were nothing short of awesome. Matt Hayden's interpretation of the day's events was that we had been stalking the South African team and when the time was right, we went in for the kill. He recruited me to re-enact a 'stalk and kill' scenario in front of the lads, complete with cream and Vegemite as 'war paint'.

Third Test, Pretoria, 21–24 March 1997

After the victory at Port Elizabeth, we had only three days to butter up for the third Test. South Africa brought in left-arm quick Brett Schultz to replace Shaun Pollock, and dropped Darryl

Cullinan and Paul Adams. The toss was a good one for the South Africans to win: they bowled us out on the opening day for 227.

Schultz bowled quite speedily, but I remember thinking that Donald was consistently quicker throughout the game. When Schultz got it right, he could swing the ball in to the right-handers at top pace. Sadly for him, his career was marred because of injuries, and he played only one more Test for his country.

In reply, South Africa took a day-and-a-half to make 384 — a lead of 157. Adam Bacher took more than seven hours to make 96, and Hansie Cronje made 79. We could manage only 185 in the second dig, and ended up losing within four days, by eight wickets.

On what turned out to be the last day of the game, umpire Cyril Mitchley made an absolute howler of a caught-behind decision against Ian Healy. Heals tried to clip Schultz to fine leg and was given out caught down the leg side off his pad. He didn't react too well, gesturing at the umpire and hurling his bat up the steps towards the dressing room as he was making his way off the ground. As a consequence Heals had to face the match referee and was banned for two One Day Internationals.

The seven-match series

After the Tests, we had to play a seven-match, limited-overs series. Adam Gilchrist was one of the players who joined us for the matches, but it took him an eternity to get to Johannesburg by plane. Rather than fly directly there from Perth, he flew Perth–Sydney–Hong Kong–Johannesburg. The Australian Cricket Board had an association with Cathay Pacific, and Gilly had to fly the long way around to keep sweet with them. How insane! In this case, commonsense wasn't used at all.

We split the first two games, and after the second, Mark Taylor decided to take a break. Ian Healy came back into the side after being suspended; we were soundly beaten by 46 runs, and we had

2–1 down and four to play. For the fourth game, in Durban, Adam Gilchrist came into the side and played one of his first major innings for Australia: he made 77 from 88 balls in our far-from-convincing 9/211. Thankfully, we bowled well and dismissed the opposition for 196 to tie the series. Gilly dropped two catches off me at slip, and even years later occasionally he brings up the moment. We managed to win the fifth game, but in the sixth we were looking down the barrel of a loss, finding ourselves at 3/58 and chasing 285 to clinch the series.

Enter Michael Bevan, who played superbly for 103 off only 97 balls and got us over the line. Bevo was such an outstanding one-day player because he could always find a gap in the field, ran a lot of twos and, when appropriate, nailed those boundaries.

Now we'd won the series, Warnie and I were rested from the last game, which we lost comfortably. Although we'd finished on a losing note, we'd done remarkably well to come away from the tour having won the Tests 2–1 and the one-dayers 4–3. We'd played some punishing cricket, and we were relieved we'd been successful. Apart from having been troubled by a few early doubts, I got through the tour without any injuries. That was a terrific bonus.

England, and the battle for the Ashes

We didn't get much of a break between the end of the South African tour and the flight to the UK for the 1997 Ashes series. We went via Hong Kong and while there played a match at the Kowloon Cricket Club against a Rest of the World Eleven. I didn't play but our captain Mark Taylor did. Again he failed with the bat and made only 4 before he was caught behind off former Pakistani paceman Mohsin Kamal. We won the match pretty easily, and from there went off to London.

My first game on UK soil was in the traditional tour opener, against the Duke of Norfolk's Eleven at Arundel Castle. I managed to get four wickets in the game — a positive way to start the tour. One thing I remember about the early part was the bloody cold weather!

Also, I couldn't believe how many 'nuffies' there were; they were at the games getting the players to sign things such as books, posters, photos and autograph sheets. There were so many of them it was unbelievable.

After the match at Arundel, we had another couple of games: one against Northants, which we won, and another at Worcester, which we got comfortably beaten in. In the three One Day Internationals against England, we got belted and the tabloid-newspaper journos got stuck into us, saying this was the time for the Ashes to come home. Ben Hollioake played a brilliant knock at Lord's and received a standing ovation when he walked off after being dismissed. Sadly, just five years later, he died in a car accident back in Australia, in Perth.

When we were heading into the first Test, to be played at Edgbaston, there was plenty of talk in the press about Tubby's form. The questions were getting louder and more frequent about his place in the team. This querying had been going on for quite a while — certainly ever since I'd been in the Test team. I'm sure the selectors would have taken many things into account when discussing the situation. However, I have to say that in professional sport, a run such as Tubby's is probably a touch on the generous side, even for a captain and quality player such as him. As a young player, I wasn't privy to much of the chat between players about this type of issue, but judging from the odd comment and players' body language, I could tell there was pressure.

Against that backdrop, we won the toss and elected to bat on what looked to be a good wicket, and amazingly found ourselves 8/54 just before lunch. A few people were suggesting we hadn't had enough First Class cricket as we were heading into the Ashes, but I don't believe it was a case of being under-prepared or a bit short of a gallop; I believe it was one of those rare days in cricket in which you nick everything and the catches get taken. England's bowlers were pumped up and did bowl well, because we eventually fell in only 31.5 overs for 116.

When our turn at the crease came, we had England 3/50 and it seemed the game could be over in about three days! However, Nasser Hussain and Graham Thorpe joined forces, and added 288 for the fourth wicket to help England a large part of the way to 9/478 declared: a lead of 360.

I hurt my hamstring after 10 overs of bowling and felt terrible because I was letting the side down and leaving us a bowler short.

Tubby in a tight corner

AFTER HIS FIRST-INNINGS FAILURE, A HEAP OF PRESSURE WAS being applied to Mark Taylor to make a score in the second innings — not only for his own place but for the fact we needed to bat for a long time to have any chance of saving the match.

There is no doubt that Tubs was feeling the pressure. For him to come out in the second innings and grind out a tremendously hard-fought hundred took a hell of a lot of character, and as a teammate I found his effort was most pleasing to see. Throughout Tubby's batting slump, the way he handled himself with his teammates, his support staff, his fans and the media was nothing short of astounding.

After he was dismissed for 129 just before lunch on the fourth day — a tally he'd made in six-and-a-half hours — at 2/327 we were almost back on level terms. Tubby figured in two key partnerships: 133 with Matty Elliott for the first wicket and 194 with Greg Blewett for the second. Blewy had played brilliantly for a ton in his first Test on England soil, emulating his feat of two-and-a-half years earlier, when he scored 102 in his debut Test knock on his Adelaide home track.

Unfortunately, after Tubby was dismissed, we couldn't find one more big partnership so we could set England a reasonable target in the last innings. After tea, we were all out for 477, so had set the opposition only 118 to win. In front of a noisy, parochial crowd, England stormed home to win by nine wickets in only 21.3 overs, so were put 1–nil up.

It was extremely disappointing to lose the first Test, but England had made us realise they'd come to play. Balancing that out, from a personal point of view, there was no stage at which I might have gone home because of my hamstring strain. I was back jogging within the week, and bowling within a week-and-a-half. However, we also had Andy Bichel and Brendon Julian injured, so Paul Reiffel was called up to join the party as cover.

Even though I had only a mild strain, I was absolutely spewing I was going to miss the Lord's Test. I was focusing on getting my hamstring right so I could play a prominent part in the series. On my first tour of England I didn't feel homesick at all, with one huge exception: I missed my daughter very much.

Second Test, Lord's, 19–23 June 1997

Despite the fact we couldn't force a win, the Lord's Test turned out to be a real turning point in the series. Paul Reiffel came into the side for me, and England named an unchanged line-up for the first time in 34 Tests. The first day was washed out, but on the second, we managed to win the toss, and because of the damp and overcast conditions, we sent the opposition in to bat. Their skipper Michael Atherton later said he'd been happy to bat in those conditions, but in the little play that was possible, England lost their first three wickets for just 13 and struggled to three for 38 before the rain came back ending play for the day.

Glenn McGrath picked up all three wickets and looked as though he was back to his best. The skies cleared on day three, and Glenn continued to maintain his superb line and length; he finished with 8 for 38 as England collapsed and were all out for just 77. Glenn's bowling was absolutely brilliant. I remember thinking there and then that I wanted to come back to England and play at Lord's to get my name on the 'five-for' honour board mounted in the dressing room.

The rain hung around again for the next couple of days, but Matthew Elliott consequently had time to make his maiden ton — a great triumph for him, after his serious knee injury back in December. Thanks to his innings, we got a lead of 136, and declared just before the start of day five in an attempt to put England under a bit of pressure. To their credit, they batted the day out fairly easily and maintained their 1–nil lead in the series. However, after Glenn's performance in the first innings, we had a feeling that the balance of power was heading back our way.

Our scheduled match after Lord's was against British Universities, but it was washed out. Thankfully, I was fit enough to play in the game leading up to the third Test, against Hampshire. I managed to get seven wickets, and Hampshire's coach, the legendary West Indian Malcolm Marshall, was kind enough to say he felt I was one of the world's three fastest bowlers.

The wicket was slow, and I was surprised that the lads thought I was bowling quickly, because the ball felt slow coming out at my end! The slips fielders were saying the nicks were reaching them at a sharp pace. I was massively relieved that my hamstring felt fine. On the downside, though, I got bad blisters from my boots during that match, but felt that at least I was back in the mix for the third Test team. The other pleasing thing was I got Matty Hayden out! Having missed out on being picked in the Ashes tour party, he was playing as Hampshire's overseas player, and I was stoked to knock him over in the second innings.

Third Test, Old Trafford, Manchester, 3–7 July 1997

When the third Test team was announced, I returned to the 11 for Michael Kasprowicz. The pitch had a strange look to it:

green and damp in the middle, and bare patches at the ends. The conditions were overcast, so the toss was again vital. We managed to win it, and decided to bat. It was a pretty gutsy move by Tubby because it looked like a good day to bowl. England started well to have us 3/42, before Steve Waugh played one of his best ever Test innings, scoring 108. On a difficult track, Tugga showed true Aussie grit when it was needed, and after a scratchy beginning, ground out what proved to be a decisive innings. Without his effort, we would have been in all sorts of trouble, and even though 235 in the first innings is generally considered a modest score, it was a reasonable effort on that pitch.

England were going along quite well in their first innings before the magic of Shane Warne came into play. Warnie spun the web that afternoon and took five wickets, reducing England from 1/74 to 8/161 by stumps. It was a vintage Warnie performance. He had some solid support from Mark Taylor, who took a fantastic catch at slip off him to dismiss Alec Stewart, and from Ian Healy, who made a brilliant leg-side stumping off Michael Bevan to get rid of Mark Butcher. Up to that day, Shane had taken only three wickets, so it was great to see him back in his best form, just when we needed it.

We knocked the opposition over pretty quickly on day three and gained a vital lead of 73, on a pitch that was still helpful for the bowlers. Unfortunately, our top order started poorly again: we lost 3/39, and Taylor, Blewett and Elliott all got out cheaply. There was a fair bit of doubt about Blewy's decision, given out by umpire Venkat caught at slip by Nasser Hussain off Robert Croft. Greg came forward to drive and edged the ball, with Hussain diving forward to attempt to catch it. According to the replays, the ball seemed to touch the ground; however, Hussain felt he caught it, and so did the umpires who after consulting gave him out.

From there, Mark and Steve Waugh had a partnership that started to turn the game our way. Mark made only 55 but played beautifully, and for the second time in the match, Steve played an innings full of guts and determination. While Tugga was batting, his hands were killing him, especially his right thumb. He needed to have our physio, Errol Alcott, massage them constantly. Thanks to the support we got from Ian Healy and Shane Warne, we ended the day at 6/282 and had a lead of 355. Tugga was unbeaten on 82, just 18 shy of his second ton of the Test.

Steve brought up his hundred on the fourth day, and we ended up declaring after lunch on a lead of 468. I even managed to bat for an hour and make an unbeaten 28, thereby sharing a partnership of 62 with Paul Reiffel.

Because we had all those runs up our sleeve, we were able to attack from the word go. After I was hooked for six by Michael Atherton, I managed to trap him plumb in front and had Hussain in a similar way shortly afterwards. Mark Butcher, who'd made a half century in the first innings, then top edged an attempted hook shot, and Glenn McGrath ran in and dived forward to take a memorable catch. England were 4/55 and well on their way to defeat.

Glenn McGrath also got in on the act: he took four of the last five wickets to fall, and half an hour before lunch on the last day, we'd won by 268 runs, levelling the series at 1–all. Steve Waugh was deservedly named Man of the Match for his two outstanding innings. I was pleased to make a contribution in the second dig although I'd had annoying blisters on my heels. Our physio, Errol Alcott, put Elastoplast over the blisters, Vaseline over the Elastoplast, and Vaseline in my sock and on the inside heels of my boots. The whole thing was quite annoying at times! I was happy to have bowled reasonably well to get some top-order wickets in what was an awesome win. In the performance, we not only squared the series; we regained the psychological advantage. The English press were back on their team's case and reopened a few mental scars. Tugga, Warnie and Pigeon were all back at the top of their games, so it was going to be a more than interesting Test match at Headingley.

In past Ashes Tests at Leeds, a few problems had occurred with the pitch, and this time around was no exception. We believed that the England chairman of selectors, David Graveney, was exerting some influence on the groundsman, Andy Fogarty. Fogarty was preparing the same pitch that had been used for the one-dayer back in May; however, the grass hadn't grown as he would have liked, so two weeks before the match, he decided to use another track. The England Cricket Board changed the pitch, and we felt that Graveney had been telling Fogarty what to do whereas what pitch should be used had absolutely nothing to do with him. The ECB members were clearly worried about the threat Shane Warne posed on a dry, turning wicket. Tubby was correct to lodge a protest, which he put in formally through our manager Alan Crompton.

Fourth Test, Leeds, 24–28 July 1997

Play started late because of rain. Thankfully, we won the toss anyway, and Mark Taylor decided to send England in. Although there was a fair bit in the track, England started well and got to 43; then, Butcher was caught at short leg by Greg Blewett off Paul Reiffel for 24. The strange part about it was that Blewy caught the ball not in his hands but between his left arm and ribs! It was a handy piece of luck, and shortly afterwards, I had my first turn at the crease. I managed to pick up Alec Stewart — a regulation catch this time for Blewett at short leg — and just before stumps, Nasser Hussain was brilliantly held by Mark Taylor at first slip off Glenn McGrath. England finished at 3/106 from the 36 overs. Michael Atherton had held up in his typical way by taking two-and-a-half hours to get his 34.

On day two, the Leeds weather thankfully improved and we started on time. We were particularly keen to knock over nightwatchman Dean Headley so we could have a crack at the middle order, before the ball got too old. Although England played and missed against McGrath and Reiffel plenty of times, Atherton and Headley hung in pretty well. When the score was 3/138, I got my first turn at the crease for the day.

I had a dream start: Headley tried to drive at an out-swinger, and Steve Waugh held the catch at backward point. Not long afterwards, McGrath bounced Atherton, who top edged a hook shot to me at long leg. Because of his wicket, we were right into the middle and lower order. Graham Thorpe hooked me for a couple of fours, but tried to do it a third time to a ball that wasn't short enough, and pulled the ball on to the stumps. John Crawley clipped a ball on to Blewy's boot at short leg, the ball popped and he completed the catch. According to slow-motion vision, the ball was very close to hitting the ground before his boot, and the crowd showed their displeasure when they saw the replay.

During that spell, I felt I was pretty lucky: I was bowling reasonably fast, not thinking too much about where I wanted the ball to go, just making sure I was hitting the crease well, and staying nice and tall when I bowled. My good luck continued when Ricky Ponting brilliantly caught Robert Croft at leg gully. Croft popped a short ball up and Punter caught it leaping high, Aussie Rules style, to give me my first 'five-for' on English soil. In knocking over Darren Gough and Mike Smith, I got 7/37 from 13.4 overs. England were all out for 172 after getting to 2/103 at one stage.

The wicket was still doing a bit, and Darren Gough and Dean Headley bowled strongly: each got two wickets and reduced us to 4/50. Ricky Ponting, who was playing his first Test for a while joined Matty Elliott at the crease and they produced one of the best batting partnerships you could wish to see. We were in big trouble. Herb and Punter counter-attacked beautifully: they added 268 for the fifth wicket and put us in control of the match. It was a triumph for Ricky, because he'd been unlucky to be dropped against the West Indies the previous summer. Matty played a magic knock: he batted for seven-and-a-half hours, hooking and pulling superbly, before a Darren Gough yorker ended his innings on 199. It was his second ton of the series and couldn't have come at a better time. When we declared at lunch on day four, Paul Reiffel had made an unbeaten 50, and even Glenn McGrath had chipped in with 20 not out. We'd made 9/501, we'd scored at a touch above four an over, and we were leading by 329.

For this Test, England had picked Mike Smith from Gloucestershire and although his county numbers were consistently impressive, we didn't think that he'd be the same threat as the man he'd replaced, Andy Caddick. Despite a dropped catch off his bowling, he went wicketless and never played again.

In the England second innings, Glenn McGrath and Paul Reiffel disposed of their top order, and at 4/89, it looked as though we were set to wrap the match up with a day to spare. However, Nasser Hussain and John Crawley stood firm: they batted for the whole last session and finished the day on 4/212; Hussain brought up his ton just before the close.

Thankfully, we made pretty quick work of the match on the final day and wrapped it up just after lunch. Paul Reiffel took 5/49. One of his wickets was Mark Ealham, who was brilliantly caught at second slip by Mark Waugh diving full stretch to his right. Mark has taken many magnificent catches over the years, but this was one of his best and he helped us finish off the opposition. Having taken two wickets in the second innings and ended with nine for the game, I was judged Man of the Match. First, however, I didn't think I deserved it, because the wicket did do a bit and I thought Matthew Elliott, having got 199, was more worthy. Second, as winner of the award, I had to give an interview to the BBC's David Gower, who was the MC for the post-match presentations.

I can still picture Gower's slight smirk every time I answered a question. Now I realise that it was because I gave him nothing; maybe it was more like a grimace and masked his frustration! It wasn't that I disliked the media; it was more that I was shy, and didn't want to give too much away and sound cocky. I'd just played in only my eighth Test match and I was still inexperienced in dealing with the media. Gower asked me what I was going to do after the interview, and I replied I was 'going to have a lot of beers, in a very short space of time'. He and everyone around cracked up. I wish I could say I was trying to be funny, but I wasn't. I must admit, though, that Gower did his absolute best to make me feel comfortable during the interview, and I really appreciated that.

Fifth Test, Trent Bridge, 7–11 August 1997

ENGLAND MADE FOUR CHANGES FOR THE TRENT BRIDGE TEST. They dropped Mark Butcher, Mark Ealham and Mike Smith, and brought in Andy Caddick as well as the Hollioake brothers; the brothers were making their Test debut. Darren Gough had a sore knee and pulled out, and Devon Malcolm took his place. We were unchanged, which I think was a true indication of how well we were going.

On a flat-looking track, Mark Taylor did the right thing: he won the toss and we batted. Tubby played one of his more fluent innings of the series: he made 76 and we ended the day on 3/302. We finished on 427 — a first-innings score that usually translates into a Test-match win; mind you, the way Alec Stewart started the England innings, it seemed he'd get a double ton before the end of the day. He smashed us to all parts, and Mike Atherton played the sheet-anchor role, as they raised a hundred partnership in quick time.

Fortunately, Shane Warne decided to take a hand in the proceedings and produced another one of his match-turning spells. Atherton (27) was the first to go; he edged a regulation catch behind, and Stewart followed to one of the more memorable catches taken by Ian Healy. Stewart (87) edged a sharply bouncing leg break, which Heals couldn't hold on the first attempt. The ball went behind him towards leg slip, and thanks to his quick reflexes, he dived back and held a miraculous catch. It was his 300th Test catch and his 100th against England and was probably one of the best he'd ever taken in his career. Hussain (2) was then bowled by a vicious-spinning leg break, which pitched leg and hit the top of off-stump, as in the Gatting dismissal at Birmingham in 1993. England had slumped from 106 without loss to 4/141, and within an hour we were back on top again thanks to the magic of Warnie.

England were all out for 313 on the third day, and I didn't have much of an influence: I didn't take a wicket in bowling 11 overs. Warnie and Glenn ended up with four wickets each. We were leading by 114, so were in sight of having our third win on the trot and wrapping up the series 3–1.

After batting consistently in our second dig, we got to 336 and set the opposition a massive 451 to win. Although they had a day-and-a-half to get the runs, they set off after the target like they had only 50 overs to get them! All their batsmen were playing with a heap of aggression, and I was getting carted around the park early on. My back was playing up to the point I couldn't bend over to touch my knees, let alone my toes. When I did try to straighten up after bending over, I felt more shooting pains in my back. Although I got smashed around, I got three wickets — for 65 — in my eight overs. Hussain chopped a half volley on to his stumps, Crawley was caught down the leg side, and I trapped Adam Hollioake leg before. I was struggling and knew I was in trouble with my back again, but my strike rate was good, and I'd taken three scalps to help us win the Test and regain the Ashes with a day to spare.

The celebrations were fantastic, but I was subdued because my back had gone again. I stayed on for the final Test at the Oval and had some scans, from which the doctor confirmed I had stress fractures in my back. I was shattered, because I felt I was starting to settle into Test cricket nicely. It was a long plane trip back to Australia even though we'd won the series and I'd had a significant role. I didn't realise it at the time, but I was to be out of cricket for most of the 1997–98 summer because of my back.

Tours, Tests and techniques

I FOUND THINGS TOUGH WHEN I GOT HOME FROM ENGLAND IN 1997. Because I'd missed the last Test as a result of the stress fractures in my back, I knew that I wasn't to start the season, and that hurt. Thankfully, I had a good deal of help in the first stages of my recovery.

A group approach to returning to form

ALONG WITH CRICKET ACADEMY COACH RICHARD DONE, A GROUP comprising then Australian coach Geoff Marsh, cricketer Dennis Lillee, physio Errol Alcott, Redbacks coach Andrew Sincock and Dr Clive Matthews helped decide how best to deal with the problem.

The consensus was that my back problems stemmed from the fact that in delivery stride, my left foot was landing too far inside the crease and I was twisting my back. Consequently, I had to learn to place my left foot closer to the return crease. Redbacks coach Andrew Sincock was particularly good at trying to help me to do this. With a good deal of effort, I managed to improve. Also, I was still filling out physically and getting stronger. I was bowling at a good pace.

Early in that season, I was lucky to have a lot to do with Dennis Lillee, who helped me work on my action. He worked with me on my run-up and tried to get me as high as possible in my action. We developed a series of cues that I still use these days when I'm bowling.

After I got to the stage of being able to bowl again, Dennis started me off by doing a drill through which I bowled off only two steps. As soon as I went to bowl from a bit further, I tended to revert to how I'd bowled before, so it was an incredibly hard habit to break. At times I still fall back into the habit in that my left foot goes much too far inside my right so I twist my back. Essentially, I still bowl with the classic 'mixed' action — the upper half of my body is front on whereas the lower half is side on — but fortunately, as time has gone on, my body has learned to adapt to the action. My back has got stronger, and I'm lucky it can handle the workload.

Up to the point in my career at which I was injured, I'd simply been running in as fast as I could and trying to let the ball go as fast as I could. Once I'd copped the injury in the 1997 Trent Bridge Test, I'd had to reassess the action and change it. I was unbelievably lucky that Dennis and everyone involved were there to help me. I was still relatively inexperienced and had to rely on these people to get me through.

In Dennis's view, I'd probably been told a few years before that I had a technical problem but I was presenting with a classic case of 'You don't listen till you break down.' I didn't agree with that proposition. One factor as to why bowlers break down is technique. But I tend to think that being strong in the right way is the key to staying fit enough to bowl. Some bowlers look good as athletes but mightn't be conditioned properly for bowling. Guys can do heaps of work in the gym, but working out mightn't be the right type of training for fast bowling. A marathon runner doesn't do a whole lot of sprint work, and a sprinter doesn't run marathons, because that other type of exercise wouldn't make sense and isn't specific to what those athletes do. I also believe it's crucial to keep your 'glutes' strong — glutes are the muscles that link your back and legs — the legs do the running, the back does the bowling and the glutes hold it all together.

As you go along in your career you learn to adapt to things. I grooved my action over many years and actually reached the point at which my body was completely adapted to the workload. Plenty of guys tinker with their action, and I'm not convinced that's the way to go.

Even though plenty of people thought I was bowling pretty fast throughout this period, I felt I was bowling only the odd ball that was genuinely quick. The odd ball was sharp, but I didn't feel I was consistently quick; I didn't quite have my action completely right.

Once I got back to playing, I didn't go flat out straight away; I took my time to get my bearings. I'd put in a swag of remedial work. A sequence of photos of me bowling appeared in a newspaper. When I studied that, it didn't appear that I had changed my action all that much.

Before Christmas, I managed to play again, against New South Wales, but after that I had to contend with some heel problems (plantar fascitis) in my left foot, which is my landing foot. When I was in delivery stride, it felt like a knife was going through my heel. In early January, I was in Tassie playing in a Pura Cup match and had an injection in my heel to relieve the pain. When the needle went in, I had to bite a towel, the pain was so incredible. It wasn't as excruciating as the pain I would later experience in 1999, when I broke my leg in Sri Lanka, but it was bad enough. After that I was okay for a while and bowled a spell of four or five overs, but when the jab wore off, I was in pain again and had to come off. From there, I had to rest and have a break, to get over the problem. The writing was on the wall: I wouldn't be able to play again that summer.

At that point in the 1997–98 season, I was deeply frustrated: I'd suffered a back problem, managed to get over it and then had a problem with my heel — both intensely annoying setbacks. I knew I had to let my body settle down and keep focusing on doing my strength work in other areas till I got my heel right. It was a case of *Patience, Jason, patience!*

People sometimes ask me how I managed to keep going through these setbacks. My motivation for getting fit again was always playing for my country and winning cricket matches. The physio and fitness co-ordinator would set me a programme to complete and I would follow it to the letter. I had faith in my rehab and believed if I did everything I should, it would give me the best chance to recover.

Australian A tour of Scotland and Ireland, August 1998

THAT SEASON, I DIDN'T PLAY A LOT MORE CRICKET. THANKFULLY, however, in the minds of the selectors I'd proved myself enough to get picked for the Australia A tour of Scotland and Ireland scheduled for August 1998. We had a terrific time over there and I got to hang out with some great guys, mainly Colin Miller and Dene Hills.

Playing in different conditions was an experience, and it was in Ireland that I first experimented with a shorter run-up. Because it was wet on and off, I thought it would be a good place to try out the new action. On the odd occasion I gave it a go but decided to put it on the back burner till the next season, when Greg Chappell was to come on board as the Redbacks coach. One day in 1998–99, we were in the Brisbane nets and worked on the action, and I used it a few times.

What's with the hair?

That trip to the UK was the time Colin Miller started to dye his hair. I had an agreement with Dene Hills that if he got an earring, I'd bleach my hair. I was confident he wouldn't get an earring but turned out to be wrong: he got his ear pierced and immediately told me I had to get my hair done. I went blond, and Col must have thought it was a good idea because he went and did it as well. It was one of the funnier things we did on the tour; we all became pretty good mates and had a good time together.

Ashes to Ashes

After the tour of Scotland, it was back to the Redbacks' pre-season in a bid to get fit for the 1998–99 Ashes series.

I was twelfth man in the opening Test, played in Brisbane on 20–24 November 1998, but the match was drawn because it was washed out on the last day. Finally my chance came in the second Test at the WACA.

It was a funny old match that was completed inside three days (28–30 November). On the opening day on a bouncy pitch, England collapsed for just 112, and by stumps we were well on top at 3/150. However, Alex Tudor bowled well on the second day, and we crashed from 4/209 to be all out for 240. Approaching the end of the second day, England was 5/67 and it seemed we'd wrap up the match inside two days.

Late on that day, I got smashed around by Hick, and at the end of it, I had figures of 0/69 from nine overs. Hick had hooked me for consecutive sixes over mid-wicket in an over that had gone for 23. I was feeling pretty dejected about the situation. However, the next morning, our skipper Mark Taylor showed faith in me: he gave me the ball first up and told me to go out and bowl and just do my thing. I had Hick caught in the slips by Ricky Ponting for 68 and finished off all the opposition with 5/88 from 15.2 overs. We won the Test match by seven wickets.

I was twelfth man for the third Test in Adelaide because of team balance. During the Test, while bowling in the nets, I developed a problem with a tendon in my right knee. Sadly, I was kept out of the Test side for the rest of the series, which we won 3–1. It was screamingly frustrating, and I had to work hard to make sure I was selected for the upcoming Test series to be played in the Caribbean. In February, I played in a Pura Cup match against Victoria. I took 4/42 and 2/30 — enough for me to get selected, although I'd played only one Test against England that summer.

Thankfully, I was on the plane to the West Indies after what had been another frustrating season.

The West Indies tour, 1999

I WAS GLAD TO BE BACK IN THE TEAM. I'D PLAYED IN ONLY ONE of the Tests that summer, and I'd developed a hunger to play. Plus we had a top destination: I was looking forward to my first tour of the Caribbean.

After we'd retained the Ashes, Mark Taylor elected to retire, having played at the helm for 50 Tests. Steve Waugh was appointed captain for the West Indies tour. During Mark Taylor's captaincy, his tremendous strength was his ability to communicate: you always knew exactly where you stood. He got across what he wanted very simply. When Mark retired and Steve took over, we realised there'd be some changes, but one thing was obvious to us all: Steve was ready to be captain and Tubby had had enough.

Before the tour, Steve spoke to each player individually, put some tour goals in place and got everything ready. Also, he gave each player a one-page outline of what he expected of them. Here's what he gave me:

Dizzy,

Enjoy the tour — your time is now.

Work with Pigeon [McGrath] to establish the best opening-bowling combination in world cricket.

Controlled aggression coupled with 'in the corridor' bowling will take wickets in the Caribbean.

Use your intimidating body language on the Windies batsmen — they don't like it.

Set the tone for their tail-end batsmen — go for their jugular — get personal, then get them out!

Work on your batting — you are capable of getting good partnerships going, which could be very important.

Keep the intensity up at fielding practice — take it into the game with you.

Be the man — make it your series.

Play well,

Tugga

As a teammate, one thing you noticed when it was a tough time in the middle was Steve Waugh the batsman made runs when faced with high-pressure situations. To me, his best effort under extreme pressure was in 1997 when he made twin tons in Manchester, despite having the sorest hands and requiring constant treatment from Errol Alcott. In the first innings, we were in all sorts of bother and he made a hundred on a fast green deck. In the second, when he could barely hold the bat, he punched out another ton to ram home the advantage against what was a stunningly good attack.

First Test, Trinidad, 5–8 March 1999

We won the first Test in Trinidad fairly easily and I found it notable for a number of reasons, the first of which was that Glenn McGrath and I had a good partnership for the last wicket. After winning the toss, we were battling at nine for 203, so needed a few more runs when, just before lunch on the second day, Glenn came in to join me. He and I always got on extremely well and I tried to keep the game simple by using a short backlift and playing as straight as I could. Glenn always tried to play as many shots as he could, and I encouraged him to put a few away and concentrate on staying in the middle. I tried to pass on the advice that a short backlift was the go but he had other ideas. We managed to add 66 for the last wicket and get to 269 all out. Through our partnership, Glenn and I not only added valuable runs, we took up a bit of time in the match. The funny thing for Glenn was that even though he batted below me at number 11, he actually outscored me: he made 39 to my 28 and afterwards ribbed me about my slow scoring!

After losing two early wickets, the West Indies were going along pretty well at 3/149 when Brian Lara went in slightly controversial circumstances. He pushed a ball to the leg side and took off for a run, but Justin Langer at short leg had actually stopped the ball and threw it underarm to Ian Healy who took off the bails. It sounds fairly 'regulation', I know, but according to the TV replay, the ball mightn't have been in Ian's glove when he took off the bails. Heals certainly thought the ball was there, as did the third umpire. From there, the Windies collapsed to the bowling of Glenn McGrath and Stuart MacGill, and got all out for 167, 102 behind — a handy lead.

Ian Healy wasn't one of the most popular guys with the local crowd at Port-of-Spain, probably because of the disputed catch that involved Lara back in 1996 in Sydney. Around the ground were a few banners on which the fans sledged Heals; one had 'Ian Healy, the mother of all thieves'.

In the second innings, Michael Slater made a hundred, and even though no one else made more than 34, we scored 261 and were put 363 ahead, a score that would take some getting. I managed my second 20 of the match by scoring 22 and was looking forward to getting stuck in with the ball, having gone wicketless in the first innings.

Heading out in the field on the fourth day, I remember that the pitch was still pretty good; there were no real demons. When we bowled, it was a mixture of good bowling and indifferent batting. The second innings was one of those days when the ball was coming out well, the batsmen were nicking it and we were catching it.

In that second innings, we bowled the opposition out in just 19.1 overs for only 51; however, the number of overs for the innings was really only 11.5 if you took out the opening partnership, which ended on the third ball of the eighth over. Glenn got five wickets and I got four — quite funny because our partnership of 66 in the first innings was more, and we thought that was pretty cool! After the match, Steve Waugh told the press that I seemed to be pretty focused and to mean business during the second innings, so in light of the written outline he'd given me before the series, I was pretty pleased.

The other pleasing thing about the first Test win was the amount of support we enjoyed from Aussie fans who'd made the trip over. Some were expats who'd come down from the United States, but a lot had made the long journey from Oz to cheer us on. Also, the Port-of-Spain ground has a beaut little drinking hole out the back of the ground, called the Cricket Wicket Bar. It's located behind the pavilion end of Queens Park and it was a popular meeting place for everyone after each day's play. Colin Miller found himself out there after one day's play, and one of the locals coined the name for him of Australia's Dennis Rodman!

Second Test, Jamaica, 13–16 March 1999

LITTLE DID WE KNOW THAT THINGS WOULD CHANGE WITHOUT warning in the second Test, in Jamaica. Windies captain Brian Lara was coming under attack from all quarters and didn't help matters by being 45 minutes late for a morning training session before the Test, having been sighted at a nightclub at 1.30 a.m. the night before. The local press were prompted to suggest that Shivnarine Chanderpaul should take over as captain, but wiser heads prevailed and Lara was retained as captain for the Test.

Lara wasn't exactly flavour of the month with the Sabina Park fans and copped some booing from the crowd when we were heading out to toss. After the toss, I heard that Lara told Steve Waugh, 'I hope this is the last time I'm gonna have to put up with this shit!' Maybe that was his way of psyching himself up, but Steve told us what he'd said, and we felt we were all over the opposition.

After Australia made only 256 on a pretty good pitch, the home side were in all sorts of trouble by the end of the day, being 4/37. Lara came in late in the day and was seven not out. I'd love to know how well he would have slept had he known that what was about to happen on day two of the Test would really shape his career.

Brian 'The Prince' Lara and Jimmy Adams batted the whole of the second day in an unbelievable performance. At stumps, The Prince was 212 not out, Adams was on 88, and the West Indies were 4/377 and 121 runs ahead. Heading into the day, we were on top, but by the end of it, the Windies had completely taken the game away from us in what proved to be the turning point in the series. Lara's method was simple: he was prepared to sit on Glenn and me while he got stuck into Warnie and MacGill. Up the other end, Adams defended stoutly and knew his place in the partnership: to hang in there, defend, and work the singles to give Lara the strike.

I found Lara to be the best batsman I've ever bowled to; I could bowl a good length delivery on off-stump and he could hit that one ball to more places than anyone else could. Other brilliant batsmen, such as Jacques Kallis and Sachin Tendulkar, play their zones well and are tricky to remove. Brian is difficult to bowl to because he's wristy and he can hit the same ball in any number of places, which puts him slightly above other batsmen.

During that second day, after Glenn and I had a crack at getting an early wicket, it was left to Warnie and Stuart MacGill to try to get a breakthrough. Warnie was struggling with injuries during this period and might have been slightly underdone heading into the series. MacGill was doing his thing, and bowled well except for a couple of spells when Lara got stuck into him.

There'd been a fair bit of speculation in the media that the two leggies didn't like bowling together, but from my perspective, that couldn't be any further from the truth. I think that Warnie wasn't at his very best and that he and MacGill mightn't have been sure how to bowl in tandem. Because we had two leggies, there was a degree of extra pressure on me and Glenn, but after all, that's what we were in the team to do.

My own plan for dealing with Lara that day was to 'bowl to two slips and a gully' on a pitch that was pretty flat and virtually rolled mud. My thought process was, Bowl right in the corridor, keep it simple, be patient, and force him to do something he doesn't want to; maybe the big drive through the off side can bring about his undoing. We knew he'd just see off Glenn, maybe try to score off me and then perhaps have a crack at the spinners. Once he got going, we tried going over and around, and to get the ball abrasive to try for some reverse swing. Adams is easily forgotten: he really hung around well that day, made 87, played the secondary role well, and frustrated the hell out of us.

The strain of making more than 200 in a day must have taken its toll on Lara because he was dismissed early on the third day; in fact, the rest of the West Indians fell rapidly, too. Their team lost 6/54 to be all out for 431: a lead of 175, so they were well on the way to victory. Our batting in the second dig was woeful: we made only 177, no one passed 30, and on day four the home side wrapped up the match before lunch by 10 wickets. The Test was a real wake-up call for us, especially our batsmen, who'd played some loose shots. To make matters worse, we were fined for a slow over rate, whereas the home side, whose over rate was as slow as — if not worse than ours — escaped a fine. Either way, by winning, the West Indies gained some amazing momentum, and headed for Barbados with their captain back on track and their whole team back in a positive frame of mind.

When we were heading into the third Test, the attention was suddenly turned to some of our deficiencies instead of those of the West Indies. Our upper order was struggling to get a decent start, and there was mumbling going on about the form of Shane Warne, who to that point had taken only one wicket — Ridley Jacobs — from 44 overs with the ball. We knew we had to re-focus on what we could do best, and that if we met our batting and bowling targets, we'd make the score 2–1 our way.

Third Test, Barbados, 26–30 March 1999

THINGS STARTED POORLY AGAIN — WE WERE 3/36 — BUT AFTER Justin Langer made an important 51, Steve Waugh and Ricky 'Punter' Ponting had a massive partnership through which they took us to 4/322 at stumps. Steve played and missed plenty of times but wasn't worried, and Punter — who'd come in for Greg Blewett because of injury — didn't miss a beat. On the second day, Ricky continued to a hundred and the captain was trapped for 199 by offie Nehemiah Perry. Both were great knocks and we ended up with 490, a first-innings score from which most Tests would be won.

We were feeling more confident at the end of the day, when we had the West Indies 4/80 at stumps, and Brian Lara was out for 8, caught behind by Ian Healy off my bowling. I banged it in short at

Lara, who couldn't do much except glove the ball behind. It wasn't a pre-planned ball, but when bowling a bouncer to Lara I made sure it was head high and right at him (it also needed to be short enough so he couldn't play a pull shot). He had to either evade or play it, not just watch it flying over his head.

Things were really heading our way on day three when we had them 6/98. However, Sherwin Campbell and Ridley Jacobs got stuck in and put on 153; Campbell got a ton and Jacobs 68. Their tail also wagged, and they reached the follow-on target at eight wickets down and were all out for 329. For the second Test in a row, we fell in a big hole in our second innings and were all out for 146, so the West Indies were back in it, needing 308 to win, on what was still a relatively good pitch.

Because we had them 5/105 in the second innings, we were really in the box seat to win the Test. However, Lara got going again, and with Jimmy Adams, put on 133 for the sixth wicket. After bowling Adams for 38, McGrath trapped Jacobs and Perry in front and to make it 8/248, and we were again in pole position to win the Test.

The big problem was that Lara was still in and again proving hard to dislodge. He was hitting the ball exactly where he wanted, and there wasn't a hell of a lot we could do about it. Curtly Ambrose was proving hard to move as well, and run by run, he and Lara were inching the West Indies towards victory.

Later in the innings, the ball was reversing a lot. The West Indies needed seven runs, and I found a nick that was heading straight for Shane Warne at slip. For some reason, Ian Healy, who was suffering from a double calf strain, dived in front of Shane and went one handed, and the chance went begging. In the same over, when they still needed six, I snared Ambrose in a similar way to that of the Lara chance; the ball was caught by Matty Elliott at third slip.

Courtney Walsh came in. I had three balls at him but couldn't knock him over. One of the deliveries was an in-swinging yorker that Courtney somehow kept out by stopping the ball dead just in front of him.

The Windies needed five to win. Glenn McGrath bowled the next over to Lara, and again we could have won it. The first ball edged by him just wide of Shane Warne at slip. Had we had another catcher in, we would have won the Test.

At the end, I was bowling when Lara hit the winning runs: a blazing drive through the off-side field. My back was gone — I couldn't bend over or stand up straight. Later it was revealed that I'd suffered a tear in one of my discs. During that last day, I'd spent a bit of time off the ground receiving treatment; however, I had to get back on to the field because there was no way I wanted to miss out on what to that point had been the best Test I'd ever played in. Glenn and I had churned through a mountain of work in that match: Glenn had bowled 77 overs, and I was bowling my 65th when the game finished.

Everyone's a critic, and there have been suggestions that our team lacked professionalism on that West Indies tour. Naturally there were times on the tour that blokes went out and had a big night, but they party all the time and always have done since I've been playing. I think the partying was more between Tests and perhaps during a tour match. From what I can remember, there weren't any especially late nights during any of the Tests. Like some of the lads, I had a beer or two after play, especially if we'd been in the field all day. It's fun to hang out in some of the many local beach bars and have a chat. Because I was very much a younger member of the squad, I didn't tend to notice the socialising too much. As you get older, you're inclined to get into the partying aspect of cricket more, and I might have been a victim of it.

As a result of injury, I'd been in and out of the side repeatedly. I was consumed with the goal of getting my game right and was in my own little bubble. I suppose I noticed the odd thing; for example, during a tour match, if a bloke was crook, I knew he'd had a big night the previous day.

In his book *Out of My Comfort Zone*, Steve Waugh mentioned that some players did have a few drinks during the West Indies tour. Maybe he was concerned because he'd just taken over the captaincy and he wanted to put his stamp of authority on the team.

Fourth Test, Antigua, 3–7 April 1999

One of the funniest things that happened in that fourth Test, in Antigua, was that Glenn McGrath hurt himself while kicking the boundary fence. At the end of one of his overs, he wandered down to his spot on the boundary and kicked what he thought was an advertising hoarding. Apparently he'd thought it was made of thin tin but he quickly realised it was painted on concrete. Initially he thought he'd broken his foot! Needless to say, he was in quite some pain as a result.

No one in the rooms actually saw the accident happen, and we didn't know anything about it at first. Before long, one of us noticed that Glenn was limping, so I went out to do my job as a 'benchie'. I walked around the rope and he described what he'd done. Pigeon's foot had blown up like a balloon. He took some pain relief from Errol Alcott, our physio, and put the foot in ice every night after play. Once we knew he hadn't broken a bone — he'd just badly bruised his foot — we took the mickey out of him, saying things like: *How stupid can you be? Not a good advertisement for fast bowlers' smartness.*

Glenn thought he was gone, and afterwards he himself thought it was bloody hilarious. Laughing at these incidents, I got through watching the match and partly overcame the disappointment of being injured again.

Colin 'Funky' Miller had a particularly important role in replacing Warne for the Test. He hit two of the biggest sixes ever; both of them were pull shots off Curtly Ambrose and one of them landed in the gaol next door. After the match, we were in the Casino Riviera, not far from our hotel in Antigua. Funky had had a few drinks, was playing the pokies and had a few hangers-on around him. He started recounting the story of the two strokes for the group and ended up spending half an hour on it. A few of us happened to be listening in while he was playing a machine and telling his tale. Allan Border walked in, Miller shouted cheekily, 'Hey, AB, have you ever hit two sixes off of Curtly?'

Like the trooper he is, AB took the remark in good spirit. Along with everyone else, he could see that Funky was living the dream, and was really happy for him. The runs came at a crucial time, and it was terrific to see Funky celebrate something he'd done in a Test.

Colin, Glenn McGrath and I had spent a reasonable amount of time together on the tour. The three of us went off and had a feed together, and then had a small punt. Glenn and I started $1 hands of Caribbean Stud. The most I ever lost was $5, because the game takes so long to play — perhaps five minutes per hand. Colin joined in and played with us, and it was good fun. Not only was it a cheap night, it did us good to have a change from the hotel.

In between games, I had no interest whatsoever in being 'Tommy the tourist', unlike some of the other guys. That distaste for sightseeing was evident when I was a kid. We'd go on holidays and Mum and Dad would want to see this and that but I had no real interest in 'this and that'. Certainly, on tour, I did have a look at some places of interest. However, I can recall being in India as an Australian Under-19 player and knocking back the opportunity to do the Taj Mahal visit because it was to take five hours. Instead I preferred to relax by kicking back and going for a swim or having a round of golf. As I've got older, I have made slightly more of an effort to go and see sights; I have had the privilege of visiting some amazing places. My attitude might change even more now my son, Jackson, is on the scene, especially if he's not into sport and he's keen on stuff I mightn't have been interested in.

I RETURNED TO ADELAIDE AFTER THE WEST INDIES TEST SERIES and on doctors' orders put my feet up for a few weeks. I wasn't named in the original squad for the World Cup, which was selected prior to the end of the West Indies tour. The selectors named 19 or 20 players and intended to reduce the number to the maximum of 15. Outside the squad, Tom Moody was brought in, at the insistence of Steve Waugh. That was to prove a particularly smart move, because Tom turned out to be pivotal in Australia's trophy win.

Not being in the squad was the least of my worries. Yet again I was injured. A long haul lay ahead of me, repairing my body and slowly slowly building back up to form. By then the art of recuperation had become all too familiar. In the immediate term, all I could do was rest up and look forward to the forthcoming 1999–2000 season.

The comeback kid

Following my return home from the Caribbean, I consulted the team physio Errol Alcott and decided to take things easy till the disc in my back was healed. My plan was to follow up a period of complete rest with a careful return to the gym and some light bowling in the nets. My aim was to be okay for Sri Lanka.

I began training with my Redbacks' teammate Mark Harrity at the SACA gym, doing some running and fitness work. As part of the official pre-season training with South Australia, the whole squad had to run up Montefiore Hill in North Adelaide. Anyone who knows the hill that leads up to Colonel Light's statue will understand how steep and arduous a task that is. We also had to do one-kilometre time trials, each one in fewer than three minutes and 30 seconds. We did them on either the 'uni loop', a running track around Adelaide University's sporting grounds, or the Adelaide Oval itself. It was taxing work, but thankfully I got through it.

Happily, I was picked for the Sri Lanka tour, which comprised some one-dayers before a three-match Test series. I remember bowling quick in those games and especially bowling Marvan Atapattu in Galle with a ball that narrowly beat him for pace. I knew I was going alright; I felt strong and good. The rewards were there in relation to my figures: in the four matches I played, I got 3/26, 2/30, 4/26 and 1/37. I hadn't made our World Cup team earlier in the year, so it was excellent to be back as part of the one-day side.

First Test, Kandy, 9–11 September 1999, and that collision

We played the first Test in Kandy, on a pretty flat deck. I remember being out there batting and wondering how the hell we collapsed to be 7/60; it simply wasn't that difficult a deck. Sri Lanka had left-arm pacemen Chaminda Vaas and Nuwan Zoysa plus offie Muttiah Muralitharan, and while Ricky Ponting was still in and batting, all I needed to do was stay in, and block and support him.

Facing Murali was not something to take lightly, but I had a plan to try to combat him. He wasn't bowling the 'doosra' but had a delivery that went straight on and was every bit as difficult to connect with. My theory was that if the ball pitched well outside off-stump it was spinning back in, and if it was on the stumps, chances are it probably wouldn't spin way down leg side; it would go straight on. I was batting on off-stump, and would attempt to get my pad outside the line of off-stump and try to smother the off break. I also managed to sweep a couple, and at other times, if I got one really full, I 'punched' a drive to score a few runs. On top of that, I had a bit of luck by getting the odd outside edge, and managed to just about make it to tea. Off the very last ball of the

Thanks to Father Christmas, I received my first decent cricket bat, a Stuart Surridge 'Oval Supercover', in 1985.

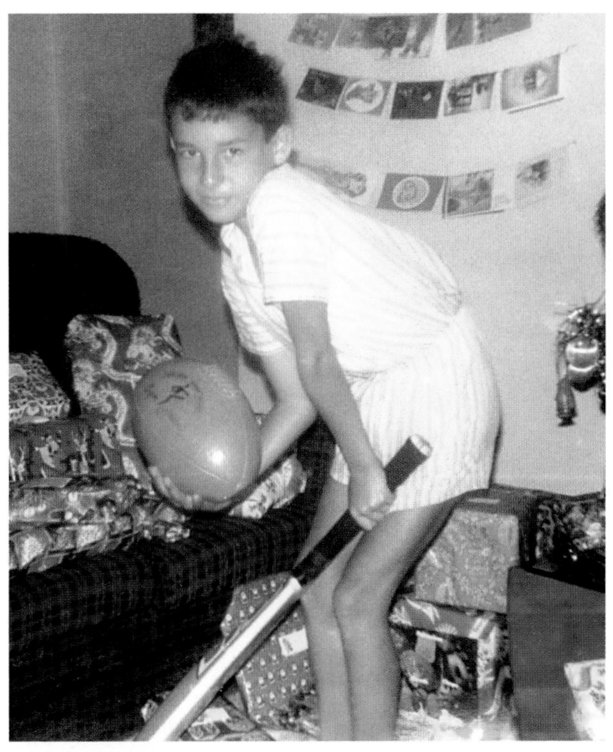

At the South Australian Primary Schools Amateur Sports Association in 1986. At that stage, like most kids, I did a bit of batting and bowling.

AAP

Dismissing John Crawley in the fourth Test against England at Headingley in 1997 during my first Ashes series. It was a pretty controversial incident – the replays showed that the ball was very close to hitting the ground before Greg Blewett caught it – and part of a memorable day for me: I took 7/37.

NEWSPIX

Celebrating after taking Graeme Hick's wicket at the WACA in the 1998–99 Ashes series. He'd smashed me the previous day, including consecutive sixes in one over.

Good times in Sri Lanka, 1999 – having a laugh with Damien Fleming and Shane Warne …

NEWSPIX

… And bad times: breaking my leg in an accidental clash with Steve Waugh. Tugga didn't come out of it too well either – he copped a broken nose.

NEWSPIX

On the comeback trail and bowling for the first time since my broken leg: South Australia v Western Australia, 19 February 2000.

NEWSPIX

Dismissing Sherwin Campbell, one of my victims in a 'five-for' against the West Indies in the third Test in Adelaide in 2000–01.

If I look happy, it's because I've just bowled Brian Lara for a duck in the fourth Test. I took the first six wickets of the innings – it was one of those great times when everything seemed to go my way.

NEWSPIX

NEWSPIX

Steve Waugh and me during our 133-run partnership in the second Test against India in Kolkata in 2001. I scored 46 in what was the highest Australian partnership for that wicket in 107 years. Unfortunately, VVS Laxman and Rahul Dravid's 376-run stand won the match for the Indians.

Another ambition fulfilled. I'd always dreamed of taking five wickets in an innings at Lord's. It happened in the second Test in 2001.

Jeff 'Bomber' Hammond took me under his wing and was a big early influence in my career, as well as a great friend.

Celebrating a big Test win against South Africa in Johannesburg in 2002. In the first innings, Adam Gilchrist scored what was then the fastest double century in Test history.

Giving some kids from the Tiwi Islands a cricket clinic in the Northern Territory. I've always been proud of my Aboriginal heritage and it's great to be able to help out Aboriginal kids who might follow in my footsteps.

NEWSPIX

Post-match celebrations with a couple of other members of the Aussie fast bowlers' club, Michael Kasprowicz and Glenn McGrath. Check out the personalised stubby holders.

Me and a few of the Australian boys in the Maldives in 2002.

session, I was trapped lbw by Murali for 41. I went back to play him after going forward the whole time — a slight misjudgement, so that was that. Ricky was last out for 96, and we managed 188 — not too foul a result after being 7/66.

On the second day, Sri Lanka was going well in reply when my Test match came to a sudden and dramatic end. I was fielding on the deep backward square-leg boundary when Mahela Jayawardene top edged a sweep shot off the bowling of Colin Miller. When the shot was played, the crowd became amazingly loud, so hearing teammates call out was almost impossible. The ground wasn't full, but a lot of schoolkids were making a fair bit of noise. After the ball was struck, I remember yelling out, 'Yeah!' to indicate it was my catch, and as I was running in, I had no idea that Steve Waugh was running straight at me from his position on the '45'. The ball hovered in the air, and I was convinced it was my catch because I was running into the ball rather than with the flight of it. Unfortunately, I didn't know that Steve was trying to take the ball till the very last minute, and given we ran into each other, neither did he! I knew I'd hurt myself pretty seriously but didn't realise how badly till I tried to stand on my leg.

Oddly enough, physio Errol Alcott was working on his laptop computer in the dressing rooms, and looked up and out just as the ball was struck. He had a premonition that something was about to happen, and from that moment till we collided, he made his way down to the boundary rope to prepare for the impending accident.

It was an amazing set of circumstances, and I was in a state of disbelief, thinking, *Here we go again: another injury*. I was carried off by our fitness man Dave Misson and security officer Reg Dickison; my wrist was killing me also, and I sensed that there was something wrong with it as well as with my leg. It wasn't till about 10 weeks later that I found out I had a fracture in my wrist. People thought I was hallucinating at the time because of the pain in my leg, but I was sure I had a problem with my wrist, too. The pain in my leg was pretty intense, and after I got back to the rooms, it wasn't long before it was time to get to the nearest hospital.

I was in the back of a car that was like an old Escort panel van — the *ad hoc* ambulance, if you like. I wasn't paying a lot of attention to the fact that my broken leg was hanging out the back of this 'panel van'. An over-keen young local, in haste for us to get going, tried to close the back door, which if it had been allowed to close would have made a real mess of my leg, if that was possible, given the leg was pretty bad already. Luckily, Errol realised what was about to happen and prevented the guy from closing the door. He then ensured I was completely in the back before the vehicle took off. From there, I had the bumpiest ride ever. Errol was there stabilising the situation, and apart from each agonising bump, which sent a jolt of pain through my leg, I don't remember a heck of a lot about the ride to the hospital.

A painful rehabilitation

Once we arrived, there were hundreds of people everywhere, and after we got through the crowds, we were transferred into a helicopter for the hop across to Colombo. Sanath Jayasuriya was extremely kind in organising the helicopter. The journey would have taken about five hours by road as opposed to the 45 minutes we actually spent in the air. I was grateful for the time we saved thanks to his fast actions.

When we arrived in Colombo, I had my leg re-set, and Steve had his nose redone — it actually came out straighter and looked better than it had before.

For a few days, Steve and I were in the same room together, both feeling sad and sorry for ourselves. I requested some pain relief at one stage and was a little taken aback when they brought in a suppository. I guess I clenched out of reflex and the pill went skidding across the floor. Steve was crying with laughter. At no stage did I feel the accident had been Steve's fault, and we certainly didn't discuss who had caused it while we were sharing the room. It was one of those rare occasions when the ball lands right in the middle of two players. Having said that, though, I can assert that the fielder running in would be viewed as having the right of way but that in the heat of a Test match, you only want to do the best for your team; you see a chance to take a catch and you have to go for it. Steve was on the '45' at short backward square leg and obviously felt he was in a position to take the catch as well. I certainly don't hold it against him, and I'm sure he felt the same way — it was nothing more than a freak incident. It might sound weird, but if I had my time over again, I wouldn't change what happened. Overall, I wouldn't change any aspect of my career: you have good days and bad ones, and this incident was part of it all.

I became a touch depressed lying in the Colombo Hospital for the best part of a week. What relieved the strain for me was that I had a steady stream of visitors from both teams, and I especially appreciate the way Russel Arnold, Sri Lanka's star batsman, took time out to come and see me while I was bailed up in bed. I had plenty of phone calls from our guys, so they also helped me get through the recuperation period.

Against doctors' orders, Steve decided he'd play in the next Test even though he still had a broken nose. He wore a helmet most of the time, even in the field. Quite a bit of rain was about the place and the last two Tests were drawn, so Sri Lanka won the series 1–nil.

After a while, I could return home, and Cricket Australia were kind enough to put me in first class on a Singapore Airlines flight. I was still in too much pain to fully appreciate it, to be honest. As soon as I touched down in Adelaide, my manager Kym Richardson had a limo waiting and arranged for me to go straight to hospital. After I was assessed there, I had to decide whether or not to have a steel rod put in my leg or retain the plaster cast. The cast went from the bottom of my foot right to the very top of my leg, and it was horribly uncomfortable. I was getting advice from a few people, and I based my final decision on the fact that my leg would waste away in a cast and that if I had a rod put in, I could shower and go to the toilet fairly normally. Given I was living in a townhouse that had stairs, if I'd had a cast on for a couple of months I would have found it a heck of a challenge to negotiate the stairs.

I decided to have a rod put in. That way I'd be able to move my leg a little and at the very least use some of the muscles in it. Former Crows coach Graham Cornes was one person who was against the idea: on the radio, he expressed the view that it wasn't the better solution, given that one of his mates had had complications after having a rod inserted and he would have been better off wearing a cast. In hindsight, though, I feel it was the right decision because I could still go to the pool and at least do something while I was waiting for the leg to completely heal. Julie Knights was helping out with the physio work at the Redbacks during that period, and she spent a lot of time managing my rehab. Much of the time I spent hanging out in a little hydro-therapy pool. It was hard work getting going again, though.

At about this time, I resumed my affiliation with Robert Crouch, whom I'd had a lot to do with when I was at the Cricket Academy. I was still working with Julie, who was giving me a lot of massage treatment that at times was extremely painful. She did a wonderful job and was one of the key factors in getting me back on track. Meanwhile, my Redbacks teammate Paul 'Blocker' Wilson was doing a lot of VersaClimber training at Crouchy's gym in order to keep his weight off, and told me that Crouchy was keen for me to give him a call. Apparently Crouchy was interested in helping me regain full fitness. Blocker's view was that Crouchy could train me and help me get strong enough to play again. Since my Academy days, I hadn't had a lot to do with Crouchy, but if I saw him at the cricket, we always had a chat. Crouchy and I had a meeting, and he suggested I try to keep the weight off my legs by using the VersaClimber and the shuttle machine for leg strengthening. He thought I should stay off my legs and that it was too soon for me to be doing running because I was still getting over the trauma of the break. The VersaClimber had a seat, and Crouchy said, 'I'll re-acquaint you with this seat, because you can't really do anything else.' He told me I'd learn to love the shuttle machine.

I was going in every morning, doing what I could with Crouchy. Some mornings weren't all that productive because I continued to be in a fair bit of pain. Even though the leg was still killing me, I got on the Versa, went easy and started slowly, and gradually built up the leg. When I got close to being fit enough to play again, I was a gun at the Versa, though never as good as Blocker, who was the 'king' of it. It was good training with him because even though he was always better at the Versa, I tried to keep up with him for as long as I could. I had someone there who was training the house down, and it was good to work with someone such as him — so much so that I was inspired to do what he did.

All I wanted was to get back into playing. The fact that Blocker had also played for Australia was also motivating; we had shared goals and understood each other well. A couple of times a week after training, we headed for breakfast at The Bakehouse, located on Melbourne Street in North Adelaide, to reward ourselves for working hard. Our discipline was second to none.

It was essential for me to take my mind off my injury. I had to focus on getting my leg stronger rather than dwelling on my misfortune at being injured. Not to be playing and training with the lads was a huge disappointment, but the building back up carefully was the best thing for me to do at the time. I know this doesn't come across as overly team-oriented, but there was no point training with the Redbacks because they were doing all the running and things I couldn't do. It was also tough for me because they were playing. It seemed best for all involved that I kept my distance from them and into some good hard training so I had the best chance of getting my leg right again.

I haven't seen the big collision on a match replay for a long time and don't need to see it again. What I do remember about watching the replay for the first time is that the injury hurt as much as it looked like it did!

Meeting Anna

IT WAS AT ABOUT THIS TIME — JUST BEFORE CHRISTMAS 1999 — that I met my future wife, Anna. Still flat out doing my rehabilitation, I'd been asked to go to the New York Bar and Grill, located in Marion, to make a promotional appearance on a Friday night. My Adelaide Grade-cricket teammate Ben Hook was to host the night, along with Channel Seven weather girl Nuala Hafner. About Nuala I thought, *She's not a bad sort — I'll go and do the night, and have a look.*

Being single, I was checking out the room and happened to spot Anna, whom I hadn't seen since school days. She looked really nice when I saw her that night. Anna was at the bar with some other people, and rather than go straight up and say, 'G'day,' I played it cool and didn't go over too quickly so I wouldn't look too keen. During the night, I was serving behind the bar and at one stage said to her, 'Hi. Remember me?' Thankfully, she did. We had a drink and chatted and I learned that she was working at a business advisory firm in the administration department, and was there that night with some of her work-mates having after-work drinks. Later that night I got her number.

I made sure I waited a couple of days before calling Anna and asking her for a date because I didn't want to come across as overly keen. We went to an Italian restaurant called Casa Mia, located in North Adelaide, and Malcolm Amos looked after us there. Most of the visiting teams go there for dinner when they play in Adelaide for Sheffield Shield matches. Malcolm put on a delicious spread, and over a glass or two of wine, Anna and I chatted easily and enjoyed each other's company. Following dinner, we went to a pub up the road called The Lion and after that we ended up in the city at a place called The Elephant and Wheelbarrow. It was a lovely first night out, and things progressed steadily from there. To be honest, I was basically 'gone' after that first date; I thought, *I can't do any better than her!*

Getting back into the Australian side

During my summer of rehabilitation, the Aussie guys were playing in Tests against Pakistan and India. Although I kept an eye on things, I didn't watch a hell of a lot of the action on television. I did try to distance myself, but when the Adelaide Test was on, I popped in to say g'day to the guys. I felt slightly uncomfortable and didn't stay too long; I only wanted to say hi and check in with Errol Alcott to let him know how I was going. At the Adelaide Oval, the back of the Members' Stand is a popular spot for a beer, and I headed out there for a couple of frosties to help ease the pain of not playing in a Test on my home ground.

After a while I started to bowl off a few steps, and things felt fine. Crouchy, Julie Knight and Errol all told me simply to trust my training and back myself. They said, 'You've done all the hard work; ease into it, and given your leg is all healed, you'll be fine.' I started to bowl, then, and slowly increased my workload week by week. I took my time and kept up the Versa along with stationary-bike training. Things haven't changed that much: I still hop on the bike and also do a lot of Versa work. I've never done a great deal of extra running. By playing and training all the time, I think I get enough running. Bowling in the nets along with participating in the fielding sessions we do; it all adds up.

When I got back into Grade cricket, I played as a batsman in the A grade. I then started to bowl a few overs here and there till I was fit enough to be considered to return to South Australia. I got back in against Tasmania for the second-last game of the 1999–2000 season. I was happy with my return and was delighted to get seven wickets in the two games.

Out comes the rod

It was hard work returning to four-day cricket, and I needed to chew a few Panadeine Fortes to get through the matches. Prescribed pain killers were a help in taking the edge off the aches and pains in my leg, and I still had the rod in. Once I had those games under my belt, I had to head back into hospital to have the rod taken out, a procedure that required an overnight stay.

Dr Kevin Angel, the orthopedic surgeon, was to remove the rod through my patella tendon (knee). He must have done a few of the operations because he was as cool as a cucumber when he mentioned that I'd probably suffer from patella tendonitis for the rest of my career. At that comment, my jaw dropped. There was no backing out of the operation, however. The doctors pulled out the 40-centimetre rod without any worries, and the lump and a few scars remain visible to this day. My leg was sore for a week or so, which meant I had to delay my trip to England to play for Rishton in the Lancashire League. Thankfully, I haven't had the tendonitis and have had no concerns about it.

A stint with Rishton

My reason for heading to Rishton for the English summer was simple: I'd had the entire summer off and I needed to get some bowling in the tank. I didn't think I was up to a season of County cricket, so thought the Lancashire League was the next-best alternative: I wouldn't have to bowl full tilt; I could ease back into the bowling; I could still train from Monday to Friday; and I could develop my strength and fitness. Good old Crouchy tracked down a gym in Rishton that had a Versa and shuttle — that's how committed he was to getting me right for the 2000–01 summer. He knew he wasn't able to supervise my training for five months but was kind enough to organise a training facility that was similar to what he had back at his gym in Adelaide.

The people at Rishton were fantastic. The secretary, John Simpson, picked me up from the airport and helped get me settled. Dave Lomas really assisted me in the early stages as well. Even though I under-achieved with the bat and made only 169 runs at 16.90, I was reasonably satisfied with my efforts with the ball there: I took 45 wickets at just 11.91. I should have scored more runs with the bat in what was a fantastic experience. The weather was okay, some of the pitches were quite impressive, and the ground at Rishton was one of my most favourite grounds to play on over there.

Those involved with the club were terrific, as were the lads I played with, but the flat I stayed in wasn't too flash. It was horrendous, actually: a small flat located above the house of a very nice couple. It was much too small but was convenient because it was over the road from the ground. Greg Blewett had played there in 1993 and his advice to me was this: 'If they put you up in the flat, don't stay there; go and get your own place.' It did the job for a while, but I needed to find another place because Anna was coming over. The two of us hadn't been seeing each other for long, so it was a fair step in our relationship. It was necessary to find somewhere nicer to live before she arrived.

I ended up in the next town, Great Harwood — about 5 kilometres away. One of the lads at the club had a house in Spain and was heading over there for a while, so offered me his place for a few months. His house had two levels — although the upstairs was only a loft that we used as the bedroom — but at least there was more room there.

I didn't realise how much I liked Anna until we were apart. I really missed her company, so I flew her over for four weeks. Not only were we still in the early stages of our relationship, Anna hadn't been out of Australia before so it was a big deal for her. Anna fitted in well at the club and got a taste for Budweiser.

While we were in England, we took the opportunity to go to Paris for a short trip, which at the time was disastrous although we laugh about it now. Our luggage was lost on the way over, the hotel room was tiny and it rained the whole time but we did get to Euro Disney (Disneyland), which was a lot of fun. Somehow I managed to eat something dodgy and was sick as a dog for a week after we got back. I was really embarrassed because we hadn't been together that long, but Anna took it all in her stride and nursed me back to health.

After the Rishton experience, I had to come back to Australia for the one-day series against South Africa at the Docklands Stadium in Melbourne. I decided against heading back to the UK to resume the arrangement with Rishton because in the three months I'd been there I'd got what I needed out of it. That suited Rishton, too, because they saved a few bucks by getting sub-pros in each week rather than paying to fly me back.

I was as pleased as punch to be selected to play for Australia again. The half season at Rishton had been enough to top up my bowling. Before I headed back to Oz, I had a final catch-up day with the team in Blackpool and had a couple of drinks. It was on a weekday, so some of the lads had to take a day off work. We had a nice lunch and enjoyed the amusement park there. The lads put a few pounds together and presented me with a spirit holder as their token of appreciation for my time at the club.

Against South Africa, Melbourne, 16, 18 and 20 August 2000

It was then back to Melbourne for three 50-over matches against South Africa at the indoor stadium at Docklands. The series was played in August, during the Melbourne winter, at the tail-end of the AFL season. The outfield wasn't in the greatest condition, and my hamstring had some problems because of it. Also, the ground was slightly loose and had some give in it. The condition of the run-ups was far from perfect, and it wasn't any easier having a drop-in wicket.

Batsmen always seem to get looked after, but we bowlers often cop a raw deal. We had to run in on a 'corrugated iron' surface that had only recently been used for footy, so the contest wasn't exactly fair and even. We won the first game, thanks to hundreds by Steve Waugh and Michael Bevan, then we tied the second and lost the third, so everything ended up all-square. I missed the first game, got three wickets in the tied match and none in the third. As luck had it, I bowled okay.

Above all, I was glad to be back in the side after almost 12 months away because of the collision in Sri Lanka. It was then time for me to head back to Adelaide to prepare for the coming summer.

A few days before the first Test against the West Indies, the Redbacks played a one-day match against New South Wales at North Sydney Oval after the four-day match had been washed out without a ball having been bowled. While I was fielding on the boundary I dived to stop a ball and felt my right hamstring tweak. While I was still warm, I managed to bowl a few overs late in the game and could still run around okay, but I knew deep down that something was up. I flew from Sydney to Brisbane to get Errol Alcott to assess the situation. Clearly there was no way I was fit enough to play. When I went to the nets, although I could bowl off a few steps, I couldn't bowl off my full run because of the twinge.

We won the Test by an innings and 126 runs inside three days: a far cry from the famous tie of 1960, 40 years previously. Once again, I suffered the disappointment of being unable to participate in a sensational victory. On the plus side, by resting and having the appropriate treatment, I managed to prove my fitness for the next Test in Perth, which was to start the following week.

Against the Windies, Perth, 1–3 December 2000

AGAIN THE WEST INDIES STRUGGLED WITH THE BAT, AND WE bowled them out for only 196. If it hadn't been for a 96 from keeper Ridley Jacobs, the game might well have been a repeat of the Gabba, when we knocked over the Windies for 82. Glenn McGrath picked up a hat-trick before lunch, and I managed to pick up the last three wickets of the innings.

When it came our turn to bat late on the opening day, I had to head in as nightwatchman. The following morning when I was batting, I got a short ball down the leg side, and gloved it to the keeper. The Windies all went up for the catch, but luck was smiling on me and the umpire said, 'Not out.' Shortly afterwards the fielders asked me whether I'd touched it. My answer was 'Yes'. In fighting terms, I'd boxed it to the keeper. Mark Waugh made 119 and we again had a robust lead, declaring on eight for 396 — 200 ahead. Again the West Indies were terrible: they made only 173, so we had another innings victory and a 2–nil lead. In the second innings, I took one wicket to add to my three in the first, so was happy with my efforts in my first Test in more than 12 months.

Against the Windies, Adelaide, 15–19 December

In the Adelaide Test match, things changed because the 'real' Brian Lara turned up. To that point, he'd made scores of 0, 4, 0 and 17 — hardly a good result for one of the world's finest batsmen. People were suggesting that his extracurricular activities were affecting his game — understandable given that he always seemed to have a young, buxom blonde on his arm.

In the tour game leading into the Adelaide Test, the Windies went to Hobart for a match against Australia A. Lara found his touch — he made 231 — and it seemed this innings was a springboard for a return to form in the Test arena.

It was hot, we lost the toss and we had to field. I managed to pick up the first three wickets, and at 3/86 it looked as if we might knock the opposition over easily for the fifth time in a row. Sure enough, Brian Lara came back from the wilderness and made a brilliant 136 on the opening day. At one stage, he hit me for three fours in a row; he made all the bowlers look second rate that day. Jimmy Adams played the sheet-anchor role in their partnership of 183, very much as he'd done in Bridgetown five years previously. I managed to get him with the second new ball late in the day, and the Windies finished on 4/274.

Early on the second day, I dismissed Merv Dillon, gaining my first 'five-for' in a Test on the Adelaide Oval. It was the first of a three-part goal I'd set myself to achieve in Test cricket: to get five wickets in an innings on my home ground, at the MCG and at Lord's. Little could I have imagined at the time that I was to achieve that goal within only 18 months.

Brian Lara finished with 182 and the West Indies ended on 391. Colin Miller knocked over the last five wickets to get himself a 'five-for' as well. Funky bowled really well, turned the ball a bit and was difficult to play, given the pace he bowls. We made 403, so had a lead of 12 and had set the Test up for a highly respectable finish.

There was a touch of controversy because of a collision between Stuart MacGill and the West Indies' twelfth man, Ramnaresh Sarwan. It was simply a right-of-way situation. Stuie had just been dismissed and was walking off when Sarwan was heading out to take some drinks to his teammates. After you walk through the players' gate, you walk through rows of seats before using a small footpath that leads into the steps of the Members' Stand and into the dressing rooms. Rather than wait for Stuie to come up, Sarwan headed off, and it was near the top of the small footpath that the collision occurred.

Now, Stuie can succumb to tunnel-vision from time to time. He would have been trying to get off quickly after being dismissed and wouldn't have meant anything by colliding with an opposition team member; he's just a particularly focused guy. If Sarwan had waited on the footpath for Stuart to go past, as I feel he should have, the players wouldn't have collided. It was the media rather than the players who made so much fuss about the incident.

In the Windies' second dig, we felt we had Daren Ganga caught behind off Colin Miller but umpire Venkat said, 'Not out,' and we carried on with the game. Not long afterwards Ganga played a ball to mid-wicket and Ricky Ponting threw it hard to Adam Gilchrist. Ganga had to get out of the way quickly to avoid being hit. Brian Lara made a bit of a deal about the action, but again we felt there was nothing in it. These two were batting quite well, and I always think that when Australia is frustrated we do that 'let them know you're there' sort of stuff. Ricky was probably grumpy that Ganga wasn't given out and wanted to send a message to him, to let him know, 'We're still out here: just because you've been out here for a while doesn't mean it's gonna get any easier.'

Eventually, Funky got Ganga and Lara out. Then the rest of the opposition fell like a pack of cards and their team were all out for 141, so had set us 130 to win. Funky picked up another five wickets to make it 10 for the game, and was named Man of the Match, ahead of Lara.

Chasing small targets can be tricky, and we were 4/48, but eventually we got there five down, early on the final day. We'd wrapped up the series 3–nil and still had the MCG and the SCG left to play at.

Reflecting on that Test, I thought it was pretty cool to get 'five-for' on my home track; however, to see my name on the honour board in the rooms along with Funky's was truly special because he's one of my very good friends in cricket.

Against the Windies, Melbourne, 26–29 December 2000

THE MELBOURNE TEST FOLLOWED MUCH THE SAME PATTERN AS the first two Tests. We made 364 and the Windies scored 165 — narrowly avoiding the follow-on. After we'd set them 462 to win, we had a few overs at them late on day three. I managed to pick up three wickets, one of which was Brian Lara for a duck.

You always pride yourself on bowling well to the outstanding players. I was lucky he misread that delivery: it was fairly straight but nipped back a tiny bit; he left it and the ball just clipped off-stump. You could say it was one of the best balls I'd ever bowled, but there was a degree of batsman error as well. You take those pieces of luck, however.

The next day, I had six for not many, and it looked as if I was a chance to take the lot. I'd be lying if I said it wasn't on my mind to take them all. I wasn't bowling anything special, only concentrating on hitting my areas; the ball was just doing enough, which is better than having it do too much. It was one of those peak times in my career, a moment when everything seemed to go my way. I got Colin Stuart out with a slower ball full toss; he didn't pick it up and was plumb lbw. When things aren't going your way, that sort of ball gets dispatched for four or six, but when it is, that sort of luck goes with you.

Colin Miller dismissed Marlon Samuels to break the sequence, and we wrapped up the match shortly afterwards to make it 4–nil. I'd narrowly missed out on 10 wickets in the game, and finished with a match figure of 9/88.

Against the Windies, Sydney, 2–6 January 2001

In Sydney, the West Indies started well: they added 147 for the first wicket but collapsed to be all out for 272. We made 452 for another big lead, but the Windies showed heaps of bottle in the second innings to make 352, and set up a tricky target of 173 to clean sweep the series 5–nil.

I only got two wickets in the match, off consecutive balls in the second innings. The ball was reverse swinging a bit at the time, and I got Campbell caught behind then Samuels lbw. Again it was a case of 'When you're hot, you're hot.' I aimed for an out-swinger, which Sherwin edged, and then went for an 'innie', which trapped Marlon. I considered I'd almost bowled at my best for the summer in that Test but didn't reap the same rewards as I'd had in Melbourne.

Michael Slater made 86 not out, so got us home by six wickets. To beat the opposition 5–nil and so comprehensively was fantastic. To finish the series with 20 wickets at just 18.4 was enough to make me proud but there was icing on the cake still to come when I was presented with the Alan Davidson Medal. Alan is a thoroughly nice fellow and was such a great player. To win an award named after him was an honour.

Looking back, I felt that things were going well, and I was happy to be part of the team again. However, I never felt really settled and fully comfortable in it. Perhaps that was a good thing, because I had to continue to strive so I kept improving and made sure of my spot in the team. The 2000–01 summer was fantastic, however, and went a long way to make up for what had happened in Sri Lanka in 1999.

8 In India and England, 2001

The Carlton One Day Series had been lined up to follow our 5–nil demolition of the West Indies. Plagued by hamstring problems, I didn't play in any of the matches. My goal was to be at full fitness for the Indian tour in one month's time. Fortunately, the hamstring came good and I was picked for the trip.

Heading into that series, we'd won 15 Tests on the trot and we were keen to add India to our sequence of victories. Because no Aussie team had won a series there since 1969–70, we knew we were in for some tough work. Although the Indians had beaten Zimbabwe only 1–nil in a two-match series before Christmas, we knew they'd be especially hard to beat on their home track, in front of their passionate supporters.

Arriving in India is an experience in itself. Once you get off the plane and head through Customs, you go to get your trolley and immediately notice everyone staring at you. It's like you're a rock star, because the Indians are mad about cricket and become pretty excited when a team arrives. When you've gone through Customs, collected your luggage and headed outside to the bus, it doesn't matter what time of the day it is: you see people everywhere; it could be two in the morning, but it doesn't matter: swarms of people just want to get a quick glimpse of the Australian cricket team. Some of the people you see mightn't have anywhere else to go, which is sad, but they're part of an enormous group who are the world's keenest cricket fans.

On the way to the hotel, you get glimpses of how people live. Some might live in a little tin shelter — not the best of circumstances. You see rubbish on the side of the road and kids playing in it — it's not all that healthy but that's the reality of life in India. Although it's all quite depressing, you can't do much about it because the extent of the poverty is overwhelming.

Against India A, 17–19 February 2001

THE FIRST GAME OF THE TOUR, AGAINST INDIA A, TOOK PLACE at the Vidarbha Cricket Ground in Nagpur. We batted first and were in all sorts of bother at 7/133. I was joined at the crease by Michael Kasprowicz, and we started to put together a partnership.

The bat I was using belonged to Justin 'JL' ('Alfie') Langer, and there's a story surrounding it. Prior to the tour, I'd been given two bats by my then sponsor Kookaburra. However, I'd brought one bat for the tour because I'd left the other behind for the Ashes and thought I wouldn't bat much on the tour — how that situation was about to change! JL had an Indian bat but wasn't using it. It had a distinct bow in it, but I liked the look of it. JL offered me the use of his Indian, which I accepted, and because I had a spare set of stickers from Kookaburra, I used them on the piece of Indian willow. It was a classy bat and felt really good from the word go. In that match, I made 57 and Kasper made 92 using his Gabba-brand bat.

It was a tough track to bat on: low, slow and spinning slightly. Kasper and I simply played to our strengths. He was the one who had all the shots: he cut, drove, swept and pulled while I nudged them around. We put on a formidable partnership. It was incredibly hot, however, which made it satisfying to score those runs when the team was in trouble during the match.

That match was our first look at Harbhajan, and there was no indication at all that he would take 32 wickets in the three-Test series. He took five wickets in that tour game, and his bowling gave none of us reason to suspect he'd have so big an impact. Harbhajan fully deserved his success and he was one of the reasons why India ended up beating us.

We managed to draw that game, and I was rested from the match against Mumbai at the Brabourne Stadium, a match that was also drawn.

The Don passes

On the eve of the first Test, to be played at the Wankhede Stadium in Mumbai, news broke that Sir Donald Bradman had died in Adelaide — cause for mourning, beyond doubt, but at 92, he'd certainly had a pretty good 'knock'. Although I hadn't had the privilege of meeting him, it was sad to hear that he'd died. His passing made the front page of all the Indian newspapers and led the TV news bulletins.

Despite Bradman's influence on the game, though, Tendulkar is the Indian cricket god — no doubt about that.

First Test against India, Mumbai, 27 February–1 March 2001

In our team meeting before the Test, rather than focus on the opposition, we concentrated on what we needed to do. If we had picked up that there was some obvious weakness in an opposing batsman, we mentioned it, but generally we concerned ourselves with making sure we stuck to our plans. For the bowlers, we decided we should bowl a foot outside off-stump and try to restrict the opposition scoring range to one side of the wicket. The idea was to try to frustrate them, be patient and wait for them to make a mistake. Looking back now, I think it might have been the wrong way to go. However, it went okay in the first Test, because we managed to get a lot of nicks and catches behind the wicket.

We bowled first and early in the match found the pitch helpful because it had a bit of pace and bounce in it, and suited me, Glenn and Damien Fleming. Before the game, Indian captain Sourav Ganguly had suggested the groundsmen prepare slow turners for the series, but the Wankhede groundsman decided he wanted to produce a track on which everyone, fast bowlers included, would have a chance to do well.

Although Sachin made 76, he received precious little support. We knocked India over for only 176, and Glenn had the remarkable figures of 19 overs, 13 maidens, 3 for 19. I managed to pick up two wickets; Flemmo got one; and Warnie mopped up the tail, getting four. Poor old Ajit Agarkar made another duck against us; he seemed to have no idea, and was caught and bowled so it was six ducks in a row in Tests against Australia.

We lost only one wicket before stumps and were therefore in a strong position at the end of the series' opening day. Things changed incredibly quickly on day two, when we collapsed to be 5/99. Both Mark Waugh and Ricky Ponting were knocked over by Harbhajan for ducks, and India was suddenly back in the match. Adam Gilchrist came in to join Matthew Hayden, and they rescued us with a partnership of 197 for the sixth wicket. Both of them made hundreds and took us from a precarious position into a strong one in only a couple of hours.

Gilly took 15 balls to get off the mark, but once he'd taken them, he just played his normal attacking game and scored freely. Matty had a plan to tackle the Indian spinners, and it came off, so the number of hours he'd put in before the Test were justified — he'd practised the sweep shot a heap — and he wasn't frightened to take on the spinners by 'hitting them over the top'. He certainly reaped the benefits, as did the team, and thanks to Gilly's and Matty's massive partnership, we got a lead of 173. Gilly got stuck into the spinners, hitting 4 sixes and 15 fours. To that point, it would have been one of the most important innings he'd ever played for Australia in a Test match. For Matty personally, that dazzling performance proved to be a springboard for a tremendous series with the bat and yielded more than 500 runs at a Bradman-like average of more than 100.

This was my first Test on Indian soil, and even though we bowled India out for only 176 and 219, the conditions were stunningly hot, humid and uncomfortable. Steve looked after the bowlers as best he could, using us in reasonably short spells. The ball loses its shine relatively early in the piece because it tends to scuff up a lot quicker, but it now started to reverse swing a bit and went quite well. The dry and dusty outfields cause the ball to hack up more, so once it lost its original shine, the idea was to keep one side as smooth as possible and let the other go rough so it would reverse.

Sachin Tendulkar made 65 in the second innings, but again the Indians' batting was disappointing and they set us only 47 to win. Rahul Dravid batted for a while, making 39, and there was a certain amount of controversy involving a catch taken by Michael Slater. Dravid pulled a short one from Flemmo, and Slats ran in, dived forward and took, in his mind, a clean catch. Neither umpire on the ground was prepared to make a decision, so it was referred upstairs for the third umpire to decide. The eventual decision was not out, and from there things got a bit ugly. Slats went over to umpire Venkat to let him know in no uncertain terms that he was sure he'd taken the catch. He believed he'd caught the ball, and felt that

Dravid should have taken his word and walked off. Dravid decided to leave it to the umpires and was well within his rights to do so. Slats might well have gone over the top with his actions but was annoyed that his integrity was being questioned; that pissed him off more than anything.

Once the decision was made, Steve told Slats to calm down. After the day's play, Dravid and Slats had a chat and sorted it out. Dravid accepted what Slats said, and they had a laugh about the incident afterwards. Dravid is a good guy and understood the pressure of the situation. Once again, the journalists' take on things tended to be over the top; without reporters having real knowledge of what had taken place, some pretty strong judgements surfaced in the media, none of which cast Michael in an especially good light. Because Michael's such an expressive fellow, the incident had looked a great deal worse than it actually was, so unfortunately he was on the receiving end of more criticism than he deserved. The cameras can zoom in on an incident pretty closely, and things that occur between the players out on the ground can look a bit more ugly than they actually are.

After things settled down, we went on to win the Test by 10 wickets, which was a magnificent effort. We'd gone at them hard, stuck to our game plan and gained a 1–nil lead in the series.

Second Test, Kolkata, 11–15 March 2001

After playing in a tour game in Delhi, we headed for Kolkata — formerly Calcutta — for the second Test. The Eden Gardens ground can hold about 100,000 people and was jam-packed for the start of the match. We won the toss and batted, and at tea, things were looking rosy: the score was 1/193, and Matty Hayden and Justin Langer were going well. After tea, though, Matty got out straight away for 97, and thanks to a Harbhajan hat-trick, we were in a bit of trouble on 8/269 just before stumps. The

'Turbanator' might have been a fraction lucky, because it seemed his third victim, Shane Warne, might have hit the ball into the ground when he was caught at short leg; however, the TV umpire thought otherwise, and he was given out, so Harbhajan was the first Indian to take a hat-trick in a Test match.

I went in to bat. Steve Waugh was still there, and the first thought was to just get through till stumps. I faced about 47 balls and managed to get through. We ended up at 8/291, which was a disappointing score because we'd been 1/193.

Early on the second day, I nicked one behind to the keeper off Prasad and was given not out. It was a big edge: the keeper had had to dive way to his right, and I couldn't believe my luck when umpire Bansal gave it not out. The fact that I hadn't looked behind or flinched or reacted must have been of help in my survival because afterwards in the rooms the lads said I'd pulled the best poker face ever. All the Indians couldn't believe it either, and after the over, they would have seen I had a stupid grin on my face because I'd been so fortunate to survive. It was a lucky break because we would have been 9/300 — a pretty poor effort given we'd had first use of the pitch.

Facing Harbhajan Singh was a challenge. My stance was a bit different from the basic 'one foot either side of the popping crease'. I decided to bat deep in my crease on off-stump. Every now and again, I batted in the usual position to try to upset my opponent's length. I didn't advance; I just stayed at home and used my crease. My best opportunity to score was to either wait for the short ball to pull or, if it was really full, try to drive through the off side. My job was to hang in for the established batsman and not take too many risks. If I'd been batting with a fellow tailender, I'd have been slightly more aggressive and played a few more shots, but I was in with Steve, so my job was to defend and score the odd run when I could.

Steve is usually a tremendously supportive person to bat with. He generally bats the right way with the tail, given he backs you in.

Reasonably early in the piece he lets you know that he'll take every run from the word go, and you're more confident as a result. In some games, though, there have been times when I thought he should have taken more responsibility and kept more of the strike. During the game in question, however, he backed me in and gave me some confidence, and I'm sure the tactic was helpful in our putting on that big partnership. I was happy with it and was positive I could handle it.

The figures were there for all to see: I scored 46, Steve made 110, and we put on 133, the highest Australian partnership for that wicket in 107 years. Glenn McGrath made 21, and he and Steve added 43 for the last wicket; they took us to 445, which was just above par on that pitch.

Yet again, conditions were extremely hot in that Test, and with the new ball we picked up some early breakthroughs before we knocked the opposition over for only 171. Glenn, after his cameo with the bat, took 4/18 from 14 overs, and the rest of us took two wickets each. Having bowled out our opponents inside the follow-on figures and in only 58.1 overs, we had to make a decision: *Do we send them in again, or should we bat again, get a massive lead, and try to bowl them out in a day-and-a-half?*

Michael Slater was dead against sending them in again; Slats wanted us to bat and set them a target. In hindsight, it's quite easy to say we should not have sent them back in. The longer I've played the game at this level, the more I've come to believe that if you have such a big advantage, you should bat again and bowl to victory in the last innings of the match, when the pitch is at its worst. At the time, in the rooms between innings, I thought that VVS Laxman (59) looked impressive in the first innings and when he came out to bat in the second innings at three, I could see he was in good nick straight away. In defence of the decision, I have to say that in the history of Test cricket to that point, not many matches had finished like this one. Hindsight is a wonderful thing, though, and occasionally you'd do things differently if you had your time over again.

At the time, I had no issues with enforcing the follow-on: maybe we'd become overconfident and got too far ahead of ourselves. Steve asked all the lads for their thoughts, and apart from Slats, everyone was keen to go out and have a crack at the opposition again straight away. Glenn was certainly keen, after the way he'd bowled in the first innings.

We were right into the Indians, too, and when I dismissed Sachin Tendulkar for 10, they were 3/115 — still 159 runs behind. At that point, it seemed as though it was only a matter of when. However, Sourav Ganguly came in and had a handy partnership with Laxman, and they added 117 — and then came the combination by which the series would be completely turned around.

Laxman and Dravid's partnership of 376 for the fifth wicket would have to be one of the greatest efforts in Test cricket of all time. We were bowling a foot outside off, but as I've mentioned, your chances of getting a 'bowled and lbw' dismissal are taken out. Looking back, it's plain to see that we should have attacked the stumps more. However, we based our plan on bowling away from off-stump with a view to drying up the boundaries and making our opponents run more between the wickets. I've never been a fan of the 7–2 off-side fields, and at this time the tactic clearly didn't work.

I'll never forget when Warnie was bowling to Laxman from around the wicket and kept getting hit in the air over mid-wicket: it was sensational batting and one of those times you simply have to give credit when it's due. Dravid played more of a sheet-anchor role but was equally as hard to get rid of. The opposition batted through the entire fourth day and took the score from 4/254 (20 behind) to 4/589 (315 ahead), so put themselves in a very good position. We used nine bowlers that day, and Slats and even Justin Langer had a bowl late in the day to try to give the regular bowlers a rest.

Eventually we dismissed Laxman for 281, and probably that had more to do with tiredness than anything else. Finally, 13 overs into the day, the Indians declared at 7/657. Dravid finished with 180, and it took a run-out to dislodge him. All the main bowlers went for more than 100: McGrath got 3/103 from 39 overs, I bowled 31 for 2/115, Kasper got 0/139 from 35, and Warnie pushed through 34 overs for 1/152.

We ended up getting set 384 in 75 overs. After being 1/106, we collapsed and were all out for 212, to lose the Test. Harbhajan went through us to get six wickets, making it 13 for the match, and Sachin Tendulkar took three, including Adam Gilchrist, who made a 'king' pair. From being so far in front in a game and on the verge of winning the series, we found it pretty disappointing to lose the match.

Third Test, Chennai, 18–22 March 2001

THERE WAS LITTLE TIME TO THINK ABOUT THINGS AS WE HEADED to Chennai for the deciding game, which was to start only three days after the stunning Kolkata Test.

Once again we batted first, and Matty Hayden proceeded to play as good an innings as you'd wish to see. He made 203 and was last out in our total of 391. Matty hit 6 sixes and was in total command of the Indian attack. He didn't get much support: we were 3/340 before the middle and lower order collapsed in a heap. Harbhajan took our last seven wickets for 51 runs. It was a disappointing effort, and I felt extremely guilty when I was dismissed, because I'd tried to slog-sweep Harbhajan and got caught. I broke my own rules of batting by trying a shot I shouldn't have tried to play; I should have been looking to bat as I'd done in the previous Test with Steve Waugh: bat defensively and try to support the top-order batsman up the other end. I had a rush of blood and made an unnecessary mistake. All it would have taken was someone to have made a 20 or 30, and we would have made 450 or 460 and found ourselves in a much stronger position.

In reply India played steadily: they made 501 and took a lead of 110. After his twin failures in Kolkata, Sachin Tendulkar found form: he made 126 and four of the team's other top six batsmen passed 60. It was a particularly tough wicket to bowl on because there was no movement at all out of the track. There was a bit of reverse swing at times but little other help for us. We tried to either put some maidens together or concede only one or two runs. It's incredibly hard to bowl maidens on the subcontinent, so the more of those overs you can bowl, the better, in a bid to put on a reasonable amount of pressure. We deserve credit for restricting the Indian batters to just on three runs per over; we bowled 41 maidens in 165 overs, so stuck to our game plan as best as we could. There was so little margin for error, and because of the fast outfields, it was a bloody slog.

When we batted again, the pitch was really starting to turn: Zaheer Khan took the new ball with Sourav Ganguly. Ganguly bowled only one over before Harbhajan came on, and Zaheer bowled a four-over spell, his only turn at the crease in the innings.

We were off to an outstanding start in making 82 for the first wicket. Then Matty Hayden was dismissed and Adam Gilchrist was sent in at number three in a bid to up the scoring rate. After his great ton in Mumbai, Gilly had made nil, nil and 1, and given he can score quickly it was thought that sending him in against a newer ball might be a good idea. Sadly for Gilly, he went for just a single: Harbhajan nailed him for the third time in four innings. From there, it was a struggle for runs and early on the final day we were all out for 264, an advantage of 154.

It was puzzling trying to figure out what had happened with Gilly. Players can suffer bad patches; he'd started in a blaze of glory by getting a ton in Mumbai and then suddenly he couldn't make a run. It certainly didn't affect his keeping: his achievements were top of the range in trying conditions. There was nothing technical we could pick up; it was just one of those things that sometimes happens in the game.

THE INDIANS NEEDED ONLY 155, SO WE HAD TO BOWL AT OUR absolute best to win the match and the series. They looked to be cruising to victory at 1/76. VVS Laxman was batting beautifully, but Ricky Ponting ran out Ramesh, and when I managed to get Sachin Tendulkar out for only 17, we got a bit of a sniff.

During that period on the last day, I bowled 10 or 12 overs straight and it was scorching hot. After the match, the photographer Hamish Blair was kind enough to say to me that it was one of the gutsiest spells he'd ever seen. After I got Tendulkar out, I had Ganguly nicking through slips and he was dropped, but fortunately I got him out shortly afterwards. That's one thing about my career that has annoyed me: I've had a few nicks go down. I've always felt I've had a bit of bad luck with the number of catches dropped in the slips off my bowling.

The atmosphere was awesome at Chennai on that last day, given the whole series hinged on what happened in that last couple of hours of play. The home crowd was going berserk and cheering every run the Indians made, and our supporters waving the flag, led by Luke Sparrow, were doing their utmost to even up the noise level when we took a wicket. Unfortunately for us, we couldn't quite get there.

For Harbhajan Singh to hit the winning runs was quite fitting, given he'd had such a wonderful series. Glenn McGrath was bowling at the time and tried to york him; it turned out to be a half volley that he squeezed out through point for a couple of runs, to see India home by two wickets. Although that was a low moment for us, we knew we'd given it everything in the field and really had a red-hot go at it. It was highly disappointing to go down so narrowly, but India had showed they were the better side.

Sensitivities

Several times during the series, India's skipper Sourav Ganguly annoyed our captain Steve Waugh for a couple of reasons: he either was late for the toss or didn't walk out with Steve to toss — a well-known protocol for skippers before a Test match. From our point of view, he appeared to be stirring the pot. I don't know why he acted that way — maybe he only came out when he wanted to come out or was living up to his nickname of 'The Prince of Calcutta'. Mind you, there was a big cultural difference between him and most of his teammates let alone between him and us. Although he was somewhat aloof, he didn't mind having a few words on the field if he thought he could upset us. Later in the series, he tried to show he could be a reasonably normal sort of bloke. At the conclusion of the third Test, he came into our dressing room: a big effort given that up to that stage we hadn't seen him off-field. I suppose he wanted to do the right thing and show his face. Some of the other Indian lads popped in, too. A few of us thought it was a bit rich given they'd just won a tight and tense Test; we were wondering where he'd been, and he hadn't been sighted after they'd lost the first Test. It's interesting, though: when you've played on the subcontinent, you realise the cricketers are a bit different over there.

In the case of the South Africans, the Kiwis and the Poms, what takes place on the field stays on the field. We Aussies can pretty much say what we like to them during the match, and still have a drink and socialise with those sides afterwards, having forgotten everything that happened on the ground. Everyone gets along fine and there are no issues. India and some of the other teams are a different kettle of fish. It seems it's not in their cultural make-up to behave that way. Now that we can see that, we Aussies have changed our ways; we've begun to understand our opponents slightly better and we are adjusting our behaviour and expectations accordingly.

Rahul Dravid was something of an exception and was one of the guys in the Indian team who understood how we played the game. He often had a few words on the ground, and we certainly admired him for the way he played the game. He'd played a bit around the world and was a well-rounded, well-travelled cricketer. He was happy to give as good as he got, and we never had any of these misunderstandings with him.

On the whole, I wonder if the Indian cricketers ever would want to fit in with that 'on-field enemies, off-field mates' approach that Aussies and players from some of the other cricketing nations share. The Indians sledge a bit, and a lot of what they say is in their native tongue. Whenever I noticed that kind of thing going on, I'd pipe up and say, 'Sledge me in a language I can understand.' At least that way, if it's something funny, I could have a bit of a laugh with them or have a crack back at them. Cultural differences occur everywhere, and no more so than in the cricket world, and we Aussies have definitely become a lot better at respecting the differences.

AFTER THAT TEST, WE WERE SCHEDULED TO PLAY A SERIES OF One Day Internationals, but I was spelled because of a problem I was having with my left foot. I was wearing a pair of hard orthotics that were causing me some aggravation, so Errol Alcott thought it would be wise for me to rest. I actually headed home before the end of the series, to give myself a chance to rest up for the all-important Ashes series that was only a few months away.

ALTHOUGH WE LOST THE INDIAN TEST SERIES 2–1 AFTER BEING up 1–nil and well on top in the second Test, the series was definitely one of the most exciting events I've been part of in my career. The cricket that was played was top quality, the crowds were sensational, and it was terrific just to be a part of it all.

Visiting Gallipoli

On our way to England for the 2001 Ashes series, we stopped off in Turkey and visited Gallipoli. The idea of visiting it came when our skipper Steve Waugh had dinner with Lieutenant-General Peter Cosgrove, who was the head of the Australian Army at the time.

It's hard to describe the place; you hear all these stories as a kid and try to understand them. You hear that a lot of soldiers died during the campaign and that it was a monumental stuff-up, and you can sympathise, but as a kid, all you want to do is hit a cricket ball and kick a footy. Those sorts of historical anecdotes don't have a massive impact early on in your life.

As you get older, you start to respect what the diggers went through more. Before we left Australia, I made the effort to do some research to refresh my memories about what happened at Gallipoli so that when I was there I could add to my understanding of what happened.

When we arrived, we had a full look around, with a female tour guide who took us on a proper tour of the war zone, and she became quite emotional when telling us about what happened there all those years ago. She told us about the battles, and mentioned that the Turks and Aussies threw food to each other at various times. We went through the bunkers that were on either side, and I found it quite bizarre actually being there. She told us about how the wounded and sick were looked after, and it made me incredibly proud to be an Aussie. It was an amazing experience, and I realised first hand how the loss of so many Australian lives there was such a senseless waste.

Knee troubles in England

After our visit to Gallipoli, we headed for the UK and were greeted at Heathrow by the usual gang of press reps waiting for us. Once we negotiated that scene, we headed for Worcester for our first tour match. I was rested from it but played in the one-dayers against Middlesex and Northants. To my dismay, my knee started to play up.

It was decided I should miss the opening matches of the NatWest One Day Series so I could get myself to full fitness. Thankfully, my knee slowly came right, thanks to treatment from Errol, and I was gradually able to bowl more and more in the nets.

My first bowl in the one-day series was against England in a day–nighter played at Old Trafford. It was a damp day, and we made only 7/208 from 48 overs.

I took the new ball with Glenn McGrath, and after he knocked over the openers, I managed to pick up three wickets as we stitched up the top order fairly easily. To get Alec Stewart and Michael Vaughan out for ducks was very pleasing; Stewart had been one of the mainstays of the team's order for a number of years, and Vaughan was in the early days of his International career. To knock England over for only 86 in that game was a fine effort, and we certainly gained a psychological advantage for later in the summer.

During the early stages of the tour, there was a problem with crowds running onto the ground. It wasn't as bad when we played England, but when we played Pakistan at Trent Bridge and Lord's, their supporters caused some hassles: at the end of the game they ran on to the ground at 100 miles an hour and the security guys did precious little. The ground stewards at most of the grounds couldn't have cared less about what was happening, and were mainly talking to their mates in the crowd. In general, the authorities seemed intent on simply counting the cash, and from our point of view, they weren't doing enough to protect everyone in the middle.

When Pakistan was batting in the match at Trent Bridge, the crowd was going nuts, and things came to a head when a firecracker lobbed on to the ground, very close to Brett Lee. When Brett said he didn't exactly feel safe after the incident, we consulted the umpires and headed off for 20 minutes to try to calm things down. After that, the game went on and we were beaten comfortably.

Against Pakistan, Lord's, 23 June 2001

It was a pretty ordinary effort by that crowd, but it was nothing compared with what happened in the NatWest Final against Pakistan at Lord's. We won the match by nine wickets in a pretty comprehensive performance. Unfortunately, the game will be remembered more for what happened afterwards. The security problem came to a head at the after-match ceremony when Michael Bevan, who was standing on the balcony, was struck in the face by a full beer can. The person who threw it must have had a great arm because it was an amazing throw and hit Bevo fair and square on the jaw. It hurt him and he was bruised, but he was more shocked than anything. The incident served as proof of what we'd been talking about; it showed that there was an issue with security. We were lucky Bevo copped it on the jaw rather than in the eye and wasn't forced to end his career there and then.

Our manager Steve Bernard had expressed his concerns to the authorities a number of times, so it was a shame it took something such as this incident for them to realise that action needed to be taken.

Against MCC and Essex, 25–27 June and 29 June–1 July 2001

The main reason we were in England was to retain the Ashes. We'd held them since 1989 and we intended to do everything in our power to make sure we kept them. We had two lead-up games before the first Test: one against the MCC at Arundel and the other against Essex at Chelmsford. I picked up a few wickets in the MCC game, and managed to get 5/37 against Essex. I bowled really well at Chelmsford: I knocked over Nasser Hussain for only 16 after he hooked me for six, and thankfully my knee didn't trouble me.

We could have enforced the follow-on, but our skipper Adam Gilchrist decided not to enforce it. Gilly had promised the bowlers we'd all get a good hit to top up for the first Test match. The Essex boys were somewhat annoyed, as were the crowd at Chelmsford, who gave us a hard time. I had a good long hit: I batted for a couple of hours for 22, and Brett Lee made 79; we put on a partnership of 61 to which I could contribute only two! Colin Miller scored 62, and even Glenn McGrath got 38, so all the lower order had the batting practice we'd been looking for.

On 'The Footy Show', London

In between the tour matches, Flemmo, Glenn and I went to London, where Channel Nine's 'Footy Show' was being filmed. Originally we were going to be watching but when Ian Botham, who was supposed to appear, became stuck on the motorway, we had to go on stage!

Prior to the show, we met Geri Halliwell backstage and around that time she was having a hit with the song, 'It's Raining Men'. When we were being interviewed, someone asked Flem what sort of music was played on the bus and in the rooms. Flem told the interviewers that we play some rock music and a bit of Aussie stuff, but then complained that Warnie loved dancing to Geri Halliwell, adding, 'How sad is that?' Wouldn't you know it but Geri Halliwell did a performance of 'It's Raining Men' on the show, which was pretty funny after Flem had bagged it. We all cried with laughter!

We got through the rest of our bit without any hassles and then watched the rest of the show from a balcony, all the while pulling faces at Warnie, who was on the panel on stage. Afterwards, a party was held in London at the Sports Cafe. We stayed at it for a couple of hours, mixing with all the 'Footy Show' lads and heaps of expat Aussies. It proved to be a brilliant afternoon.

From London, we headed off to Birmingham for the first Test. Damien Martyn was back in the mix for a spot in the top six after not playing in India, so someone would have to miss out. Justin Langer was the unlucky one, so Ricky Ponting was put back to number three after his stint at six in India.

First Ashes Test, Birmingham, 5–8 July 2001

Going from the hotel to the Edgbaston Ground for the first day of the first Ashes Test was an unusually casual affair. Flemmo and I kicked back at the rear of the bus and listened to music, some lads played cards, and others simply chatted away. I must admit I had hardly slept the night before. I was bursting with excitement, although I get excited before every Test!

We won the toss and decided to send the opposition in — a reasonably bold move on the opening morning of an Ashes series. I think Steve Waugh felt that because Ian Ward and Usman Afzaal were in the other team, they had a bit of inexperience in their line-up and it might be a good idea to try to put them under the pump straight away.

I managed to dismiss Marcus Trescothick with my first ball of the game. From there, though, Michael Atherton and Mark Butcher played well, and just before lunch, England were 1/106, so we thought we might have erred in sending them in to bat. However, in the over before lunch, Shane Warne picked up the wicket of Butcher, and after the break, I managed to get rid of Atherton for 57, just when he was starting to look dangerous. Their middle order fell in a heap, and when they were 9/191, we were pretty pleased about the fact we'd sent them in.

Then, however, Alec Stewart found an ally in Andy Caddick, and England added 103 for the last wicket and were able to finish on 294, still a bit short of par.

When we batted, Michael Slater set the tone: he smashed Darren Gough for 4 fours in the first over, and the rooms were really buzzing. It was such a positive start, remarkably similar to what Slats had done to Phil DeFreitas in the opening over of the Gabba Test in 1994–95. We finished the day on 2/133, and 427 runs had been scored in the day's play — not bad entertainment for the spectators.

On the second day, Steve Waugh cashed in on England's untidy bowling, and reached a hundred just before stumps. As always, Tugga was brutal outside off: he kept the good ones out and scored off his pads when given the chance.

THERE WAS HARDLY ANY PLAY AFTER TEA ON THE SECOND DAY OF that Test, because of rain. During those delays it can be a challenge to keep yourself occupied. Warnie, Pigeon, our team manager, Steve Bernard, and Punter always played cards, whereas most of the other boys sat around and listened to music and relaxed. Slats and Brett Lee had dusted off their guitars and were belting out some tunes; I noted that Slats was in need of some more practice that particular day. On the whole, though, I have to say that it can be frustrating sitting around waiting for the clouds to blow away.

Damien Martyn reached his ton on the third day and stuck to his game plan, which was to play very straight. He was in the second phase of his career. In his early days, he'd played flamboyantly and dynamically but been dropped after the Sydney Test against South Africa in 1994. After a lengthy absence, he'd started to play differently and become more measured and methodical. In all the years I've played with Damien, I'd rate him as the best timer of the ball I've ever seen.

Adam Gilchrist played a remarkable knock and really drove home the advantage, making 152. His batting with Glenn McGrath at the end of the innings was exciting to watch; Glenn scored only one run in a partnership of 53. We had 576 on the board and were in the box seat to go 1–nil up.

In the second innings, England again got into a reasonable position at 1/99 before they crumbled to be all out for 164. The wicket still had something in it; I remember that while bowling from the Pavilion end, the track had enough to keep the bowlers interested. I hit Nasser Hussain in the fingers, so he had to retire hurt and missed the subsequent two Tests. After that we coined the nickname for him of 'Poppadom Fingers', because he seemed to hurt his fingers or break them every time he got hit when he was batting — either that or his gloves were no good. In some ways, the recurrence of the injury was comical, but in reality it was rotten luck he had such brittle fingers.

I picked up three wickets in the second innings and felt really good bowling; it was a solid effort at the start of the series. After the match, Steve Waugh was kind enough to say he felt I was as good a bowler as he'd seen.

In the column that I was writing at the time for *The Independent on Sunday*, I took the bull by the horns and got stuck into England for the way they played. Here's an excerpt of what was published in the paper on the Sunday of that Test:

> *England can be a very good team, but they need to get some shit in them. You see reports about how they're aiming to compete with Australia. That's frogshit. When you're playing for your country, you should be trying to win, not trying to compete. Why play? They're going to cop flak ... anyway. They might as well go out swinging.*

The celebrations were plentiful and enjoyable. We didn't leave the change rooms till 9.30 p.m. and by then they were in an ugly state! Funky Miller was the star of the show at the local Walkabout Hotel later that night; he served behind the bar and tried his best to re-create scenes from the movie *Coyote Ugly*. It was a memorable night.

Watching Wimbledon!

HAVING WON THE TEST IN FOUR DAYS, WE WERE GIVEN THE opportunity to attend the Wimbledon Men's Singles Final between Pat Rafter and Goran Ivanisevic. The match had been delayed for a day, so we headed back to London, hoping Pat could break through and win his first Wimbledon singles title.

Tugga came up with the idea that to show support for our countryman, we should all wear the baggy green cap to the match. Although not everyone was keen on it, it was a case of 'If you wear it, I will', and in the end we all wore our caps. I must confess I felt a bit silly. Prior to the game our skipper went into the dressing rooms to wish Pat all the best on behalf of the lads. To attend a Wimbledon final was a real highlight. I was lucky to go again, in 2005, and we met Roger Federer in the rooms beforehand — a memorable experience. The match itself was an absolute epic, of the same calibre as the Bjorn Borg versus John McEnroe match of 1980. It ended up 8–6 in the fifth set. The atmosphere was electric, with heaps of Aussies there to cheer on Pat, but despite his valiant efforts the result didn't go in his favour. One day, I'd love to spend a few days at Wimbledon without having cricket get in the way.

Life at Lord's, and the second Ashes Test, 19–22 July 2001

I WAS STOKED TO BE FIT ENOUGH TO PLAY AT LORD'S, HAVING missed out in 1997 because of injury. To play in a Lord's Test will always rank as one of the high points of your career. It's amazing that Lord's is so successful a ground for the Australian Cricket Team. I think we lift because of the tradition of the place, the fact that it's the home of the game. However, I wouldn't say it's my favourite venue — although it has the best lunches going around, and its showers are sensational: each one has a massive head, which is excellent for recovering quickly after a long day in the field. What makes those lunches at Lord's phenomenal is the fabulous array of food to choose from. There are platters of peeled prawns with dipping sauce, three choices of main course, and sweets that can include strawberries and ice-cream.

The ground itself has a fair slope and so is unique. Bowling from the Nursery end, you get the impression the ball will shape away from the right-hander, because at that end the slope runs from your right to your left. I've always thought that the help you get at that end is a bit overrated. Over the years, Glenn has preferred the Pavilion end because the slope runs the other way and is of help to his off-cutter. I reckon it's all a myth, but on the odd occasion you do get the feeling the slope has a bit of impact.

AFTER ENGLAND HAD LOST SO EASILY AT EDGBASTON, THEY had a shocking lead-up to Lord's. Nasser Hussain was out injured and neither Alec Stewart nor Mark Butcher was keen to fill in the role, so the captaincy fell back to Michael Atherton, who'd given it away back in 1998. There's no doubt he wasn't keen to do the job, but no one else could do it. Perhaps with this in mind and because conditions were a bit overcast and quite dark, we sent England in to bat for the second Test match in a row.

England struggled in the play that was possible on that opening day, and finished on 4/121. We again stuck to our areas, and the wickets came before play was called off, before tea. I was bowling from Steve Bucknor's end. Although he doesn't say much, he has a fine sense of humour, so when he does have a chat, he usually leaves you with a smile on your face.

DURING ONE OF THE DELAYS, DUE TO RAIN AND BAD LIGHT, WE all met Her Majesty the Queen. One of the traditions at Lord's is for the Queen to meet the teams during the tea interval of the Ashes Test matches. When Funky Miller was introduced — surprise, surprise — she asked him about his pink hair (Funky changed his hair colour like most people change their underwear). Funky just laughed and continued with some small talk. The Queen showed that she also knew about another long-standing tradition. Fans of the 'Test Match Special' radio programme, broadcast on the BBC, have been sending cakes to those in the commentary box for many years, and that day the Queen presented the announcers with a cake to mark 40 years of Ashes commentary.

ON THE SECOND DAY, ENGLAND SHOWED LITTLE RESISTANCE and we knocked them over for 187. Glenn McGrath found his way on to the Lord's honour board by again taking 5/54, and I managed to take 2/56 — still a bit away from the coveted 'five-for' I'd been looking for.

This was the series in which the raising of the ball started after a five-wicket haul. Before the first Test, the bowlers on tour had a meeting and decided it was time we did something akin to what a batsman does after reaching a century. Consequently, raising the ball came in, and because Warnie had taken five at Edgbaston, Flem had done the same in the tour match at Somerset and Glenn had done it in the first innings at Lord's, we had built up momentum for our idea of getting acknowledgement for the bowlers' milestone.

In our innings, we lost a couple of early wickets before Mark 'Junior' Waugh began what turned out to be a gem of an innings. This knock was a special, high-quality one in which Junior played his role as a pure entertainer superbly. Over the years, he's been an interesting character and it always seemed that the main thing on his mind was to go out and bat with the sole purpose of entertaining the fans. Junior has always come across as a somewhat casual bloke, and you often got the impression that when there was no crowd, he might have suffered from lack of interest. This characteristic perhaps showed up after he finished his Test career and was playing for New South Wales in front of small crowds. On those occasions, he had no one to entertain — that might be why he didn't make many runs in his final season of First Class cricket.

Mark has always had all the shots in the book, but it's that flick shot from middle and off stumps that many people remember him for. It's an amazing cricket shot, one that no one else can play at that level. To be honest, I never really wanted to bowl to him in the nets, he was that good at times. I tried to bowl well outside off-stump to him and get him to play through the on side, hoping he'd miss it or edge in onto his stumps. Sometimes you could get him out early bowling straight, because he was often half asleep. Like I said, he's a pretty relaxed sort of bloke.

Although they're twins, Steve and Mark were total opposites as batsmen. With Mark, you bowl outside off, whereas with Steve, you aim at the stumps. You had to be much tighter to Steve, who was more an offside player than Mark, and so you had to bowl straighter to him. It was always excellent practice to bowl to the brothers in the nets.

On the third day, Gilly got stuck into the Poms in much the same vein as he'd displayed in Birmingham. He had a bit of luck on his side and was dropped several times in making 90. Butcher put him down on 13 at second slip off Darren Gough, a mistake that was extremely costly. We ended up with 401 and a lead of 214, so were put right on top at the halfway point of the game.

In the second innings, Butcher and Ramprakash were our only two opponents who showed any fight. I managed to pick up both of them on my way to figures of 5/53. I was pleased because I wanted to get my name on the honour board in that Lord's change room. I'd reached my goal of getting five wickets in an innings on the Adelaide Oval, at the MCG and at Lord's. Personally it was a very proud moment when I got to hold the ball up in the air to acknowledge the crowd. However, I felt a bit guilty because Mark Waugh had taken the catch to get my fifth wicket and in doing so had broken the world record for most catches in Test cricket. In raising the ball, I took a bit of the limelight away from Mark whereas he deserved most of the applause for breaking the record. I was a bit selfish, and if I'd been a bit more aware, I'd have taken more of a backseat.

We won the Test by eight wickets and had quite a few drinks afterwards to celebrate the win that put us up 2–nil. Although Mark had already made the honour board for his ton in the first innings, he managed to find a marker pen and some ankle tape so he could put it up on the board that he'd broken the record for most catches — not quite a hundred runs or five wickets, but a Test record at Lord's which was significant.

It was a special occasion and great to see some ex-Aussie players afterwards. Merv Hughes and Paul Reiffel were there with their tour group, and Ian Healy with his. It was good to have those guys over there and to catch up with them and seek their advice.

Third Test, Trent Bridge, 2–4 August 2001

Heading to Trent Bridge, we needed just one more win to regain the Ashes. England again had some fun and games with selection issues. Paceman Chris Silverwood pulled out at the last minute because of back strain, and his replacement, Alex Tudor, was struggling with stiffness in his side. Tudor lined up and was to have a fair impact in the match.

We also had a minor drama of our own: the so-called leaking of information that was for the Australian team's eyes only. I think the journalists made a mountain out of a molehill. It wasn't for their eyes but was accidentally put under someone else's door; surely they could have returned it knowing it wasn't for them to view.

The opening day of the Test was quite freaky in that 17 wickets fell. It was an overcast morning, and for the second Test in a row, Glenn took five wickets in the first innings. England's middle order gave them little: their team collapsed from 4/142 to 185 all out. We started well before Andy Caddick and Alex Tudor ripped through us, and at stumps we were 7/105 and in a fair bit of trouble.

England bowled extremely well, and Caddick had the most amazing spell in helpful conditions. I found him particularly tricky to face because he hit the bat quite hard and was pretty quick at times. His numbers on the radar didn't do justice to his pace. He hit his areas, and it was difficult to know whether to come forward or back to him. Late on that opening day, he was in the middle of a triumphal spell: he dismissed Steve Waugh, Damien Martyn and Shane Warne all in rapid succession. Alex Tudor finished with five wickets, having not played for England for two years.

Things brightened up on day two; the sun came out and conditions were slightly easier. However, Brett Lee got out early, so at 8/122 it was up to Gilly and me to put in some solid effort and try to get close to England's first-innings score.

They rightly believed they had us on toast. When I went in to bat with Gilly, I was really pumped up, thinking, *How did we get in this position?* We had to find a way to take the advantage back. I was facing the bowlers in the early stages of my innings and remember yelling to Gilly a few times, 'C'mon! Let's get into them!' I don't know what the England boys thought, seeing me facing up and getting all excited. For me, though, it was all about trying to get the positive vibe happening again. Also, I wanted to make it clear we were there to fight hard and make our opponents earn our last couple of wickets.

We added 66 for the ninth wicket and were put in the lead. Those runs proved to be surprisingly important in what turned out to be a low-scoring game.

In their second innings, England got to two for more than a hundred before they had another middle-order collapse. Mike Atherton's dismissal for 51 was the start of it, and by the end of play the opposition were 6/144. Warnie dismissed Craig White off the last ball of the day to take another five-wicket haul. Early on the third day, I quickly picked up three of the last four wickets including my hundredth in Test cricket — Caddick caught behind by Gilly — so we needed only 158 to retain the Ashes.

We didn't have any real worries chasing those runs, apart from when Steve Waugh's leg packed up. Watching from the rooms, we all thought his leg had been hit by a sniper or something. It was a pretty serious injury because he went off on a stretcher. Chasing small targets can be a worry, but we made the runs in only 29.2 overs. In winning the Ashes after 11 days of cricket, we showed up the difference between the two teams.

After the game, we all celebrated with a good guzzle. Unusually, we had to work out who should take home our second-innings ball, because I'd grabbed my hundredth wicket and Warnie had taken 6/33. Under normal circumstances, he'd have automatically received the ball. Everyone was asking, 'Who keeps the ball?' I strongly put my case forward, saying you get your hundredth Test wicket only once in your career, but Warnie insisted with equal passion that he was entitled to keep it. Up to that point, he'd had about 20 'five-fors', so had a bag of milestone balls. Anyway, as a more senior player he overruled me. His final words were, 'I got six wickets and I'm having it.' I was spewing — but in a good-natured way — but Shane, if you happen to find it, I want that ball back!

Post-Ashes, and a downer for Flemmo

With the Ashes all wrapped up, the English journos were suggesting we had it all over our opponents psychologically — especially Atherton, Butcher, Hussain, Thorpe and Stewart, all of whom had played quite a few series against us. For my part, I had a different view, though, because most of those guys had made runs against all the other nations. We totally respected all of them, and for me personally, to get any of those scalps was terrific. Atherton was always a prized wicket, and to get him out was awesome for me; I had the utmost respect for him. They were terrific servants for English cricket, but at certain times they couldn't quite do the job against us when it counted.

Every upside in the game has a downside, and for Damien Fleming it was a pretty tough tour, which was a pity. There was no way he was going to get a game, because the selectors seemed to want to keep Brett Lee in regardless of anything else. Binga wasn't bowling that well and also wasn't taking a heap of wickets, and was going for a few runs each over. He probably needed more time to be fully fit. It appeared he was still becoming match fit in the Tests, although I have my doubts about that. Early in Flemmo's career he had been earmarked for big things, and there's no doubt he's always been an outstanding talent. On that tour, he was coming back from injury; he was easing himself back in. Since playing the Test series in India, he hadn't been getting a game, and the frustration of that built up in him.

After the third Test, Flem played in a game against Sussex at Hove and looked like he was purely going through the motions. It seemed he wasn't really putting in, and at the end of the first day, over a beer, I asked him, 'What was going on out there today?' He replied, 'Well, I'm not going to get a look in because they'll play Binga no matter what.' I could see his point; historically the selectors were unlikely to change a winning side.

Flem had every justification for thinking that way. In the past there'd been precious few instances in which winning teams had been changed. It happened later in the series when Slats got dropped for Justin Langer.

At one point, Ricky Ponting said he got the feeling that Flem wasn't putting in, and when I heard him say it, I stuck up for Flem. Regardless, Ricky was convinced that Flem wasn't putting in. I could empathise with Flem because he knew he wouldn't be getting a game. Unfortunately, that's just how the cookie crumbles sometimes.

Fourth Test, Leeds, 16–20 August 2001

Steve Waugh was out injured for the fourth Test, to be played at Headingley, and Adam Gilchrist became skipper. We batted first, and Simon Katich made his Test debut. Ricky Ponting was under a bit of pressure because his last 10 innings had brought only 77 runs. He'd had a tough tour of India, and to date he hadn't done much in England. His luck was about to change, because he survived an appeal for a catch at third slip from the third ball he'd faced, and went on to make a brilliant 144. Damien Martyn also made a ton and with 447 on the board, we looked well on our way to winning 4–nil.

England made 309, and in another superb performance, Glenn McGrath took another seven wickets. We had a chance to build a big lead, but a rainy fourth day put paid to it. We therefore declared and set the opposition 315 to win on the last day.

We had them 2/33 and looked like we were going to make it 4–nil. However, Mark Butcher came out and played the innings of his life, and steered England to a six-wicket win. He'd never batted as well and he wouldn't get close to playing as well again. I don't want to take credit away from him, because he fully deserved it. We tried everything possible: we bowled over and around, bowled him bumpers and then went back to bowling good length. He smashed us all over Headingley and with good support from Nasser Hussain and Mark Ramprakash, England won the match. We were disappointed because it was the end of our chance of a series whitewash. We'd felt that 315 would be a tough ask, and England did extremely well to win the game. The rain on the fourth day definitely caused a change in the game, because if we could have played on that day we'd have set our opponents 400 and put them out of the game. In the end, though, we were happy setting them that target and thought it'd be our best chance to win. We always tried to play the game for a result, and even more so when we already had the series sewn up.

About an hour after the game, a few of us ventured into England's rooms and were amazed to find that hardly anyone was left. I was reminded of the time I'd had a chat to Andy Caddick at the end of the 1997 Ashes series. England had just won narrowly at the Oval, and I asked Caddick where they were going to celebrate the win when they left the rooms. He replied that he was about to head off onto the motorway because he had to play for Somerset the following day. I found the lack of interest in celebrating quite baffling, because winning is one of the reasons you play and you must savour those special moments in your career. You can always have a game for your county, but winning a Test is special and you need to enjoy the victory. Mark Butcher had batted his heart out for England, yet just one hour after the game, hardly anyone was left to celebrate with him. Thankfully, Australia doesn't take that approach: we enjoy our win every time we have one.

Exit stage left for Slats

WE HAD ONLY A FEW DAYS' BREAK AFTER LEEDS AND HEADED TO the Oval for the final Test, keen to atone for our loss. Little did we realise that Michael Slater had played his last Test for Australia. Before the Test, we had a meeting out on the ground and there was a feeling of tension in the air. I didn't know the ins and outs of the situation, because I stay out of the more complex discussions, and simply play. However, I could tell something was brewing: the vibe on the bus was somehow different, and at the ground, the atmosphere didn't seem normal. At the meeting, it was announced that Slats was out of the team and that Alfie was back in. Slats was dreadfully upset and immediately said to the skipper, 'Tugga, tell them why I'm dropped; I'm happy for you to tell them why I'm dropped.' He was extremely emotional.

It appeared to me that the decision was related to off-field issues and had nothing to do with anything that had taken place on the field. Things became heated between Steve and Slats, and thankfully Gilly, the voice of reason, stepped in and said, 'Nothing can be resolved now; go and have a talk later.' Slats stood up, walked out with his gear and went straight back to the hotel. Warnie chased after him to check he was okay. It was all pretty dramatic.

My instinct was to get away from the place, so I grabbed Funky Miller and we went for a lap or two around the Oval, hoping things would have cooled down by the time we came back. Everyone felt slightly uncomfortable. Thankfully things had simmered down when Funky and I got back. It was a case of 'Shit, what's happened here?'

Personally, I hadn't noticed anything to suggest that Slats's behaviour off field had gotten out of hand. Slats is a unique personality, and I hadn't observed anything out of the ordinary till that morning the team was announced. I suppose he'd been smoking a bit — but that's not a big deal because some blokes can go through those sorts of phases.

Fifth Test, the Oval, London, 23–27 August 2001

Steve Waugh somehow overcame his injured calf and proved he was fit to play in what was to be his last Test match in England. He did the right thing by winning the toss, and Matty Hayden and Justin Langer got us off to a brilliant start.

It was the start of a period of some big opening stands, and from a bowler's point of view there's nothing better than seeing them. You get maximum rest, and scoreboard pressure is provided, through which opportunities are created in turn. Matty and Justin batted well: they added more than 158 and set things up beautifully for the rest of the innings. Alfie took his chance and ran with it, making a hundred. He had to retire hurt shortly after he reached it, because he was hit on the helmet, by Andy Caddick.

Tugga's unbeaten 157 in that match was testimony to how determined he was. After he was injured at Trent Bridge, he worked hard with Errol and got around-the-clock treatment in a bid to be fit for the Oval. Leading into the match, he never looked as if he'd make it, till Errol worked his magic. He really willed himself to play in what was to be his final Test in England. I think he felt he had to play, otherwise it would be an anti-climactic end to his career. Whether that was best for the team, I'm undecided, but he played well: we won, and he made a hundred in his last Test on English soil. By the end of his dig he could barely move and wasn't in the best shape. Nevertheless, for us to win by an innings and to win the series 4–1 was a high note for him to finish on, and no one can ever take that away from him.

Parting company with Kym

TOWARDS THE END OF THAT TOUR, UNBEKNOWN TO ME, MY manager, Kym Richardson, put a rather obscure advertisement in the papers back in Australia. It read, in part, *Jason Gillespie is now available for exclusivity, endorsements, advertising, speaking engagements, a role in a movie, etc.*

The ad was first brought to my attention by *The Australian* cricket writer Malcolm Conn. Looking for a comment on it, he slipped a copy of it under my door. He was surprised, and I couldn't believe it myself. As well as feeling let down, I was embarrassed. My place in the team was something I had to fight for, and never did I feel I had a mortgage on it. I didn't want my position in the team to be jeopardised because of something such as this ad. If Kym was keen to market his client, he should have done it in a more professional way.

I was so annoyed about it that I ended up having a heated phone conversation while on the team bus. By the end of the call, I was yelling so hard that everyone was looking back at me wondering, *What's made Dizzy so angry?*

It was inevitable what the outcome would be, and Kym and I parted company shortly after the altercation. That's all water under the bridge now; Kym is a nice fellow. He's since moved on. He went from being a former policeman who managed cricketers to being a politician. In all sincerity, I hope his new career works out for him.

In the final Test, I hadn't been able to get a wicket and had never really looked like I would. I'd been either too full or too short and was struggling unsuccessfully to find the balance. My areas had been poor. In my impatience to get home — and in my private life I had so much to get home for — maybe my foot had slipped off the gas slightly. After being in India and then England, I was counting down the days to head back to Oz.

I'd finished with 19 wickets at 34, and having taken 17 in the first three Tests, I found the score a shade disappointing. However, at least I'd made it through a complete five-Test series for the first time in my career — and a comprehensively victorious one at that.

Anna had been in England for the final three Tests and we travelled to Amsterdam for a brief holiday before returning home. It was great to get away from everything and we caught up with Colin Miller and his then girlfriend, Christi, who was Dutch. We had planned to travel to New York as I've always wanted to see a live World Wrestling show but I was also really keen to get home so we cut our trip short. We arrived home on 6 September, five days before the devastation of the terrorist attacks on September 11, 2001.

A busy 2001–02

AFTER THAT LONG AND TIRING TOUR OF ENGLAND, IT WAS fantastic to come home and have a rest. Anna moved into my townhouse in Norwood at this time. We had been together for almost two years and things were going really well. The new season came around quickly enough, though, and before I knew it, I was playing in the Pura Cup for South Australia against Victoria at the Adelaide Oval (17–20 October). I bowled quite well in the season opener, picking up five wickets. After that match, we headed to Sydney to play against New South Wales (26–29 October).

We sent the Blues in on a moist pitch and knocked them over for only 188. I snared 8/50, the best figures in an innings on the ground by a South Aussie, since Tim Wall snared 10 for 36 back in the 1930s. Adding to the significance of the score, I got to play with Tim's grandson, Brett Swain, who bowled left-arm swingers for

South Australia. A further coincidence is that his now wife, Bec, was our masseur on the 2001 Ashes tour.

I bowled well and extracted a deal of help out of the track. It was decking around a bit, so I pitched the ball up a tad more than usual. I also bowled more at the stumps, and the result was that five of the eight dismissals were either bowled or leg before. To bowl out Mark Waugh was a highlight, especially on his home ground.

Unfortunately, our batting in reply was woeful: we were knocked over for just 142 and were back bowling again that night. To rub salt into the wound, I thought I had Michael Slater plumb lbw, but it was given not out. Had I picked him up, I would have had nine wickets on the day, which would have been a decent sort of effort. At least in the second innings I picked up another two wickets to snare my only 10-wicket haul in First Class cricket. Glenn McGrath was the last of the 10, so to get him out for the milestone wicket gave me a kick.

After those two Pura Cup matches, my body was feeling quite good, although I had an issue with my back. My facet joint, in the lower back, was slightly on the sore side, so I had an injection to settle it down. Thankfully, the needle did the trick, and I was primed and ready to go for the summer ahead, when New Zealand and South Africa would be visiting for three Tests each.

ABOUT A MONTH OUT FROM THE FIRST TRANS-TASMAN TROPHY Test at the Gabba, former Queensland and Aussie Test batsman Peter Burge passed away without warning. As he'd also been an ICC match referee, we all wore a black armband for the match as a mark of respect. Before the first ball was bowled, we all stood out on the ground and paid tribute by having a minute's silence.

First Test against New Zealand, Brisbane, 8–12 November 2001

THERE WAS DRAMA IN THE FIRST OVER, WHEN CHRIS CAIRNS went up for an lbw shout against Justin Langer. It pitched on middle and straightened, and would have taken middle and leg stumps without any worries at all. Umpire Daryl Harper gave it not out and the game went on. JL had been amazingly lucky to survive. Back in the rooms we all said, *That's out.* I put myself in Cairns's shoes and thought that if it was given not out to my bowling, I'd be pretty upset. It was a spot of bad luck for the Kiwis, because from there, Justin and Matty Hayden went on and added 224 for the first wicket. Had that lbw been given, who knows what might have happened on that opening day. The Kiwis hung in there well, and once Hayden had gone, wickets fell at regular intervals, and by stumps, we were 6/294.

Rain caused some problems over the next few days, and by stumps on day four, the Kiwis had reached 5/186 and were chasing our 9/486 declared; the match was destined for a draw unless they had a massive collapse on the final day.

On the last day, Stephen Fleming declared the New Zealand innings closed once their team had reached the follow-on mark, and the decision was suggestive to us that he and the team were up for a game. I don't think there was any official arrangement; it was the fact he'd declared that did it.

We went in and batted for an hour and then declared, setting them 284 in two sessions. In that situation, our thinking seemed to be, *Let's set them a target and play to win.* We didn't want to shut up shop and just bat the day out; we felt we were a chance to bowl them out in four hours of cricket. Even though they got to within 10 runs of the target, we tried to play to win the match. We certainly didn't think we were giving them a chance for an easy Test victory — none of us viewed it that way at all. It was good for the game and kept the public interested right to the end. Both teams gave the crowd who'd bothered to turn up on the final day an exciting bit of cricket. We felt that playing out a boring draw was no good. In the end, it was a thrilling draw, because New Zealand batted well — something positive had come out of what we'd done.

Second Test, Hobart, 22–26 November 2001

BAD WEATHER MARRED THE NEXT TEST IN HOBART; ONCE MORE, the rain caused its fair share of problems: no chance was allowed for an exciting finish. We made 6/411 on the first day, which was an amazing effort. We batted really well, and the opposition's bowling was a bit indifferent. They over-attacked and pitched up, and when the ball didn't swing, they got smashed. JL got off to a flyer and made another century. He and Matty Hayden had another big opening partnership, which was a terrific effort.

In that game I was in form with my bowling, getting through 28 overs to finish with 3/45. My left side was bothering me, but despite it I was happy with the way I bowled. In general, there were many Tests in which I wasn't 100 per cent fit and had some sort of niggle. Over the years, Michael Kasprowicz had always referred to something he called the 'niggle worm'. According to his theory, it starts in the ankle, finds it way to a spot behind the knee, and at some stage works its way to your hammy. From there, it can sneak up to your shoulder and go across to your lower back. That was simply his humorous take on the fact that when fast bowlers are playing cricket, they are never without some little issue with their body.

From my experience, if you asked most quicks, they'd say they didn't feel completely at ease with their body all the time. When my son Jackson gets older and hopefully grows up to be as tall as his old man — 6 feet 5 inches — I won't encourage him to be a fast bowler; I'll say, 'Play golf or tennis, or if you're playing cricket, be a batsman.' I'll be really happy if he becomes a golf professional so I can go and watch — but my advice is to stay away from bowling unless you like being stiff and sore a lot.

After day two of that Test match, umpire Steve Davis managed to injure himself when he tried to scale some temporary fencing to get out of the ground. He'd been to a function after play, and thought all the gates were locked. He hadn't realised there was an open gate right near where he'd attempted to get over the fence. He hurt his knee, and it was bad enough for him to spend some time in hospital, so local umpire John Smeaton had to take over. We all found immense humour in the situation. Steve is well liked in cricket circles, and we all thought in a fun sort of way, *What a bloody classic!* Thankfully, he was over the injury fairly quickly and back umpiring later in the season.

Third Test, Perth, 30 November–4 December 2001

THE SERIES WAS STILL LOCKED AWAY AT NIL ALL, AND WE HEADED to Perth for the deciding Test. Lou Vincent was brought into the side to make his Test debut and did brilliantly, making 105. He had terrible luck to be dismissed as well: he drove and missed a massive leg break from Warnie, and the ball went to slip; according to the replays, he missed it by a fair way.

It was a shame he didn't stay with us here in South Australia, where he'd played most of his junior cricket — so, Louie, if you ever want to come back, mate, you'll be more than welcome with the Redbacks! It was a quality effort, and he showed what a fine talent he is. On a very good pitch, Stephen Fleming also made a ton, and by the end of the day, the Kiwis had reached 7/293.

The Kiwis had a long batting order and batted well into the second day, making 9/534. Nathan Astle was in sparkling form and made a hundred, as did Adam Parore; they added 253 for the eighth wicket.

I've always liked the way Astle plays and he has always had my respect; his wicket is always hard earned. Over the years, he's been somewhat underrated, and has had to contend with some tricky wickets. New Zealand often play fairly early in the season, when the pitches tend to deck around slightly. In Test cricket, anyone who makes a 200 off only 153 balls *can* play — no doubt about it.

Adam Parore strikes me as an interesting character — he's always shown plenty of aggro out on the ground. Some of his opponents would say he's an annoying person, but I think he's just a competitive bloke. He seemed to be fiercely proud to play for his country; he dished a bit out verbally and never cared whether he received any of it back. I liken him to the Redbacks batsman and sometime wicketkeeper Shane 'Deitzy' Deitz. Deitzy cops heaps on the field, and is more than happy to take it and give some back. Although he could be a pest, it's always good to have one of those types of bloke in your team. Parore was much the same, but the really good thing was he never took it any further; he had a beer with us after the game.

Chasing their big score, we were in a bit of bother at 6/192 and looked like we might follow on. Shane Warne batted solidly and looked as if he'd get a century. He took us past the follow-on, and found himself on 94 when he was joined by Glenn McGrath late on the third day.

He made his way carefully to 99 and then decided to loft Daniel Vettori to try to bring up his ton spectacularly. Unfortunately, he skied the ball to the deep and Mark Richardson took the catch, running in from deep mid-wicket.

Having discussed it with him, I can say that not a day goes by when Warnie doesn't think about that 99, wishing he'd been smarter and a shade more patient. Years later, at the Allan Border Medal presentation night, Channel Nine found some footage in which it was shown that it was a no-ball, and as a result, more salt was rubbed into the wound. Warnie had been playing so well, we thought he was a monty to get the ton, and when he played the shot off the fourth ball of the over, it was a shame. He reckons he tried to place it and actually over-hit it. It's very funny looking back on it now, but at the time we all felt for him. As you'd expect, he was not a happy man when he came in after his dismissal.

New Zealand batted well again and ended up setting us 440 to win. Late in their second innings, Brett Lee bowled six bouncers in a row to Craig McMillan. Also, he pointed Shane Bond towards the Pavilion when he bowled him and got fined about $8000 by match referee Jackie Hendriks.

I remember thinking how ridiculous it was; I'd always felt there's nothing wrong with a bit of banter, a bit of pointing to the Pavilion — I think it adds to the game and the spectacle. Cricket Australia and the ICC want players to show a bit of exuberance and a bit of passion when we play, so when we do, they turn around and fine us and/or suspend us — amazing. They seem to believe you can do it in some way, but I think it has to be heaps more clearcut so the players have a chance to show some more personality. In recent times showmanship has definitely gone from the game, to my way of thinking. If you think back to the era in which Merv Hughes played, I'd say most of those players would recall the times when Merv gave them a send-off with good humour. None of them could say he wasn't a top bloke and a mighty competitor; they wouldn't think he was the worst fellow ever. Some of what he did out on the ground significantly added to the spectacle of our great game.

We had to do some serious batting to save that match in Perth. We started the day on 2/69, but thanks to some good, positive batting, we were 5/339 at one stage and still an outside chance to win. Steve Waugh and Adam Gilchrist were putting together a decent partnership when Gilly smashed one back off Daniel Vettori. It flicked his finger and rolled on to the stumps, and Steve Waugh was run out backing up too far. From there, the tail had to hang on for most of the last hour with Gilly to ensure a draw. Things got a bit tight because I had to bat with him for 40 minutes to save the series.

The Kiwis gave it a good whirl, and their efforts in that last Test had a lot to do with the splendid captaincy of Stephen Fleming. One of the reasons he'd been so effective is that he knew his players so well. He'd always known his team members' capabilities; he was prepared to play attacking cricket; and he tried to match the players up as best he could with Australia's. It was man for man, and he and his team didn't mind getting stuck in. The Kiwis are always revved up when they play us; it's a case of 'little brother versus big brother', David versus Goliath.

They played very well in that series. Although the weather had an impact, they performed strongly in Perth, where they outplayed us.

After the drawn series with New Zealand, the South Africans came out to play three Tests, and given their strong record over the previous 12 months, it seemed likely they'd be tough to beat.

First Test against South Africa, Adelaide, 14–18 December 2001

Thanks to a hundred from Justin Langer and Damien Martyn, we made 439 in the first innings of the first Test against South Africa. They showed plenty of fight in their innings and were 6/355 before getting all out for 374. Matty Hayden got in on the act in the second dig, making 131, and we set our opponents 375 to win.

We went through the opposition with relative ease and won with about a session to spare. After not getting a wicket in the first innings, I bowled pretty well in the second and got a couple. Although I was bowling well, my shoulder was starting give me some trouble and I had to have a jab. Throwing started to become a big issue, and then bowling became a worry, so I knew I had a problem. Once again, I found myself battling injury and was forced to sit out the next couple of Test matches.

Missing out — and getting back in

To miss out on both the Boxing Day Test and the New Year's Day Test was a bitter pill to swallow because my bowling had been good in the Adelaide Test. After taking off a few weeks to recover, I had to fight to retrieve my spot in the side. To do that, I played for Australia A against South Africa in Adelaide and logged some solid achievements. My next engagement was in the Australian one-day team for the VB series.

I returned for the match at the MCG on 13 January and had a 10-over spell of 2/28. I was happy to come back strong, but we lost the game, and losing became a regular occurrence because we missed the finals of the one-day series that summer. We managed to beat South Africa most of the time but had trouble with the Kiwis, who beat us in three of the four qualifying games. We beat them on the MCG when Michael Bevan made a brilliant ton despite the fact we were gone for all money. However, we didn't win enough games and missed out on the finals for the first time in ages.

Tugga bowls again — and goes

The 2003 World Cup was looming, and the spotlight was on Steve Waugh's place as captain of the one-day team. One strange thing that happened towards the end of that summer was that he decided to resume bowling. In one game, he came on and had a long bowl, which was a surprise because he was hardly bowling towards the end of his career and suddenly he was bringing himself on. I don't know whether the selectors had put him under the pump. I had to wonder, *Did he work it out for himself that he should bowl again to add some versatility to the side?*

After we missed the finals, I remember hearing that Steve had been left out, and feeling totally shocked. I thought back to that game and wondered whether he'd been put under the pump by the selectors. Despite all the conjecture in the media, the decision wasn't something that I'd been expecting. I was in a bit of a bubble trying to get myself alright after missing the Melbourne and Sydney Tests. Looking back, I think the selectors made the correct decision: Australia went on, turned things around and won the 2003 World Cup in South Africa.

AFTER THE UNSUCCESSFUL VB SERIES, WE WENT OFF TO SOUTH Africa for a three-Test series. Although we'd thrashed the South Africans 3–nil in Australia, the series was being billed as the 'world championship of cricket'. If South Africa managed to beat us, they'd be placed on top of the ICC points table.

The Wanderers Ground in Johannesburg is an intimidating place to play because the crowd give you heaps. As a professional, though, you don't worry about them; you simply go out on the field and get on with it. While I'm on the crowds, I have to say that South African and New Zealand fans are the ones who abuse you the most. The UK crowds were mostly good, and although we copped some flak from time to time, it was usually good-natured banter. Despite the fact I've copped my fair share in England, I've found the Poms okay. I've been to New Zealand only once and I couldn't believe how full-on the crowds were there — especially in Auckland. Even though they weren't far behind in South Africa, the South African crowds weren't as bad as the appalling crowd at Eden Park in Auckland: they threw stuff and the abuse was terrible.

First Test against South Africa, Johannesburg, 22–24 February 2002

WHEN MATTHEW HAYDEN MADE A HUNDRED ON THE OPENING day of the first Test at Jo'burg, we were off to a promising start. However, it was Adam Gilchrist in his innings on the second day who really stole the show: he batted beautifully at the Wanderers and was pumped up to do well because of some terrible stuff that had been doing the rounds before the game. On an Internet site, it was being suggested that Adam wasn't the father of his own child. What was worse, it was alleged that the father was actually Michael Slater. Adam was clearly distressed about the questioning of his son's paternity. The crowd had read all about the claim and were giving Gilly a hard time about it. When he was punching out that double ton, he was exceptionally emotional. At the time, it was the fastest 200 ever. However, the record didn't last long because Nathan Astle broke it several days later.

Gilly hit 8 sixes and smashed the South Africans all over the place. One of his sixes just missed a sponsor's sign for a bar of gold; if he'd hit it, he'd have won an ingot worth about 1,300,000 rand or $A150,000. It was amazing he was so close, because the sign was well over the mid-wicket boundary about 100 yards away. Gilly's knock was brilliant, and we declared late on day two at 7/652.

Andre Nel played in that Test and bowled quite quick, taking two wickets. He didn't carry on as he carries on when he plays now. Sadly for the South Africans' Allan Donald, this was to be his last Test match because he broke down with a torn hamstring and had to go off; he'd been the team's spearhead over the past decade. He was a fantastic bowler over the years; I was lucky enough to play against him and see how he went about it. I know for a fact he's always been Brett Lee's hero. I really admired him for the effort he used to put in, day in, day out, for South Africa. Unfortunately, I didn't get to know him all that well. When he came off after being injured, someone in the crowd yelled out some colourful abuse, and you have to wonder why. He was a pretty hard player: he ended up with 330 Test wickets at just over 22 and is quite rightly viewed as being one of the greats of South African cricket.

In Johannesburg, we stayed at the Sandton Hotel in the city's central business district. Johannesburg is considered to be the world's most dangerous city but the CBD is quite a lot safer than elsewhere. Nevertheless we were advised not to venture out too far from the hotel. The Sandton was very good, and everyone more or less stayed in, even though the city has quite a few places to go out and relax in. It didn't make any difference to me because I was happy to stay in and eat at the bar.

South Africa followed on in that Test and capitulated in the second innings to give us a massive win. Statistically, it turned out that the defeat was the second-worst ever in their Test history. We bowled them out for 159 and 133, and headed to Cape Town with rising confidence.

Second Test, Cape Town, 8–12 March 2002

On the opening day of the second Test, played at Newlands, we bowled out South Africa for 239. We thought we were going to bowl them out cheaply for the third time in a row when they were 6/92, but their tail wagged well and debutant Andrew Hall made a plucky 70 from number eight. We'd been in a good position early in our innings, but our middle order fell in a hole and we got to 6/185. Adam Gilchrist came to the rescue and played another blinder of an innings, making a hundred off 91 balls. He spanked all the South African bowlers, including spinner Paul Adams, and at one point hit him for 36 in two overs. Shane Warne made 63, and through their partnership, we got to 382, a lead of 143. Thanks to

Gilly's unbeaten 138, he'd made 342 runs in his first two hits and had yet to be dismissed!

It was Warnie's hundredth Test match, and he had flown his family over for the big occasion. Although he had a leg problem, he managed to bowl 70 overs virtually unchanged in the second innings; he just kept on bowling and bowling. After we took the new ball in the second dig, he bowled from one end while we rotated from the other, and he finished with 6/161. After the match, he was kind enough to sign a beautiful panoramic photo of the ground for me; it's a stunning photo — there's a wonderful view of the Newlands ground and the Table Mountain in the background, and it hangs over my bar at home.

In the second innings, South Africa's batsmen finally found form and batted well to get themselves back into the match. Gary Kirsten and Graeme Smith made runs, and Neil McKenzie played well, making 99.

The unspoken code regarding banter and sledging

Neil McKenzie was a highly superstitious fellow and never stepped on any of the creases when he was batting because he believed he'd have bad luck otherwise. It was even suggested he went as far as to have all the toilet seats up in the dressing rooms because it had happened once before and he made runs.

We sledged him for being so pedantic about stepping on lines and got stuck into him about a couple of other things. He was really keen on keeping the area around the batting crease neat and tidy. Gilly stirred him a bit by dropping pebbles and dirt in his area, all the time trying to put him off. Then we said, 'Hey, you stepped on a line!' It was all good-natured banter, and Neil took it well because he could see the funny side. When Gilly was stirring him up it was pretty hilarious. South Africa batted for a long time, so the banter helped to break up the day, and thankfully Neil took it in the right way. He deserved a ton, but was run out by Damien Martyn for 99.

South Africa finished with 473, and set us a challenging target of 331 to win the match and the series. It looked as if it could have been a few more, because they were 5/431 before they lost their last five batsmen for just 42.

Graeme Smith also made his debut in this Test and made 68 in the second innings. After the series, he came out and complained bitterly about the sledging he'd received from some of our players. He named Brett Lee, Matthew Hayden and Glenn McGrath as the ones who'd particularly got stuck into him. He claimed that Lee had threatened to kill him when they'd had a small collision mid-pitch. He suggested it was Matthew's job to attack him verbally while he batted, and said Glenn was like a grumpy old man and didn't stop cursing.

It was a real pity that Smith had gone against the unspoken agreement that had operated in the past — the notion that what goes on on the field stays there. It's fair enough to allude to it in the press, but he really went to town in complaining about what had been said.

Smith came out and made these big statements, and maybe he had his own agenda. The whole thing came across quite poorly; I believe most people thought so. Everyone in our camp was really disappointed about it and felt that Smith should have pulled his head in. Maybe he'd been baited by a journalist who was looking for a big story: it's easy to believe that was what happened. And then there was his age. Given he was only 20 at the time, who knows whether he'd have handled the situation better if he'd been a few years older. Judging from some of the stuff he said later on when heading into the 2005–06 series, it appears that Smith completely forgot about what had happened a few years earlier. I can't see how he could say what he did at that time when he was trying to take the heat off his teammates; it was quite ridiculous.

In that second innings, I felt I bowled as well as I could have and was really happy with my effort. The conditions were highly comparable to the ones we have in Australia, and suited me. The South Africans play hard and fair, and their grounds are much the same. As a rule, they're a good bunch of blokes to play against. Playing against South Africa is a good, fun tour, and despite the social issues, I can't speak highly enough of the place.

Chasing a target of 331, we were cruising along at 1/201 before we lost a few wickets in the middle order, and we still needed about 60 when five wickets were left. Ricky Ponting was batting well, and with four wickets in hand, pulled a six to win the match. In pulling the six, he brought up his hundred and clinched the series for us 2–nil. Warnie was there at the end, and thanks to his runs and terrific bowling was named Man of the Match.

The celebrations were huge. Matty Hayden was one very excited player because he'd had another good match, making 63 and 96. We were heading up to Table Mountain in a cable car, and Matty somehow found his way up to the top of it wearing an Australia flag as a cape. The wives and partners met us up there and we sang the team song — a great moment to share with them after we'd won that Test match and the series.

Third Test, Durban, 15–18 March 2002

In the last Test, played in Durban, the old dead-match syndrome came in. I think we've always had a problem with it. I'm not sure why, but in the past we've taken our foot off the gas; we might have been plain tired from playing many games in a short space of time. I've always believed that if I'd been a selector, I wouldn't have played me in dead matches; my record has never been that good in them.

Here are my figures from seven of those games:

Fifth Test in Sydney in 2001 against the West Indies:
0/44 and 2/57; Australia won
Fourth Test in Headingley in 2001 against England:
0/76 and 2/94; England won
Fifth Test at The Oval in London in 2001 against England:
0/96 and 0/38; Australia won
Third Test in Durban in 2001–02 against South Africa:
1/25 and 0/58; South Africa won
Fifth Test in Sydney in 2002–03 against England:
1/62 and 1/70; England won
Fourth Test in Antigua in 2002–03 against the West Indies:
0/56 and 1/64; the West Indies won
Third Test in Sydney in 2004–05 against Pakistan:
0/47 and 1/39; Australia won

Out of those seven Tests, we won three and lost four. My figures, 9 for 826 at 91.77, which is not the best of returns, is it?

We don't go off the boil deliberately; it happens subconsciously. After we'd made 315 and bowled out South Africa for 167, we should have won the Test and taken the series out 3–nil. However, we batted poorly in the second innings; we made only 186 and set our opponents 335 to win the match. Herschelle Gibbs and Gary Kirsten got them off to a fine start of 142, and they went on to win by five wickets.

Playing, travelling, promoting

We'd played nine Tests in four-and-a-half months, which is a lot of cricket in anyone's book. There are always questions about how much cricket is played. It's not only the matches we play that are tiring; it's the constant travel. Also, Cricket Australia is always big on having the players appear at functions. There's always pressure to try to look after sponsors, appear at sports stores and go on TV ads. The people I feel for the most are the guys who play in both forms of the game, lads such as Ricky Ponting, Brett Lee, Glenn McGrath and Adam Gilchrist. These guys who play both Tests and one-dayers are the big names; they get asked to do much more and on top of that they have their own personal matters to take care of. Even when I was playing in both forms of the game for a while, I wasn't one of the 'big boys', so wasn't under that same off-field pressure. For that I count myself lucky. I slipped under the radar, which suited me fine. Outside the game I didn't have too many things to do.

Cricket Australia has to respect the players because they're the game's biggest asset. They need to look after the lads to make sure they can focus on playing and maintaining the high standard of play.

LOOKING BACK ON THAT TOUR, I THINK SOUTH AFRICA AS A country had changed a good deal from when I first toured there, in 1997. Certainly, my game had changed: back in '97, I was very young, I was single and I could go out and have a good time. I was just running in and bowling as fast as I could. Five years later, in 2002, I was older and wiser, and thought about my game more. Comparing the two visits is like comparing apples with oranges.

The touchy issue of quotas

WHEN THE SOUTH AFRICAN TEAM IS BEING PICKED, A QUOTA system comes into the picture. What it boils down to is that there has to be a particular racial mix in the team, irrespective of talent. I lean towards picking your best team. Skin colour shouldn't matter, but in South Africa, that's the system they've brought in.

Not surprisingly, occasionally it blows up in their faces. During the Sydney Test back in January 2002, all hell broke loose when Jacques Rudolph was selected to play, but Percy Sonn, the president of the United Cricket Board of South Africa, ordered the selectors to pick Justin Ontong, who is coloured.

It seems that at the time, from the South African selectors' point of view, a short-term loss in selection could translate to a long-term gain. However, where does that leave players of European origin who are better players according to merit? A lot of guys get lost within the South African system and choose to find somewhere else to play.

Gerard Brophy, who kept wicket at Yorkshire in 2006, has been the Free State keeper and skipper. Because of the quota system in First Class cricket there, he was forced out. He now plays in the UK, and fortunately has the advantage of having a British passport, which sees him considered as a local after a year of residential qualification. Others from South Africa play under the 'Kolpak' rule, which came about when Maros Kolpak, a Slovakian handball player, won a court case for restraint of trade to play in Germany and not be considered a foreigner. The Kolpak rule now applies in English County Cricket, so a European Union passport holder can be classed as domestic, as long as he's classed overseas in his home country.

Martin van Jaarsveld, who played nine Tests for South Africa, is a top-flight batsman playing at Kent but now feels he won't get a go at home for the same reason. He therefore chose to stay with the club so he can make a decent living playing County cricket. Former South Africa all-rounder Lance Klusener has been in a similar boat in the past.

Deon Kruis, who was also at Yorkshire in 2006, is another player who believes there's no point in staying in South Africa. There's not a lot of money in the game there, and it's especially difficult to get a game because of the quota system. If you're of European origin, you have to be the absolute best player available, otherwise you won't get a game. Deon has captured 240 First Class wickets with the Eagles in South African domestic cricket, but he couldn't be guaranteed a spot, so decided to take up an offer at Yorkshire.

Don't forget that South Africa's biggest defection has been their batsman Kevin Pietersen, who went to England. What a start to his Test career he had. Kevin couldn't get a regular game with his province in South Africa due to the recently introduced quota system. This meant half the team had to be of 'coloured' origin. He says the change of rules was the sole reason he left. Now he's one of the English stars in both forms of the game. I hope the situation is eventually sorted out: plenty of South African cricketers aren't getting the opportunity to play because of the rules in their country.

Tests against Pakistan and England, 2002

WHEN WE RETURNED FROM SOUTH AFRICA, WE HAD A BRIEF BREAK before playing a three-match one-day series during the Australian winter. Two of the matches were scheduled indoors at Melbourne's Docklands Stadium, and one was to be played in Brisbane at the Gabba. Because we'd been relatively successful in the series we'd played against South Africa in 2000, it was thought we should have another try. However, it was Melbourne in June and the middle of the AFL season, and practically no one turned up. I think only 28,000 spectators made it along to the two Melbourne matches and only 11,000 bothered to come to the Brisbane one. We won the first match easily but Pakistan beat us in the next two. Shoaib bowled a devastating spell in the last game, taking five for 25, and it was the first of a couple of sensational spells he was to bowl to us in the space of four months.

Security scares, safeguards and silliness

AFTER THE WINTER ONE-DAYERS, WE WERE SCHEDULED TO TOUR Pakistan in October, but it was deemed too dangerous to visit. A bomb had gone off when New Zealand were touring the country in May; they'd left as soon as the bomb exploded outside their Karachi hotel. Fourteen people had been killed. None of the Black Cap touring party were badly hurt, but it frightened the hell out of the team, and you couldn't blame them for wanting to catch the first plane home.

Some major things were happening around the world at that time, and when it came to travel, security had become the main priority. Cricket Australia and the Australian Cricketers' Association did all the relevant checks, and found that things weren't safe enough in Pakistan for a tour to be held there. The Australian Government also advised us against going there. Because we were due to play Pakistan under the ICC's scheduling, which was that we must meet every five years, it was decided we'd play one Test in Sri Lanka and then play back-to-back Test matches in the emirate of Sharjah. Interestingly, although Sri Lanka was undergoing a civil war at the time, it was viewed as being a safer place than Pakistan to tour.

In the months leading up to the trip, the cricket authorities monitored happenings between Iraq and the United States. If their assessment was that it was too dangerous to play in Sharjah, which is quite close to Iraq, we were to stay in Sri Lanka and play the remaining two Test matches there.

Heading into the series, the Pakistan team had their fair share of problems. Wasim Akram and Saeed Anwar announced they were unavailable because they were worn out from playing too much cricket. To top that off, Inzamam and Yousuf Youhana were out because of injury, so the team had four of their best players unavailable.

First Test against Pakistan, Colombo, 3–7 October 2002

Before the first Test against Pakistan, their skipper, Waqar Younis, had asked the groundsman to prepare a pitch that suited their team. They had a similar line-up to ours, so the request seemed strange. Our captain, Steve Waugh, commented that what Waqar had tried to do was a disgrace. According to Tugga, if groundsmen were going to prepare the pitch to suit the home team, the visitors should be awarded the toss to even things out.

In the first innings we dominated the opposition with the bat. Thanks to a hundred by Ricky, we made 467 even though we lost our last five wickets for 10 runs. In their first innings, we seemed to have the game well under control when we bowled them out for 279. Warnie was on fire again and took 7/94.

Australia were reigning champions in both forms of the game, and Ricky and Shane were in good form, so it was amazing that hardly anyone was at the match. Sri Lanka weren't involved, so hardly any of the locals were interested in the outcome. However, you'd think that because such quality players were involved there'd be more than 500 spectators each day. The atmosphere was sadly hollow — a real shame.

In the second innings, we were cruising and trying to set them a big target. Then Shoaib Akhtar fired up and took a few wickets in a hurry. He bowled Ricky Ponting and Mark Waugh, and then knocked over Steve Waugh leg before for a duck. However, he saved the best ball of the lot for Adam Gilchrist: a searing yorker from around the wicket that smashed into Gilly's stumps before he could complete the stroke. We lost our last 10 wickets for 66, and before we knew it, were all out for only 127 and had a lead of 315.

They didn't have a speed gun there, but from what I can remember, it was just about the fastest bowling I'd seen in a match

I'd played in. Facing Shoaib is a tough task at the best of times, and when I faced him it was purely a matter of survival. In some one-dayers, I went through a patch of facing five balls from him and he got me out three times. He either knocked me over with a yorker or got me lbw or bowled, often so I was humiliated.

Suspect actions

While I'm discussing Shoaib's action, I have to say I think he was breaking the laws of the game such as they stood at the time. His action was doubtful back then, but because of the laws that are now in place and the new 15 per cent rule, the action is now legal.

The biomechanics experts reckon they know more than me, but even when you look at Shoaib with the naked eye, he looks suspect. Not so long ago, my former Aussie teammate Damien Fleming came up with an appealing commonsense theory about throwing. He said that if you lined up a sportsperson who'd never watched or played cricket, say an American, and you picked out three bowlers for the person to look at, such as Muttiah Muralitharan, Dan Cullen and Shane Warne — or you could go with three quicks, such as Shoaib, Glenn McGrath and Steve Harmison — if you asked the American to pick who had the dodgy action, for sure they'd be able to pick it out. It's not the case that I mean any malice towards Shoaib or Murali, but bowling actions are a fact of life. They're tough to judge, but you almost feel that the ICC change the rules to keep specific players in the game.

Whether we like it or not, there's a hell of a lot of politics in sports such as cricket, and it's one of those issues that won't go away. From the batsman's point of view, the other way you need to look at it is that some of the bowlers who have a suspect action are ending the career of some of the players they're dismissing — you rarely hear anything said about that aspect. If Adam Gilchrist had been on a bad run of form when he was bowled by that yorker and then had been dropped, how would he have felt?

Still on the topic of suspect actions for pacemen, I have to say there's a chance that a major injury will occur from a bowled bouncer that's a throw. If during a game someone ends up badly hurt from a suspect delivery, that would have to be a problem, so what's the legal standing? One day, could a batsman sue a bowler for breaking his jaw because he threw his bouncer? At this stage, the legal aspect hasn't been tested, but there might come a day that it will be. In some ways, because of the interest they create, I'd hate to see the likes of Shoaib and Murali forced out of the game but the ICC can't continue to ignore the problem. Regardless of what Murali achieves in cricket, there'll always be a question mark over the wickets he's taken, because of his action.

I can see a further problem occurring in the future: in relation to the existing law, where do you draw the line? What's the difference between 14 and 16 degrees, and how can an umpire tell the difference? Will there be a time when a bowler has an action that's at 18 degrees? What will the cricket authorities do: change it to 20 to allow the guy to play? It's madness, and as far as I'm concerned, not satisfactory.

On the final day of the match, things were becoming tight: Pakistan were in sparkling form: they'd reached 3/179 heading into their final day and they were chasing 316 to win. It looked as though they'd get there with their under-manned line-up. They opened up well, and at 4/230 they needed another 86 and were right on track to win the match.

Fortunately, Warnie got out Younis Khan. His wicket was a signal for a collapse, and with about 40-odd to get, I had the ball in my hand and we needed one more wicket for victory.

Not again!

It was right at this pivotal time that I injured my right calf muscle. Bowling the ball before I actually tore the muscle, I'd felt a twinge and suspected some sort of stiffness. It didn't bother me; I put it down to being the last day of the match added to which I'd put through a good number of deliveries. However, I became aware that not all was well as I was stretching when walking back. I bowled the next ball and knew I had a problem after my follow-through. I limped off without finishing the over. Fortunately, we got the last wicket shortly afterwards and thereby won that tight Test match by 41 runs.

Afterwards I found out I'd suffered what in technical terms was classed as a 'grade 1½ tear', which meant I was out of the game and would be unable to play for a while. Tearing my calf was quite a painful experience; it's always painful when you tear a muscle. It was a tremendous disappointment to get injured, because I'd managed to play 20 out of the previous 22 Tests for Australia and my bowling had been going well.

It was decided I should go to Sharjah to stay with Errol, who could ensure I'd receive the correct treatment. He didn't want me to make the long trip back to Australia because I might cause more damage and perhaps suffer from deep-vein thrombosis. 'Hoot' also didn't want me to fly back because he wanted to get stuck into the injury during the early stages to ensure I recovered as quickly as possible. The Ashes series at home was around the corner, and I needed to make sure I'd be ready in time for it. Thanks to Errol's treatment, it wasn't that long before the calf muscle started to feel good again. However, there was no way I'd be playing in the last Test of the series. Errol didn't want me to fly home too soon because of the risk of getting deep-vein thrombosis, so I hobbled around in Sharjah for a few days, and after treatment the muscle started to come good pretty quickly: I was walking without pain in about a week. I started jogging and jumping around.

Second Test, Sharjah, 11–12 October 2002

I WATCHED THE SECOND TEST, WHICH WAS PLAYED IN WHAT were some of the hottest conditions imaginable. The heat was searing and unbearable. Andy Bichel bowled the gutsiest spell I've ever seen. He bowled seven overs in a row, and it was just silly bowling in such hot conditions. It was easily the hottest game I've ever been to or played in. Apart from the Bichel spell, the Test was memorable for the fact that Ricky Ponting got hit on the jaw by Mohammad Sami. The weather was much too warm for any batsman to wear a helmet, and Sami half bounced Ricky and hit him. Ricky had decided he wouldn't hook, because the pitch was slightly up and down, and I guess he paid the price for not wearing a lid by copping one. Presumably, if he'd batted as normal and hooked them anyway, he would have been okay. As it was, he had his jaw checked out and kept batting.

It was Matty Hayden who starred in that Test, however: he made 119. When he batted, the temperature was about 50 degrees. He later said it had been like batting in an oven, and wondered whether hell was any hotter. We won the Test in only two days, which was a blessing, because five days of playing in that sun would have been a shocker.

My one and only disagreement with Hooter

AFTER THE TEST, I HEADED HOME TO GET MYSELF FIT AND READY for the Ashes series. Sure enough, it came around fairly quickly, and thankfully, when I hopped on the flight to Brisbane, I was fit and rearing to go.

I made my way to the Gabba and was doing plenty of bowling in the nets. My spirits rose because my calf pulled up well after each session, and I'd be okay to play. The day before the Test, an odd thing happened — in fact, looking back on it, it seems astonishing, and it was the only time I'd ever had a difference of opinion with physio Errol Alcott. He wanted to see how much of a weight load my calf could take, so suggested he sit on my back and get me to do some calf raises to test it out. I'd never done anything remotely like that in my life, so why would I do something like it a day before a Test match? Somehow, Errol persuaded me to do it, and I got through it okay.

The trouble was, on the second day of the Test, when we came out to bowl, my calf tightened up. I attributed the problem to the stupid calf raises. That's when Errol and I had words, but he stuck to his view that we needed to know the calf could withstand the workload. Although I understood where he was coming from, it still seemed crazy. Rather than applying that artificial stress to test the repair, surely bowling was a better way to go. I felt that because I'd been bowling freely in the nets, I had been fine to play before he insisted on applying that ridiculous stress. Throughout the many years of our association, that was the only time I'd had a difference of opinion with big Hooter.

During the match, the muscle tightened up lower down in the calf rather than where I'd torn it in Sri Lanka. It was only stiff, so I had it treated, and as the game went on I got better and better. Despite the dreadful worries I'd had on the second day, I was 100 per cent the next day.

Unfortunate judgement

Before the Test started, England Skipper Nasser Hussain came out and said publicly that he felt there'd be something in the wicket for the bowlers and he wanted to get it for his team. That came as a surprise to us. When Channel Nine's Ian Chappell spoke to Nasser, we were in the rooms and had assumed we were going to be bowling. When Steve came in and signalled we were batting, we jumped for joy. Everyone makes mistakes, and Hussain's decision to bowl proved to be a bad move for his side. Of course we posted a massive first-day score. Nasser's decision at the toss wasn't just bad but it looked bizarre. He 'dobbed us' on that pitch.

There's no doubt that Nasser's decision at the Gabba in 2002 and Ricky's at Edgbaston in 2005 were the two biggest mistakes I've ever seen at the toss of the coin.

EARLY ON THE OPENING DAY, ENGLAND PACEMAN SIMON JONES badly hurt his knee while trying a slide save in the field. He caught his left knee in the turf, and his body twisted, which caused his right knee to hyper-extend and his anterior cruciate ligament to rupture. It was a shame for Jones because that injury caused him to miss over a year of cricket.

Quite unexpectedly, because of Jones's injury, I won the Spirit of Anzac Medal. I was the first recipient of the award and I'm not even sure it still exists. It all came about because I just happened to be standing near the boundary when Jones was hurt, so I went over to him and tried to help out — not that I could do that much. The judges or the people involved in awarding a medal must have seen the gesture, and that was how I won the medal. I simply thought it was the right thing to do when a player had been hurt.

As for diving on the field, I'm not a fan of it at all. I understand it's part and parcel of the modern game, but there have been times when trying to dive has cost me personally. I remember diving during a domestic game in 2000–01 and doing my hamstring, and as a result I missed the first Test in the West Indies series that season.

From then on, I only rarely dived in the field. For starters, I can't dive properly; also, diving is particularly hard to practise if you're not a natural at it — either you can do it or you can't. My biggest problem is I find it really difficult to time a dive; I find it the trickiest thing to do on the cricket field, so I avoid doing it at all costs.

A number of other incidents have occurred in which players have hurt themselves with their dives: Shane Watson hurt his shoulder diving, Brad Young banged his knee in a fence and was out for a while, and Ricky Ponting injured ankle ligaments in 2000 and had to miss six months of cricket as a result of diving. I think too much risk is involved for the sake of saving a run or two. My approach to the task is to work on my speed — I'm not the quickest runner around — I'd rather try to get to the ball quicker so I don't have to dive.

First Test against England, Brisbane, 7–11 November 2002

MATTHEW HAYDEN PLAYED A SUPERB KNOCK ON THE OPENING day of the Gabba Test. We got a hundred from Ricky Ponting and were on top at 2/364, so Nasser Hussain's decision to send us in looked all the worse.

Midway through the third day, we'd ended up with 492 and England were going well at 3/268. Thankfully, after the dramas with my calf on the second day, everything was going alright. I managed to get a couple of wickets with the second new ball, so we really turned the game and put the opposition under pressure. When Hussain was well set he nicked one behind to Gilly and then as Stewart tried to let one go, the ball just clipped his bat as he tried to leave it and it went on to the stumps. Glenn picked up a few wickets at the other end, and we bowled England out for 325. After that day, Glenn was kind enough to compliment me on my bowling, when he said in the papers, 'He's quite a bit quicker than I am, so I tease them a bit that I am a bit slower so that if I do something off the wicket, the batsman's got time to chase it and nick it, whereas if it does something off the wicket for him, it's actually past him before it's actually moved.'

We set the Poms more than 400 to win in the last innings, and they didn't play well: they capitulated for only 79 to give us the win inside four days. As had happened a few times in past encounters, we knew we were on top of them again early in a series.

Second Test, Adelaide, 21–24 November 2002

NEXT UP FOR ME WAS MY HOME TEST IN ADELAIDE, AND BECAUSE I didn't have to play in South Australia's Pura Cup game in Sydney the week after the Gabba Test, I had a bit of extra time to rest and recover.

England didn't waste the toss this time: they decided to bat first and had a good first day, making 4/295 and having Michael Vaughan score 177. Fortunately for us, Andy Bichel dismissed him in the last over of the day. If Vaughan had made it through to stumps and had a night's rest, he might well have gone on and scored a double ton the next day.

EARLY ON THE FIRST DAY, PASSIONS WERE INFLAMED WHEN Justin Langer claimed a catch when Michael Vaughan was on 19. Vaughan drove a ball from Andy Bichel in the air to cover, where Alfie seemed to take a low catch. All the lads gathered around him to celebrate the catch, but Vaughan stayed there — because he's entitled to till the finger's raised. Umpires Bucknor and Koertzen consulted and referred the decision to third umpire Steve Davis up in the stand. He gave it not out, probably because of a lack of evidence.

I think that's where the big issue lies in relation to the Langer catch. Camera technology isn't good enough, and probably never will be. Two-dimensional television pictures can't tell you conclusively that a low catch has been taken. Ninety-nine per cent of the time, the player knows whether he caught it, and the fielders in the area also know whether a catch has been taken properly. As far as I'm concerned, you should leave it to the player. If a fielder says he's not sure, if there's any doubt at all, it should be not out. A similar thing happened to me later in the series when I caught Nasser Hussain in Melbourne and he stood his ground, even though I was adamant I caught the ball. I was absolutely fuming at the time when it was given not out, because I knew I'd caught it, but unfortunately that's the way cricket is now.

Batsmen definitely have a right to stand there and question the decision, but I'd like to see them ask the fielder whether he caught the ball or not. You'd like to think the batsman could ask, 'Are you 100 per cent sure you caught it?' If the player answers, 'Yes, I am,' that should be the end of it. Let's face it: if it shows up on the TV replays that it wasn't caught, the player will be vilified in the media for being a cheat, and the opposition will lose a lot of respect for him. Therefore, I'd rather see the decision left to the players — but, unfortunately, it seems unlikely it will be.

Ricky Ponting has tried to get other teams to comply, but other skippers are reluctant to and are well within their rights not to. However, I know the situation annoys Ricky no end; it niggles him that no one else is prepared to take the fielder's word for it. Yet that's the way the modern game is now, and the whole thing is quite sad. The day after Alfie's catch, *The Australian* ran the headline 'RIP: The day the game lost its very soul'. To my way of thinking, that sub-editor summed up the general feeling quite well.

THE NEXT DAY, WE KNOCKED THE POMS OVER PRETTY QUICKLY for only 342, which was way short of what they needed on the Adelaide pitch. Having not taken a wicket on the opening day, I managed to take four wickets on day two and was extremely pleased. It was as well as I've ever bowled in a Test, especially when I delivered five very good balls in a row to Craig White during one really good over. From memory, the over went:

Ball one: Bowled an off-cutter that White tried to play forward to. He was beaten between bat and pad, the ball just flicked the pad, and we went up half-hearted for the catch behind.

Ball two: Almost identical to the previous delivery: beaten between bat and pad. This time, the ball went straight through the gap between bat and pad, and just missed the top of the stumps.

Ball three: White pushed half forward to a ball he might have just hit before it crashed into his pad. We appealed for lbw because the ball looked quite adjacent. However, Steve Bucknor said, 'Not out', obviously thinking that White had definitely hit the ball first.

Ball four: Just outside off-stump, right in the corridor of uncertainty, where you're not sure whether to play or leave it. White decided not to play at it.

Ball five: Very similar to ball four: nice line, and the right length. White elected to leave this one too.

Ball six: A bouncer. White took the bait and hooked at it. However, he couldn't get on top of it to control it, and holed out to Andy Bichel at long leg.

Everything went to plan, and it was thoroughly satisfying to set up a batsman and to see the plan come off. As I've said before, it was probably one of the best overs I've ever bowled in First Class cricket.

Dismissed by his brother-in-law — again!

Having knocked the opposition over, we'd gained a massive lead of 210 and were put right on track to make the score 2–nil. Darren Lehmann was the only player who failed in the innings: he got out in front of his home crowd for only 5 — a disappointing result for him. It was the second Test match in a row in which he'd been dismissed by his brother-in-law, Craig White — an 'honour' that I think is unique in Test cricket. Darren had married Craig's sister, Andrea, and having your brother-in-law playing against you would have been a weird feeling, to say the least.

In the second innings, England again put up a disappointing effort and we won the Test pretty easily. We had them three for 36 at the end of the third day, and on the fourth day, apart from the work of Michael Vaughan and Alec Stewart, they put in a fairly token effort. The sad part for them was that rain marred most of the scheduled final day, so if England had batted better, they might well have saved the match.

A couple of thousand dollars for every metre

In their second innings, Glenn McGrath took one of the most remarkable catches I've ever seen in Test cricket. For starters, he was way out of position down at deep backward square leg, where he was fielding. Steve Waugh always says that Glenn was nowhere near where he was supposed to be, and that when the print of the catch was sold, Glenn made a couple of thousand dollars for every metre he was out of position. He was about 20 metres away from where he should have been, made a big run and dive, and took an amazing catch in his left hand before he secured it in his right. He then carried on like a good sort — a pretty funny sight. Another bonus was that it was the crucial wicket of Michael Vaughan, a quality player who'd batted so well in the first innings. To knock him over like that was fantastic.

In the second dig, I managed to pick up the wicket of Marcus Trescothick and finished up with five victims for the match.

For the second Test in a row, we'd beaten the opposition in four days — particularly satisfying, given they'd been in a strong position late on the opening day.

HEADING TO PERTH FOR THE NEXT TEST, I TOOK A LITTLE TIME to reflect that the ball was coming out very well and I was hitting the deck hard. I wasn't bowling at express pace but was making a contribution to a winning side. It was only really early in my career, for about 18 months, that I'd bowled 90 mph (144 kph) consistently. I don't think I've ever been an out-and-out genuinely fast bowler. I might have the odd fast spell, but I was bowling more fast-medium than flat-out fast; it was only every now and then I cranked it up. The ball was coming out consistently fast at that time, which is all you can ask for.

Third Test, Perth, 29 November–1 December 2002

ENGLAND'S BATTING IN THE PERTH TEST WAS WOEFUL, AND WE beat them by an innings to wrap up the Ashes pretty comfortably. Each of our bowlers chipped in for a few wickets, and even Damien Martyn picked one up: he got Robert Key to drag a ball on to his stumps.

When we batted, Craig White managed to pick up five wickets and at that stage of the series was England's leading wicket taker. He had to carry the attack at the WACA because Chris Silverwood injured his ankle after managing only four overs.

Late in the match, Alex Tudor got hit in the head by a bouncer. It really hurt him, and I think he was rattled by it for a while. I'm not saying it's the reason he hasn't made it back since, but I'm sure it's affected his career. He's now moved from Surrey to Essex, and he's had a bad knee — a shame, because he was a highly talented cricketer.

When Tudor was struck, it was unfortunate and quite ugly. You don't bowl a bouncer to try to hit blokes. On that bouncy WACA pitch, Brett bowled a short one to get him out or put him on edge rather than to hit him and knock him out. You hope you unsettle a batsman and that you'll get a wicket shortly after you bowl a bumper by bowling in the right areas. To see a guy get cleaned up like that is upsetting, and you don't wish an injury on anyone.

When we're playing in Perth, I think the reason the opposition do so poorly is that they try to play at too many balls. Australian bowlers tend to get a heap of nicks as a result; it's the same as batting at the Gabba in a Pura Cup match. The pitch is a 'greentop' for most Shield matches, but the principle's the same: you have to let a lot of balls go. You can learn a lot from watching how the Western Australian fellows such as Langer and Martyn bat. They wait for the right balls so they can push straight or work off their hip to the on side. They minimise their risks and know that once you're set, it's a fantastic place to bat. For the first 15 or 20 minutes it can be the hardest place to bat, but after that it can be one of the best.

Boxing Day Test, Melbourne, 26–30 December 2002

After we'd hammered England in Perth, we had a small break before we headed to Melbourne for the fourth Test. The lead-in to the Boxing Day Test is always especially enjoyable. We usually arrive before Christmas Eve and have our main training session on that day. We all get together for a big Christmas lunch with our families, and the whole set-up is wonderful. We have an optional training session on Christmas Day, so some of us go and have a hit; others might have a swim and 'fill the boots' ahead of the opening day of the Test.

We won the toss and batted. Justin Langer made 250 in our first-innings score of six for 551 declared. He and Matty Hayden pummelled the England bowlers: they added 195 for the first wicket. Alfie has been such a hard worker over the years and deserved every bit of his success. He's extremely thorough in his preparation; he loves the game and loves batting. His concentration is phenomenal and has been one of his greatest strengths during his career. He's never that flamboyant, but he always pushes the score along. At times, Alfie could be classified as one of those batsmen you could term ugly, but he manages to get the job done. He works bloody hard on his concentration, and the bottom line is he has the runs on the board.

When England had their turn at the crease, I thought I caught Nasser Hussain at mid-on when he was on 14. As I mentioned earlier, I told Hussain I caught it, but he declined to walk, and the umpire decided to refer the decision upstairs. As soon as he referred it, I knew it wasn't going to be given out. Fortunately, we dismissed Hussain shortly afterwards for 24, but it was a disappointing situation that could have been avoided had Nasser believed me. Once England were out for 270, we made them follow on, an interesting move given the weather was pretty hot during the match and we had the Sydney Test straight after it.

Craig White made 85 for England, and it was his first score of the series. In a way, he was playing on his 'home' ground, because quite a few members of his family who were living in Victoria were coming to watch the innings. He'd made his First Class debut with Victoria and then headed to England to forge a career with Yorkshire.

When England followed on, Michael Vaughan made a superb hundred and set us a tricky last-innings target of 107. Steve Waugh came in to bat for the last time in a Test on the MCG, and we needed about 50 to win.

Nasser Hussain tried an interesting tactic: he gave Justin Langer a single to get Steve on strike. I thought it was a good idea because it was something different, a smart move given that Tugga was suffering from a migraine. It was certainly outside the square of thinking. The same thing happened when Martin Love was batting. England wanted to have a go at Steve, and given he'd played 160 Tests up to that stage, it got up his nose a bit because he didn't think England were being respectful.

Tugga nicked one behind, and England didn't appeal till they saw the screen. Shortly afterwards, Tugga was caught at mid-off, but it was a no-ball. Had that wicket fallen, the move might have almost paid off for them, but they didn't set us a big enough target, and although we had the jitters, we made it home by five wickets and went 4–nil up.

Hookesy weighs in

It was at about this time that David Hookes got stuck into Steve Waugh, saying it was about time he retired. I think Hookesy got stuck in by saying that Tugga had slogged his 77 in the first innings and also went on about the fact that Tugga was demeaning the Australian team by continuing to wear his baggy green cap, which looked dirty and untidy.

David spoke his mind, and I for one respected him for the fact. It seems as though many modern-day players take criticism badly and can't handle it when former players come out and make statements. They're happy to take the praise when it comes their way, but suddenly, when a bit of criticism is floating around, their critics are bad blokes. Everyone hops into former champion Aussie batsman Neil Harvey, and it's probably true that he might've overstepped the line from time to time. However, you can look at it from the point of view that a former player is getting a bit of work on the speaking circuit and staying in a job.

Hookesy would say that there's nothing wrong with having an argument about things that occur during a game. He used his media role to keep cricket in the minds of people by generating debate, so people in turn started thinking about the game. In Melbourne, an AFL town, he continually kept cricket right up there as a topic for discussion — a good thing. Just because someone like him states his opinion that a spot in the team is up for grabs, there's no need to have the shits with him.

In my Test career I've always found it quite hard work to play a back-to-back Test in Melbourne and then Sydney. You often get only two days off at best, and that includes travel. As a bowler, I've found this schedule quite difficult and I don't think it's right, especially because a summer day can be quite warm, which it was for that Boxing Day Test. There should be a minimum of three days between the Test matches, but because the scheduling is traditional, the cricket authorities won't change it. If they started the Sydney Test on 3 January, I don't think it'd make a lot of difference. The players deserve the extra day, and not only the pacemen but the batsmen — they all need to recharge their batteries.

I don't want to take anything away from England, who played very well in that final Test match. Andy Caddick took 10 wickets and bowled magnificently. Michael Vaughan made a brilliant 183 in their second innings. Steve Harmison started to hit his straps, and bowled fast and well.

Tugga brings up a ton

On the second day of that match, one of the most exciting ends to a day's play ever seen on the Sydney Cricket Ground occurred. In front of a packed house, Steve Waugh brought up a hundred off the last ball of the day's play. On 95 at the start of the over, Steve blocked the first three balls and then played a square drive for three runs, and moved to 98. Two balls were left, and Adam Gilchrist managed to find a single to give Steve a chance to get his ton off the last ball. Gilly has since said it was probably the most important single he's ever scored. Steve then duly hit Richard Dawson's last ball for four and brought up his ton. The crowd went nuts, and I'm sure the estimated 2.1 million fans watching the match on TV did as well.

It was terrific to be part of it all. The atmosphere in the rooms was truly tense as Tugga was approaching the ton. We were all sitting back and holding our breath, hoping he'd get there. When that last ball of the day went flashing through the covers for four, everyone in the rooms went ballistic. When Steve came in, he was dumbfounded by it all. His family was there, including his father, Roger, and it was nice for them to be able to celebrate the moment with Steve. We were chuffed for him, and it was a perfect end to the day.

ABC funnyman Andrew Denton also happened to be in the rooms. He'd paid to be in there as 'assistant coach' for the day. He couldn't have picked a better day to be in there with the Australian team. He's quite an interesting and intelligent fellow and is obviously passionate about the game. I think he later described it as the best day of his life.

Early on the third day, Steve was dismissed reasonably early, so probably felt a bit let down from the previous day's high. Gilly stepped up to the plate and made a fantastic century. It was a typically aggressive innings by Adam as he smashed England to all parts of the SCG. I managed to hang around with him for a while: I made 31 as we added 72 for the ninth wicket, and helped us to 363 — a lead of one run.

My left elbow

In the second innings, I managed to get injured again. This time it was a ligament in my left elbow. The groundsmen had been repairing the footholds with part-cement and part–pitch soil, and in doing so had made the footholds as hard as a cat's head. I slipped on one of them, and as I landed, I tried to stop my fall and landed on my left elbow, injuring the ligament. I couldn't move my arm, so I had to go straight off, and that was the end of the series for me.

Thanks mainly to Michael Vaughan's innings, England set us the mammoth task of scoring 452 to win. We had a terrible start to the innings in that we copped a few bad lbw decisions.

Spitting the dummy

Justin Langer was unlucky, as was Matty Hayden. Matty was really angry; he either hit or kicked the door in the rooms and broke a glass panel. It was unfortunate the 'dummy spit' was captured on television, because he was fined $2200 for it. Although it was a pretty ordinary decision, he'd have done better to release his anger somewhere in the rooms where no one could see the outburst.

In one way, Matty's outburst is indicative that we're good front runners but that when things don't go our way, we lose our rag a bit too much. I think we've set such a high standard over the years that when we don't get the rub of the green, we carry on and spit the odd dummy. I think that was evident during the last session of play on the fourth day of that Test match.

Andy Bichel went in as a very early nightwatchman, so attracted some attention. He played skilfully to be 49 not out at stumps but was fired out lbw early on the final day by Russell Tiffin. In my belief this was a wrong decision, and I must say he didn't have the best of games. He and I have had a few beers in the past, and he's a nice fellow. However, on this occasion he might have been suffering somewhat because he'd also umpired the MCG Test and he was perhaps finding it all too much, having to umpire 10 days of Test cricket in the space of only 12 days. My argument for a three-day break between Tests applies to umpires as well: they're under a heap of pressure to get all the decisions right.

ENGLAND DESERVEDLY WON THE TEST AND THEREBY AVOIDED the whitewash. Michael Vaughan was named both Man of the Match and Man of the Series, based on his 633 runs and three hundreds.

Darren Lehmann missed the last two Tests of that series because he had a serious leg infection. It was a bizarre situation. He'd felt something funny in his upper leg, something that felt like a sack of marbles near his groin. It was ugly for him: he'd picked up a nasty infection from God knows where — maybe a pair of dirty socks. I popped in to see him, and he was diagnosed as having a staph infection, which turned out to be somewhat serious. Thankfully, he recovered after a while and was soon back in the middle. He just had to spend some time in bed to recover and was pumped full of antibiotics to try to rid his body of the infection.

Although I'd taken 20 wickets in the series, I couldn't snare a five-wicket haul in it. I don't know how many 'four-fors' I've got during my Test career, but there've been a bloody lot of them. Really, though, I wasn't all that fussed, because I had bowled well and contributed without too many worries. If you could get four wickets an innings, you'd take them every time.

Fortunately, my left elbow recovered pretty quickly and I was on the plane for the World Cup coming up in South Africa. Having won in 1999 over in England, we knew we'd have to put in some massive effort to make it back-to-back titles.

Cricketer of the Year

In 2002 I was named Wisden Cricketer of the Year, which was unexpected and certainly gratefully accepted. Apart from the honour of that title, the other lovely gift I received was a leather-bound copy of the *Almanack* for that year, which is now part of my treasured memorabilia.

World Cup 2003, the Windies, and other important engagements

Our 2003 World Cup campaign was to be played in South Africa, Zimbabwe and Kenya. It got off to a highly dramatic start when Shane Warne called a press conference to announce he'd taken a diuretic his mother had given him. Warnie had been routinely tested and his sample had come up positive — a shock to us all, to say the least. Obviously, he hadn't realised the diuretic was on the list of banned medications, and when quizzed, he admitted what had happened. It was massive news and wasn't the ideal way to lead into our first match against 1999 runners-up Pakistan.

When the story broke, I was getting some treatment from an acupuncturist in Johannesburg. The shit had hit the fan, and Warnie had had to explain the situation at a team meeting. Once that had happened, he was out of the World Cup and on the plane home.

We were disappointed and felt bad for Shane. He'd explained the situation to us, and we had no reason to doubt that what he'd said was true. Later on, a few theories flew around as to why he took the diuretic, but I believed his explanation — nothing more, nothing less. I'm a strong believer that if someone who's a mate looks me in the eye and tells me something, I take him at his word.

It was a blow to team morale that Shane wouldn't be turning out for us in our defending of the World Cup. He'd played such an important role in getting us back from the brink in 1999, and to not have him was a massive disappointment. We knew the repercussions of being subject to a positive drug test: what can happen in relation to the suspension and the baggage that goes with all that. At that point, we had to re-group. We knew we had to play the tournament without Warnie, so we had to move on and focus on the matches ahead.

Shane had made a massive mistake because he should have known that the drug he used was on the banned list, and he acknowledged as much. For him, though, I think one underlying message came out of the incident: not long after it, he came out and said he truly knew who his mates were. Many people had a real crack at him publicly — people from everywhere, not only cricket media types. All sorts of individuals suggested he should be banned from playing cricket for life and said he was a disgrace to Australian sport.

As soon as someone does something wrong, all these sports reporters come out and nail him — no ifs; no buts; no maybes. Apparently that's good journalism. I've never been able to understand why print journalists do it. Fair enough, Warnie's done the wrong thing, it's a major story and it's 'got legs' — so the newspapers will run off the shelves — but I think that at times, reporters and their editors could handle the news a lot better. Shane has done many good things for charity over the years, and plenty of that stuff goes unreported. I guess those positive things aren't worthy of being a big news story.

Against Pakistan, the Wanderers, 11 February 2003

We didn't have much time to sit back and worry about what had happened, though, because in our opening match of the tournament, we had to play Pakistan at the Wanderers. Batting first, we were in a fair bit of trouble early in the match: we were 4/86 when Andrew Symonds came in and played a spectacular innings. From the word go, he came out and timed the ball beautifully. It was almost as though he'd picked out the areas he wanted to hit the ball to. Symmo scored a lot of runs through cover and wide mid-off, with some fierce drives. I can still picture him smashing Shahid Afridi through that area a number of times — he gave the appearance of being a player with a concise plan.

Over the years, the perception has arisen that Symmo lacks planning for his batting. However, in that knock of 143 from 125 deliveries, he definitely showed otherwise, and it seemed to be that if Pakistan bowled anything outside of off-stump, he'd have a real crack at it. He worked the ball around the field nicely, and given he's a pacy runner between the wickets, he did his best to turn as many singles as he could into twos. Symmo absolutely nailed the ball a few times; it was one of the best knocks I've ever seen in International cricket.

It was a turning point in his career and gave Symmo the impetus to believe in his own ability. Also, after that knock, he seemed to feel more that he belonged in the team. He'd always had a potential tag as a bits and pieces player, but with this knock, he overcame a big hurdle in his limited-over career.

Before the lead-up to the tournament, Ricky Ponting had pushed hard for Andrew to be in the squad. Ricky really believed in

Andrew's ability and must have seen his qualities, because he badly wanted him to come to South Africa. There's no better endorsement for a player than having the captain want you in the team that much. Ricky must also have given Symmo immense confidence. His faith was repaid instantly, and Andrew helped us get 8/310 — a tremendously good score.

We ended up bowling Pakistan out for 228 and had a comfortable win.

Against India, Centurion Park, 15 February 2003

After we'd won at the Wanderers, we ventured north of Johannesburg, to Centurion Park, for our match against India. They batted first, and I didn't take the new ball; instead, I came on first change and in my first delivery got the wicket of Rahul Dravid. Everything progressed smoothly from there. The ball was coming out really nicely, and I had a feeling it'd be a good day when Dravid played on. It was just one of those days: the ball wasn't coming out at any extra speed; I was simply hitting good areas. The ball nipped a tad early, but it wasn't as though I was unplayable. We got a few wickets early, and thanks to a combination of good bowling and tight fielding, we bowled the opposition out cheaply. I finished with 3/13, and the score was obviously a factor in our winning a vital game. In actual fact, I bowled my 10 overs straight through. Thanks to the three wickets Brett Lee also took, we bowled India out for only 125. To walk away from that game having chalked up figures such as those in a World Cup match was a big personal highlight. The Indians' batting line-up was especially strong, so for us to have a performance like that was terrific.

We knocked over the runs fairly easily, so we'd had two wins from two games — a rousing start to the tournament.

Against Holland, Potchefstroom, 20 February 2003

Rain affected our next game. We played in Potchefstroom, South Africa, against Holland. I bowled only three overs and got 2/7; it was like stealing candy from a baby.

A few media reps in South Africa had been questioning whether the Dutch should even be in the World Cup. But it's not just the guys from the Netherlands, the issue is much bigger. I'd like to see the ICC rethink how the World Cup is organised. I think the qualifying process that the minnow teams have to go through is okay, but that the main tournament has a couple of sides too many.

Although we Aussies want to spread the game globally, when the early stages of the tournament have games like that which are a foregone conclusion, frankly, it ends up being a joke. While these sides do need to have a carrot dangled, dropping them into a one-sided situation doesn't help anyone. No one enjoys these no contests; there are no winners. It seems unfair to put them into the cauldron of a World Cup in which they're more likely to sink than swim. They won't get within a bull's roar of making the next round.

Okay, there is the odd exception. In 2003, Kenya were lucky and made it through only because New Zealand wouldn't go to Kenya to play them because of concerns about security. Kenya beat Sri Lanka, so they'd improved, but essentially they fluked it to secure a berth in the semi-finals.

I can see some good options for trying to help them out. Rather than have these beginner-type teams in the actual World Cup, I'd like to see them play more against A sides in the various full-member countries. It'd be better if the ICC invested money in a team such as Holland by getting them to play some cricket in Australia against A sides, State teams and Second Elevens. It would get them used to other conditions, because at present all they do is play cricket in their own country and participate in the occasional tournament that involves other teams at their level. The sides need to experience various types of conditions in order to improve. The ICC could do things like bring them out here to play on our tracks, send them to India to experience turning wickets, and get them to tour places that have different pitches from theirs, to help them experience a wide range of cricketing situations.

Why can't these teams go to South Africa and play against some of that country's provincial teams? Why can't they come to Darwin and Cairns to play some matches when our Centre of Excellence members are up there? Another possibility for helping to grow those teams is to get them over for a hit against Club sides. Give them some experience and get them on tour! If the ICC wants to spread the game, it has to spend some money in the right areas to facilitate initiative.

After we'd won against Holland, we had a few drinks with them, and I remember that one of their guys, Henk Mol, was desperate to swap shirts with one of us. However, it was only early in the tournament and we still had a few games to go, so we thought we'd need all the shirts we had. The Dutchies were dying to swap, and Damien Martyn was being cornered by this bloke, Henk Mol, who wasn't taking no for an answer. Marto eventually swapped with Henk, for whom we coined the catchphrase 'Molly! Molly! Molly!' So, Marto now has this shirt from Henk Mol. No disrespect intended, but Henk isn't one of the more recognisable names in International cricket, so I think he did slightly better out of the deal! Henk now has a 'D Martyn' shirt, and has probably framed it and placed it in his bar at home — and good luck to him.

Against Zimbabwe, Bulawayo, 24 February 2003

Because of the terrible political situation in Zimbabwe with dictator Robert Mugabe, plenty of people were saying that, on moral grounds, we shouldn't make the trip to Bulawayo to play our scheduled match against their national side. England had declined to go there. We were concerned both about the morality of the decision and about security within the country. People were constantly experiencing problems there because of the food and petrol shortages, and because the government was kicking farmers off their land.

To protest against the government's human-rights abuses, Zimbabwe players Andy Flower and Henry Olonga each wore a black armband during the team's opening match in the tournament in Harare. Also, they issued a joint statement to mourn 'the death of democracy in their beloved Zimbabwe'. They took a huge personal risk by making a stand, and were highly courageous. Olonga didn't play in the World Cup again, and the selectors were going to drop Andy for allegedly not trying against India; however, when the rest of the team threatened to boycott the match, the selectors kept him in the team.

At the end of the World Cup, both players left the country, and as far as I know have never been back. Andy played a year in South Australia, and although he didn't do that well, he enjoyed the place and was a good bloke to have around.

In hindsight, it was a mistake to go to Zimbabwe to play. The ICC assured us we'd be safe and was really keen on having us go, for reasons only it would know. Safety was the biggest issue, and we were fortunate in that our security officer, Darren Maughan, was a Zimbabwean who actually came from Bulawayo. Nicknamed 'Pirate', Maughan was a man you could respect, and because he guaranteed we'd have no problem, we were more than satisfied. We put our faith in his judgement, and the game went off without incident.

One of the other biggest issues was whether Mugabe was going to come to the ground and, if so, would want to meet us and shake our hands. I'm sure that most if not all the blokes, me included, wouldn't have wanted any of these three things to happen. Politically, too, it would be a disaster for him if he turned up — at least that's what we heard from the locals — and there were sighs of relief all round when we heard we wouldn't be faced with that situation.

GIVEN ALL THE PRESSURE THEY WERE UNDER, ZIMBABWE BATTED quite well in the game: they made 9/246, and Andy Blignaut blasted 54 off only 28 balls. At one stage, he smashed me for three fours in successive balls, and he then hit Brad Hogg for two big sixes over long-on in the one over. Brett Lee came back on and bowled Andy a full toss, which he hammered back at Brett, who somehow caught it, to preserve his own safety more than anything else.

Andy was a handy all-rounder and eventually left Zimbabwe to try to make a First Class career in Tasmania. It's a shame that things didn't work out for him there, and given the situation in his home country, it's unlikely he'll play any more International cricket — very sad.

We ended up having a comfortable seven-wicket win in Bulawayo and left the country that night, as per our security arrangements.

WE ACTUALLY WENT BACK TO ZIMBABWE 12 MONTHS LATER AND played three one-dayers. Believe it or not, it's been one of my favourite places to visit. We were there for only seven days, so we played the three games and fitted in some hunting on two days and bass fishing on the other two days.

Not only did I have a great time in between games but I was named Man of the Match in one game and Man of the Series. I loved Zimbabwe! But not for one second do I agree with what's going on in that country; I don't think anyone agrees with it. Everyone just wants the country back to what it once was.

Out of the game — that sinking feeling

THINGS WERE GOING OKAY FITNESS-WISE RIGHT UP UNTIL I bowled my last ball in the nets before the game with Namibia, in Potchefstroom, 20 February 2003. I felt something strange in my right heel but thought nothing of it. I was walking around okay, and it wasn't till the next morning that when I went to push off and break into a jog, I couldn't do it. I went to Errol and told him the situation, and that was it: I was out of that game. Little did I imagine that I wouldn't be bowling again in the tournament. For the next week or so I stayed around trying to get the heel right, but the way the recovery was going, it seemed that the earliest I'd be available was for the semi-final. The selectors were right in not wanting to carry me through the rest of the tournament.

It was a long and lonely flight back to Adelaide because it was such a disappointment for me to be coming home early. It was my first, and what turned out to be my only, World Cup, and I'd been bowling well. If I wasn't making a contribution on the field, I didn't want to hang around. It would have been nice to be there with the lads, but I've always felt it's better to make way for someone who can be fit to play. I feel I made the right decision to head back.

Back in Adelaide, I watched the Final at the Oyster Bar, on East Terrace. A group of South Australian cricket lads were there, and the owner Jason Bernardi looked after us really well. The trouble was, everyone kept coming hassling me all night: 'Dizzy, you should be there!', and I was thinking, *No shit — thanks for that.* I had a couple of beers, a few oysters and a chat to a few of the lads, but I left before the end of the game because I was a bit sick of the attention: I couldn't handle it and the fact I wasn't in Johannesburg playing. I ended up watching the end of the game at home. That was the other hard part about being injured this time around: you're missing out on creating history in a tournament that comes around only every four years.

Luck was on my side and I recovered fairly quickly. As soon as my right heel came good, I was on the plane for the West Indies tour, which followed the World Cup. I played in all the lead-up matches in Georgetown before the first Test; I was fit, bowled well at training and got through nine overs in each innings of the last tour match, so in my own mind I was ready to go for the start of the four-Test series.

Stories from Georgetown, Guyana

I'd never been to Georgetown before, and it surprised me how much of a Third World country it appeared to be. I'd assumed it would be much more prosperous. We stayed at the Pegasus Hotel, which was a nice place, and they looked after us extremely well. However, all around Georgetown, things weren't that flash: there were whole streets that were run-down and open sewers, for example.

Security was a genuine concern, so much so that when I wasn't playing in the Test, I didn't leave the hotel. With my general lack of enthusiasm for sightseeing, that arrangement suited me fine. At night time, I would head down from my room, find a table by the pool and have dinner there with whoever was around — that was my Georgetown routine.

Steve Waugh, however, had to have a look around; he has this incredible curiosity about different places. On a previous tour there, he was escorted by one of the big crime bosses, to ensure he was safe, when he went to one of the more dangerous parts of town.

The guy took Tugga to the worst part of the town, where he was well respected and had a bit of power. Going to those places like that outside the hours of play has never been my cup of tea, and I was more than happy to stick with the security advice of staying in and around the hotel. I was content to just chill out in my room or have a swim.

DURING TEST MATCHES IN THAT PART OF THE WORLD, YOU HAVE one or two room attendants who look after you during the breaks in play. They might fetch you a drink, a towel or whatever. After one match during this tour, we were all sitting around having a few beers when our 'roomie' grabbed a bottle from one of the Eskies in the rooms and necked it in a few seconds flat. A few of us who'd noticed what he'd done had a brainwave and offered him a few bucks to do it again. We suggested that he drink a six-pack in 10 minutes, and all chipped in a few US bucks each to watch him do it. The Caribbean is a pretty poor area, and guys like the roomie don't earn much, so we thought the dare was an okay thing to do. The poor guy started in a blaze of glory and necked the first couple, but after that he got into a spot of trouble and ended up being sick. Obviously, having a lot of beers in a short space of time isn't the best idea, so even though he didn't quite complete the half dozen, we paid him the money anyway.

By chance, we found out how the story ended. Our skipper, Steve Waugh, was out shopping the next day and ran across the guy with his wife. Apparently he still didn't look too well. Despite that fact, the roomie's face broke into a big grin when he saw Steve. He told him he and his wife had bought a new couch with the proceeds of the bet! His wife was delighted by it all, so it was nice that some good had come out of getting our roomie to try to skol those beers!

First Test against the Windies, Georgetown, Guyana, 10–13 April 2003

The Bourda Ground in Georgetown is quite rickety; most of its stands are made of wood, and it's quite old-fashioned in appearance. Each stand is named after a famous Guyanese player — people such as Clive Lloyd or Rohan Kanhai, who are legends of the game in the West Indies.

It's a quirky place to play: it has a flat wicket and an extremely fast outfield. It's the home ground of Shivnarine Chanderpaul, and in this first Test he got a hundred runs off 69 balls yet didn't play a risky shot at all, despite reaching the milestone so quickly. He didn't slog or do anything silly; instead, he played each ball on its merits, and suddenly had a hundred — it crept up on us and was a bizarre situation. He hit good-length balls, by punching them past mid-off and mid-on. When he reached his ton, he kissed the pitch, which seemed a bit ridiculous but I suppose he was caught up in the moment. He fully deserved the achievement, though, because he'd played extremely well. I suppose if you make a 69-ball hundred, you can do what you want.

After centuries to Justin Langer and Ricky Ponting, we had a lead of 252, so were set up for a win. In the second innings, Stuart MacGill and Brad Hogg opened the bowling. It's not too often that two spinners open the attack, but it was late in the afternoon and we were threatened with going off through bad light, so if we wanted to play on we had no choice. The next day, both Daren Ganga and Brian Lara made hundreds after sharing a long partnership through which they gained some chance of setting us a decent fourth-innings target. To that point, Ganga had barely averaged more than 20, so it was a real breakthrough for him to make a hundred. Lara always seems to save his best for us. However, that day he was unlucky when he tried to hit a leg-side ball from Hoggy with one hand and clipped the stumps in his follow-through.

After he was dismissed, we bowled the Windies out early on the fourth day and won by nine wickets.

In the second dig, I managed to take 5/39, including my 150th Test wicket: Vasbert Drakes, whom I snared lbw.

WE PLAYED FIVE BOWLERS IN THAT FIRST TEST, AND DID SO FOR the rest of the series. Our thinking was that wickets were going to be as flat as a tack and painfully slow, and that we definitely needed the extra flexibility in our attack. We were proven right: our thoughts had been to back the top six to make enough runs, and we'd ended up being totally justified in doing so.

Asoka de Silva was one of the umpires in that Test and had to that point managed to acquit himself well on the ICC Elite Panel. Unfortunately, he had an inconsistent match — the worst thing for the players.

Second Test, Port of Spain, Trinidad and Tobago, 19–23 April 2003

DARREN 'BOOFER' LEHMANN MADE A HUNDRED ON THE OPENING day of the second Test — his maiden ton in Test cricket. He was pretty delighted to finally crack three figures, and in his innings, he set things up nicely. His knock was brilliant: he took on the Windies bowlers and played well. If anyone deserved a Test ton it was Darren, and later on in his career, he went on to score a few more.

When Boof was dismissed, Steve Waugh sent Adam Gilchrist in at five, and in the end, Steve didn't bat at all in the match — an extremely rare occurrence. Steve 'slid down the greasy pole', as we liked to say, because he seemed to have something wrong with his hand. His argument seemed to be, 'If I don't need to bat, I won't.' The decision was rather strange, because he almost seemed to be playing the game as skipper only. I'm pretty sure before he took on the captaincy, he would never have agreed if someone else had done as Steve was doing if that player was in charge — it didn't really add up.

As far as injuries were concerned, during that game, I was having a few worries of my own because my achilles tendon was playing up. I'm not sure whether the injury was related to the problem I'd had during the World Cup, but it was extremely painful. Each morning, I got out of bed and would struggle to walk, so I'd hobble down to the hotel pool to try to stretch the leg and warm it up before I got to the ground. Prior to the match I kept my warm-up minimal, and the only running I did was when I was actually in the field bowling.

This approach was effective, because I bowled really well in that game and I guess I was lucky to get through it without breaking down.

In each innings, I picked up three wickets and managed to keep Lara very quiet, even though I didn't dismiss him on his home ground. I felt I bowled really well to him despite being worried about my achilles tendon. I did, however, get Devon Smith out for a pair, caught behind in the first innings and lbw in the second. It was a dead flat deck, as were all the decks on that tour, so every wicket was hard earned.

We set the Windies 407 to win, and on the last day, Brett Lee went head to head with Lara during a spell of about 40 minutes. Binga bounced him a few times, and Lara played some brilliant hook shots. The crowd went into a frenzy. Brett was bowling extremely fast without having a lot of luck, and it was sparkling Test cricket, because neither player gave an inch. Brett bounced him, and Brian left one and then hooked the next. Both players were going hammer-and-tongs at each other. After lunch, it was a bit of an anti-climax for the local fans, because Stuart MacGill eventually got Lara for 122 and we ended up winning the Test by 118 runs.

A disco in the grandstand

The West Indian spectators are amazing in that most of them are thoroughly knowledgeable about the game and understand it well. The support they show for their team is very parochial and is the focus of their attention; they don't tend to direct it too much to you as a visiting player. At some of the grounds, they even set up a disco. At Port of Spain, they had a disco dance floor, complete with strobe lights, up in the grandstand. It was an outdoor nightclub, and people were up there drinking beer and rum while dancing around enjoying themselves.

Trinidad is one of those places where as a player you'd like to return, purely to watch a Test match up in the stand; the lads are always talking about a couple of places they'd like to visit to watch a Test match at the end of their career.

For me, pretty much anywhere in the West Indies would fit the bill. The fun and frivolity of the Caribbean are terrific. Adelaide is also one of those places. Everyone places Adelaide high on the list because the ground is in beautiful surroundings, and the Members' set-up out the back is extremely popular.

Third Test Bridgetown, Barbados, 1–5 May 2003

For the next Test, our hearts sank when we had a look at the pitch in Bridgetown, Barbados. It was a hell of a flat track, so once again, we'd be using five bowlers. In years gone by, the Kensington pitch had been known as one of the world's fastest, but sadly, in recent times, it's become slow, and lost all its pace and bounce.

We nutted out a strategy that involved four pacemen and Stuart MacGill; Andy Bichel was selected to bat at number seven. 'Bic' really stood up to the plate to make 71; it was phenomenal the way he took that responsibility and embraced it. Steve Waugh had complete faith in him, and Bic responded by giving a fantastic account of himself. Tugga seemed to have recovered from what had bothered him in Trinidad: he and Ricky Ponting notched up a century apiece.

In that innings, I hit two sixes, both off their spinner Omari Banks. I came in with the score at 7/580. A declaration was pending, so I thought I'd better play some shots, because if ever there was a chance for me to hit a six in a Test match, this was it. They were both over 'cow corner' — mid-wicket — and I gave Omari a severe touch-up: the poor guy ended up going for more than 200 runs. Up to that stage of my Test career, I'd hit only one six: Craig White, over cover in the 2002–03 Perth Ashes Test, so it was pleasing to get a couple away over the fence in Bridgetown.

In India, we'd been burned by making the Indians follow on. In this game, however, we ran out of time so we had to enforce the follow-on, because we felt it was the best and probably only method we could use to win. We'd picked five bowlers so we'd have enough firepower up our sleeve to field for three days.

Having made them follow on, we did have to bowl a heck of a lot of overs — we actually fielded on four of the five days of the match. At one end we rotated the quicks while Stuart MacGill wove his magic from the other. We decided that Stuie would have a rest for half an hour in each session but would still end up bowling his 12-over spells in the two-hour period. We planned it like that: four-over spells for the quicks to keep them fresh, and we'd simply bore and grind them out.

We bowled really tight, Test-match lines. For the second match in a row, my figures were fewer than two runs per over — 4/68 from 49 overs. It was one of those games: we all bowled well on the flattest pitch ever. We were stoked to win that Test.

I'll never forget how, after that win, we went out onto the pitch and sang the team victory song there. Tugga said it was one of the most satisfying wins of his career because we'd managed to get the Windies out twice on a track that had definitely lost its former fire and pace. Even the locals were disheartened by the state of the pitch. During the 1980s and '90s it had been a trademark of the West Indies' phenomenal success.

Even though that wicket was too flat by a country mile, we stuck to our guns and achieved what we'd set out to do.

'Frank Drebin' and friends

WHEN WE WERE IN BARBADOS, WE WERE INVITED TO ATTEND A function with Winfred Peppinck, who was the Australian High Commissioner. When you visit these sorts of places, you have to sign a guest book, so this time I decided to have a bit of fun. I signed in as *Frank Drebin — Police Squad*. The American actor Leslie Nielsen had played Frank in a number of the *Naked Gun* movies and been extremely funny in the role, and because I'm a fan of the character, I thought I'd sign in as him. I think everyone knew it was me, because I'd signed in as 'Frank' a couple of times before, and Anna, who was with me, had signed in on the line above. I certainly didn't think I could get into any trouble over it. Thankfully everyone had a laugh and saw the humour in it. It'd become something of a running joke, because over the years, I've left tickets for 'Frank Drebin' at quite a few Test grounds.

Somebody else I've left tickets for on the odd occasion is my Adelaide Cricket Club teammate Erin Bernhardt. He was always one for saying he'd turn up unannounced at a Test ground one day and expect to be able to get in, no matter where the game was. After he started the joke, for about the next two years I used to arrange to leave a single ticket for him in an envelope marked 'E. Bernhardt', just in case he turned up.

The former Australian off-spinner Tim May used to leave tickets at matches for 'Mr F. Flood' ('Flash Flood') and 'Mr R. L. Downpour' ('Rather Large Downpour'). Another recipient was 'Ferris Bueller', the lead character in the movie *Ferris Bueller's Day Off*. It was quite funny at the end of the day's play when the room attendant would come back in with the leftover tickets and let me know, 'Ferris didn't use the tickets you left for him.' I'd respond by saying that it was probably Ferris's day off and he must have had something else on. Without fail, the 'roomie' wouldn't have seen the movie and didn't get the joke, but we all had a bit of a guffaw at that one. I probably took it too far, but you have to have a bit of fun sometimes when you're involved in a long tour or series.

Fourth Test, St John's, Antigua, 9–13 May 2003

We had a 3–nil lead in the series and headed to St John's, in Antigua, for the fourth and final Test. Antigua is one of the world's most picturesque places; it has beautiful beaches and a fantastic climate. We batted first and the Windies bowled us out for only 240, thanks to their paceman Jermaine Lawson, who took seven wickets. Jermaine had a slightly suspect bowling action, and the umpires later found he didn't quite conform to the laws of the game.

When it was the Windies' turn to bat, Brian Lara came out to bat early on and immediately had a confrontation with Steve Waugh. Lara started carrying on, then Steve retorted and got a bit back for his trouble. I've never had any issues with Brian as a bloke, but things change when you're on the ground. That day several of us had a few things to say to him. Basically, we told him to stop carrying on like a baby and to concentrate on his batting. His response was to tell us to go and get nicked, which he was well within his rights to do.

During the last innings of the match, tempers became frayed and quite a number of clashes occurred on the ground. Ramnaresh Sarwan and Glenn McGrath had what was, at the time, an obvious disagreement out on the ground.

There are various accounts of that altercation but the following is my version of what happened. Glenn had been bowling quite well but was getting frustrated and decided to sledge Sarwan. He asked him, 'What does Lara's c—- taste like?' Quick as a flash, Sarwan answered, 'I dunno; why don't you ask your wife?' He wasn't aware that Glenn's wife, Jane, was battling cancer. Glenn had been helping Jane to get through her awful time. Anyway, the remark caused Glenn to go off his brain: his eyes started to spin and he was instantly unbelievably upset. He responded by walking up to Sarwan, his eyes spinning, and declaring, 'If you ever talk about my fuckin' wife again, I'm gunna fuckin' rip your throat out!' That's what he said, word for word; I was right there. All of a sudden, I was thinking, *Here we go; anything could happen.* Funnily enough, however, as bad as it looked on TV, it wasn't quite as bad out there in the field — but it's all about perception, and I must admit it didn't look that good.

Sarwan had little to say in response to Glenn's tirade. He virtually went to water after that and decided there and then he'd finish contributing to the conversation. His original comeback had been sensational, though, and even Glenn couldn't believe he'd come up with such a quick response in so short a space of time. The beauty of it was that after the West Indies had won the match, the two guys were in the rooms and spent about 40 minutes together having a beer and a chat. In Sarwan's defence, he'd had no idea about Jane's illness and he was sticking up for himself when he was being sledged. It was another one of those situations in which things end up alright, because what happens on the field stays out there. In different circumstances, I reckon Glenn might have had a laugh, but because the sledging centred around his wife, it was too sensitive an issue. Cricket Australia raked Glenn over the coals for his role in the drama: naturally they had to be seen to be doing the right thing and not to be supporting playing the game in the wrong way.

Taking the rough with the smooth on the road

LOOKING BACK ON THAT MATCH AND HOW IT WAS PLAYED, I wonder whether the tiredness factor had anything to do with the fact that so much sledging occurred. We'd played a whole summer of cricket in Australia, then had the World Cup in South Africa and after a few days headed for the Caribbean. After the World Cup win, the lads hadn't had a chance to celebrate and unwind a whole lot. That might go some way towards explaining the grumpiness in that Test in Antigua.

Before the West Indies tour, I'd had a chance to go home and have a reasonable break, so the tiredness defence couldn't apply to me too much. However, I know that a lot of the guys who play in both forms of the game were cooked by the time they played in the One Day Internationals in the West Indies. Adam Gilchrist was 'gone'; he needed to get away and have a break, having had enough of playing cricket. He was physically and mentally 'shot', and couldn't wait to get home and recharge his batteries. It's amazing how good you feel again in a short space of time if you can have some kind of a break.

Travelling around the West Indies is also taxing. The pace of life over there is laid back and everything is done slowly. What isn't helpful is that some days there's only one flight from A to B. Sometimes, for a half-hour flight between islands, the routine starts at 8 a.m. and you don't make it to the hotel till 6 p.m. Getting around the Caribbean can be a laborious and tiring process.

Players' gear has a tendency to go missing fairly easily, too, in that part of the world. On this tour, a taxi driver nicked some of our stuff. Later he got caught out and ended up being arrested and thrown in the lock-up. To our relief, some of the stuff he'd stolen turned up; however, disappointingly, a few guys lost some of their equipment. I was very thankful I got all my stuff back.

In 2003, plenty of Aussie supporters were in the West Indies. I'm mates with Luke Gillian from wavingtheflag.com, and occasionally after stumps, he joined me for a beer to discuss the day's play.

Over the years, I think that Luke and his crew have gotten a bit of a rough deal. Cricket Australia never helped them out all that much, and it was a shame because the 'wavingtheflag' boys were the really diehard cricket fans. They went everywhere and tried to set the campaign up, but this didn't get a whole lot of support and it fizzled out. On the subcontinent, where not that many Aussie supporters would go, I'd have thought that Cricket Australia would be more than happy to have some loyal Aussie presence in the stands. Luke's a staunch team supporter, always clapping partnerships or little milestones that were important for the team. He was there waving his Aussie flag in one hand and his bat in the other, showing major support for the team.

People within the team tried to offer support. Steve Waugh is good friends with Luke, and did his best for him and the gang. Adam Gilchrist is another player who went out of his way to match Luke's loyalty. The Australian team manager, Steve Bernard, always helped them in getting tickets, too. When it came to big matches, I always tried to help Luke get tickets when I could.

Darwin and Cairns come on-stream

WHEN WE'D RETURNED FROM THE WEST INDIES AFTER THE ONE-day series, which we won 4–3, we hosted Bangladesh for some Test matches in Darwin and Cairns. These were new venue cities for

International cricket, and all the fans in the two areas were looking forward to having some top-class cricket up there. The Marrara Ground in Darwin is a good set-up for Australian Rules but to that stage hadn't been used for cricket, whereas Cazaly Stadium in Cairns had an extremely good wicket and outfield, and was more than ready to have a Test match hosted on it.

Although Marrara had a nice grandstand and outfield, we had to play on a drop-in pitch, which as I've said can be a real disadvantage for the bowlers. The run-ups leading in to a drop-in wicket are never the best: you're running in, and then you hit the 'join' between the edge of the pitch and the outfield. You can be thrown off balance in your delivery stride. Also, the 9.30 a.m. start for TV was difficult for both us and the Bangladeshis: we had to get up so early to get ready for the start of the game. There's no such thing as a sleep-in when you play Tests that start at 9.30.

HAVING TO START SO EARLY CAUSES ME A SIGNIFICANT DISRUPTION in my routine. No matter what time we start, before I play I always like to have a solid breakfast. To my mind, breakfast is the most important meal of the day. Food-wise I try to keep things varied. I've always loved my bacon and eggs, sausage and tomato with HP sauce. Cereal with fruit, or toast with Vegemite (I always take plenty of Vegemite when travelling overseas) is another breakfast I don't mind. I will try most things. After that I'll head for the pool to loosen up if I possibly can. So for a morning game I have to get out of bed with the larks to get all that under my belt. Whether it's a batting or bowling day, it makes no difference, as long as I eat an hour before the warm-up at the ground.

THE FUTURE OF INTERNATIONAL CRICKET IN NORTHERN AUSTRALIA has wonderful potential. The first attendances for these Tests proved not to be huge, but the one-dayers attracted good crowds despite the fact the fixtures were going to be one-sided. The Top End had been crying out for some quality International cricket for a while, and given that their teams play when it's winter in the southern states, I think an enormous opportunity exists to host more games up there.

The ICC could help out by scheduling some more A tour games up there; in doing so, it wouldn't benefit only the cricket fans by giving them some quality cricket, it would help develop some of the weaker nations by having them play against quality First Class opposition. Let's see Kenya, Bangladesh and Holland play games up there in our off-season to help them improve their ability.

Darwin has only about 80,000 people, so it will be a struggle for it to ever have a team in the domestic competitions. I wouldn't agree with any suggestion that it use excess players from other states to boost its team. The Darwin Grade competition isn't strong enough, and for the time being, the odd player who shows he's good enough to play at First Class level has to head to another state if he's going to pursue a First Class career.

Tasmania has about half a million people, and has finally broken through and won a Pura Cup after all these years, taking the title in 2006–07. Despite having waited a long time to win one, it's proven it can support a competitive State team, even though the team also struggles a bit with depth.

What I would like to see at some point is some sort of Twenty 20 competition or tournament in which more than one side from each state play. You could have Country Victoria and City Victoria, a team from the Western Districts of Sydney and perhaps incorporate a team from the ACT as well. The ACT have proved they have some good youngsters by going so well in the Under-19s in 2006–07, and many of their players, such as Mark Higgs and Brad Haddin, have progressed through the ranks.

Against Bangladesh, Darwin and Cairns, 18–20 and 25–28 July 2003

We flogged Bangladesh well inside the three days, but they put up a much better showing in the second Test. They won the toss and managed to bat the opening day out. All their recognised batsmen are quite short, which isn't really helpful, but they played with pluck and put together almost 300 in their first innings in Cairns. Their game plan was to let anything outside the stumps go; they trusted the bounce at the Cazaly Stadium, which is one of Australia's best pitches — it has terrific carry and is an excellent ground. The Bangladeshis played their zones, were extremely patient and did well. They adjusted from the slow, low wicket in Darwin and learned from their innings loss in the first Test. We were always going to be all over them because they didn't have a bowling attack, but to their batters' credit, they did better than they'd done in Darwin.

A surpise wedding

Anna and I were married in Port Douglas, Queensland, on 20 September 2003. There was no defining moment or big planned proposal when we decided to get married; it was more of a mutual decision. We had been together for three and a half years and knew that our relationship was strong and long term. We had a great deal in common and shared similar views and values. Anna has always been a great influence in my life. Her support and positive attitude throughout my career has been the backbone of my success. Earlier in the year, some of our close friends had announced their engagement and it brought up the question: if we did get married, when could we fit it into the very busy cricket schedule? At that time it was either September (only three months away), or the following April, or the following September, or …

We both came from similar traditional family backgrounds and had spoken previously about how important marriage was to us, especially as a foundation to starting a family. We spoke at length about what kind of wedding we wanted. The idea of trying to come up with a guest list was a daunting task and didn't appeal to either of us. Anna wasn't keen on the big white traditional wedding anyway, which I was pretty relieved about, although I would have done it if that's what she had wanted. One other factor we had to consider was the media attention. We wanted something different and intimate and so had to come up with a solution that would ensure our wedding wasn't splashed on the front pages of women's magazines.

We knew it would be impossible to keep our wedding quiet in Adelaide, so we decided to get married interstate, and Queensland could almost guarantee good weather. Then we thought by having the ceremony on a moving boat, it would limit any photographers or interested bystanders taking photos, just in case it did get out. From these discussions we decided to go for it and started planning the wedding for three months' time.

With wedding plans under way, I still hadn't officially asked Anna to marry me. I'd already been up to Anna's parents' house to ask them whether I could marry her. Ronan and Jenny are lovely people; I called and spoke with Ronan and asked whether I could pop up for a feed. I don't know whether he had any inkling of what I was going to ask him, but I thought the request would be pretty straightforward. Off I went by myself, and we sat down together for dinner. It was a nice evening. When I asked Ronan and Jenny for permission to marry Anna, they seemed slightly taken aback, but I did think to myself, *Why else would I come up here by myself for dinner?* The situation was quite comical, I suppose, but they gave me permission to marry Anna.

I officially proposed to Anna over a romantic dinner at Casa Mia. I didn't exactly get down on one knee; I told Anna that she was the best thing that had ever happened to me and I wanted us to share the rest of our lives together. During my little speech our friend and restaurateur Malcolm Amos came past our table to give us the progress score of the AFL game that was on at the time, not knowing he was interrupting one of the most important speeches in my life. He had a good laugh about it when we told him later.

When we got into the car to drive home, I gave Anna an engagement ring. She had been shopping to buy it herself, because I didn't want to be seen buying it and maybe give away our secret, but she still got all misty-eyed and teary. Anna couldn't wear it in public until the wedding, but I caught her wearing it at home a couple of times while she was vacuuming.

In the days leading up to the wedding I was on a Redback 'boot camp' at Woodside in the Adelaide Hills. I remember lying awake at night worrying that I was going to get the flu and be unwell for the wedding because we were sleeping out in the rain and living on rations, etc. Luckily, I came away unscathed.

Part of the excitement of the wedding was keeping it a secret from everyone. We told our immediate family before the event but not our close friends.

We flew our chosen guests — Damien and Wendy Fleming, Sue Carmichael, Greg McEvoy (Anna's brother) and Greg's girlfriend, Cherida Palmer — to Port Douglas on Friday, 19 September. My heart sank when we were collecting our luggage and I saw a TV camera pointed at us. It turned out that they were waiting for the local football team who were also on our flight, and when they saw me they thought they'd get some token footage while they were waiting for the team. They had no idea why we were there. Phew!

That night we had our stag and hen's night, but as there aren't many pubs and clubs along the Port Douglas main street, we kept running into each other.

The following day we set sail on a catamaran we had hired (with two crew) and cruised for a couple of hours along Four Mile Beach before dropping anchor. Our captain took the speed boat back to shore to pick up the celebrant. I have to admit that my heart was pumping very hard when I heard the boat returning. Anna walked down the side of the boat to a saxophone instrumental rendition of 'Sea of Love' in bare feet — she looked so beautiful. I had the biggest lump in my throat. After the ceremony we sailed out to Low Isles for a spot of snorkelling and a lazy lunch. That night we dined at Nautilus restaurant and enjoyed a 1998 Grange to mark the occasion.

Anna and I stayed on for another two days to enjoy the sunshine. I had to insist on getting home to Adelaide as I didn't feel comfortable missing too much training, so I promised Anna that Port Douglas was the first of a four-part honeymoon. I still owe her one!

After the wedding we sent out lots of text messages to our extended circle of friends. It was a lot of fun hearing everyone's responses. Our friends knew we were going away for a few days but expected us to come back engaged — not married.

On our return to Adelaide, we wanted to put our wedding photo in the weddings section of the *Sunday Mail*. They decided to put it on the front page on Monday morning. Anna couldn't understand why it was deemed front-page news, and was a little embarrassed about it.

Upon speaking to a photographer about the wedding, he assured us that had they known about it they would have followed us and they would have been there. I guess we made the right decision. I believe a very small grainy photo of us on the boat was published in a local Port Douglas paper but thankfully we got the private ceremony that we wanted.

Our friends were very supportive about the way we got married, and some were jealous that they hadn't done the same thing. Still, to make up for it, we threw a big cocktail party at the National Wine Centre just after the Adelaide Test in December.

Against Zimbabwe, Perth and Sydney, 9–13 and 17–20 October 2003

We had a decent sort of break and then played the Zimbabweans in a series of two Test matches. The first Test, played in Perth, was on a particularly flat track. Matthew Hayden took advantage of the conditions: he made 380 and broke Brian Lara's Test-record score of 375, which Lara had set in 1994 against England. At one stage in the rooms, Matty was eyeing 400. However, sadly, he got out, more through tiredness than anything. We won the game by an innings that was memorable solely for Matty's innings. Little did any of us know that about six months later, Brian Lara was to break his record by making a mammoth 400 not out!

During the Perth Test, I sprang another injury, this time by doing the intercostal muscle in my side. We'd had very little cricket leading into the Test, and my lack of bowling fitness might well have had something to do with the injury. I remember having two for not many in the second innings, having incurred the injury with the actual ball I took my second wicket with.

Stuart MacGill broke down with a calf problem during the match as well, and Brett Lee was injured in the next Test, in Sydney. It just goes to show that heading into a Test, you need a few overs under your belt, regardless of how strong the opposition is.

Tests against India, 2003–04

HEADING INTO THE TEST SERIES AGAINST INDIA, A FEW OF US had an enforced break. Brett Lee, Stuart MacGill and I had all suffered injuries against Zimbabwe, and now had to get ourselves fit and ready for a series of four Test matches against the Indians. Thankfully, I managed to get a five-wicket haul for South Australia in a Pura Cup match against New South Wales, played in Adelaide on 18–21 November 2003, so was fit to go for the first Test, to be played in Brisbane.

We played strongly to win that match, and in it, Mark 'Cossy' Cosgrove emerged as an exciting young talent. He peeled off 118 for the Redbacks against a seriously decent Blues attack and in the knock showed he had the ability to be a top player.

First Test against India, Brisbane, 4–8 December 2003

Given the strength of the Indians' batting line-up, it seemed they had a side that would push us hard. Sachin Tendulkar was in the side, as were Rahul Dravid and VVS Laxman, who were seeking to repeat their brilliant batting of the 2001 series played on the subcontinent. Their attacking opener Virender Sehwag was there at the top of the order, so it seemed our bowlers would have plenty of work to do.

The first Test against the Indians was scheduled to be played in Brisbane, and before the match got under way, Steve Waugh announced it would be his final Test series. As a player I felt that because Steve was saying it was his last series, the selectors were under immense pressure to keep him in the side. Speaking for myself, I sometmes felt it was overshadowing what the team was about and that it was almost Tugga's retirement tour.

Here's an example of what I mean. On the opening day, Justin Langer made a fine century, and when he was dismissed for 121, he started to head off. Normally, under such circumstances, he would have received a standing ovation. However, in his eagerness to start his innings, Steve was out on the ground well before Justin reached the gate. As a result, the crowd responded to Steve's entrance to the Gabba, and Justin's departure from the ground after his sterling performance wasn't properly marked. Don't get me wrong; I think Steve deserved a welcoming ovation as he headed out to bat in his final Test in Brisbane, but because he came out early, Justin missed out on the crowd's full focus.

To be fair, the run-out that involved Damien Martyn was Steve's fault, but that was an unfortunate situation. The journalists made a big deal out of it, but it was just one of those things that happen in a Test match sometimes. A stack of run-outs have occurred in the history of Test cricket, and it certainly wasn't the first time one person was more to blame than another in a run-out situation.

IN OUR FIRST INNINGS, WE COLLAPSED AND FINISHED WITH ONLY 323 after at one point being 2/268. When India batted, I managed to knock over Sachin Tendulkar lbw for a duck, third ball. Front on, it was one of those lbw's that looked quite good, and after a long look, umpire Steve Bucknor gave it out. Side on, it seemed to be a bit high, which was unfortunate for Steve. Sachin was disappointed with the decision but took it on the chin and headed off as soon as he was given out. That's the sort of person and sportsman he is: he takes the rough with the smooth, and this time it was the rough.

The side-on replays didn't look good, and he was unlucky. Overall, in your career, things even out, and I'm sure there've been a few times when Sachin received some good luck when he might have been given out.

Hawkeye versus the umpire

AT THAT TIME, THE HAWKEYE TECHNOLOGY WAS JUST STARTING to come in, and it was generating a good deal of debate among the players, media reps and cricket fans in general. It makes for interesting viewing and is a powerful tool for giving the punters an insight into where the ball is heading when there's an lbw appeal.

I don't think the technology will ever be used to make lbw decisions in Test matches; in fact, I don't think it should ever be used to make decisions in any International matches. If it were, there'd be a lot of quick games because if a batsman were hit on the pad and the ball was shown via Hawkeye to be just hitting leg stump, the appeal would have to be given if it were referred to the third umpire. When an umpire thinks the ball *might* be clipping leg stump, he usually gives the benefit to the batsman. According to the letter of the law, if the ball was shown via Hawkeye to be clipping the edge of leg, the decision has to go in the bowler's favour. Height is another consideration, because there are plenty of times when the ball is shown via Hawkeye to be just clipping the top of the stumps. I think a can of worms would be opened, and being a bit of a traditionalist, I love the fact that the umpires out in the middle always make these sorts of decisions. Most of the time they get it right, and despite the fact they sometimes get it wrong, I like maintaining the human element in the game. I hope the umpires are retained for many years to come.

A positive element of making these touchy decisions is that people keep talking about the game: the blokes down the pub having a beer and the office workers around the water cooler have something to talk about. The journos perhaps overdo the analysing, but at least when people are talking about the game, their interest in it is heightened. The good umpires will always shine through, and if they make only the odd mistake, the players usually tolerate it.

INDIA'S CAPTAIN, SOURAV GANGULY, MADE 144 WHEN THEY batted, and though it was a pretty good knock, we didn't bowl that well to him. Our plan was to bowl fairly straight, either over or around the wicket, and not to give him any room. For some reason, we all bowled a bit too wide and he took full advantage. He was slightly streaky at times, and rode his luck and got away with a lot. He hit a number of those backfoot drives in the air, through which the ball could have ended up in the hands of a fielder. However, he managed to keep piercing the field. Full credit to him, because he played very well.

At about this time, former Australian cricket great Greg Chappell was helping Sourav with his batting; I think Sourav flew him to India for some personalised help before the series. I've always felt that Greg was particularly good at coaching people one-on-one at that level. He coached the Redbacks for five years, and I think that compared with someone who plays State Second Eleven or Grade cricket, he's always identified better with the top echelon of players.

Zaheer Khan bowled extremely well in that match. In the first innings, he took 5/95 and caused all our batsmen a bit of trouble. He was able to swing the ball into the right-handers and away from the left-handers, so was a tricky proposition. At the other end of the scale, Harbhajan Singh had a shocker of a match: he took only 1 for 69. He ended up incurring an injury and heading home, so wasn't anywhere near the player he'd been in the 2001 series in India, in which he took more than 30 wickets.

The match ended as a draw, because there'd been so much rain it was impossible to reach a result.

Second Test, Adelaide, 12–16 December 2003

THE INDIANS HAD PUT IN A DAZZLING DISPLAY WITH THE BAT IN Brisbane, so there was plenty of interest during the lead-up to the second Test match, to be played in Adelaide. It turned out to be one of the best games ever played at the ground. We won the toss and got off to an absolute flyer. We finished the day on 5/400, with Ricky Ponting having made an unbeaten 176. He was in top form in that series and played superbly on a pitch that suited batting.

On the second day, I came in to bat with Ricky when he was past 200. I managed to get to 48 before he was dismissed. Brad Williams and Stuart MacGill then went immediately, so I was left stranded, with a potential 50 nipped in the bud. When tail-enders bat with a top-order player, their job is to support their partner, but when they bat with each other, the idea is to push the score along as much as possible and keep the game moving forward. Therefore, I didn't have too much of an issue with their getting out. Although it would have been nice to get my maiden 50 at my home ground, we had 556, which would usually be enough to win a Test match.

Early in the Indians' innings we had them in trouble at 4/85, but Rahul Dravid and VVS Laxman batted to stumps and the next day went on to put on a triple-century partnership. They just batted, and batted, and batted. The wicket wasn't any use for the bowlers at all, and a couple of catches went down that also weren't very helpful. It was a hot day, and the Indians played well, as they had in Kolkata two-and-a-half years earlier. Dravid batted for almost 10 hours for his 233, Laxman six for his 148. It was a brilliant partnership and, because of it, India were well and truly back in the game.

When we went in for our second dig, Ajit Agarkar took 6 for 61 and knocked us over for only 196. In the first innings, I was able to keep running the ball down to third man off him to score runs. In the second dig, I was thinking, *Why can't I do it again?* However, Ajit was swinging the ball, and because I was trying to do the same thing, it was a dangerous mix — not the smartest idea. I made only 3 and then nicked one behind, to give Ajit his fifth wicket. I don't think he's bowled that well either before or since. Wow, he really caught us on the hop when he started to get the ball to swing. We batted badly and had no excuses whatsoever.

After that day's play, our coach, John Buchanan, made some comments to the media reps to the effect that he was less than impressed about the way we'd batted. Then what he did was slip under each player's door a dossier in which he referred to 'the spirit of the baggy green'. It's interesting to think about exactly what a coach's role is. I suppose it's to get us motivated, to try new things and to make us ready, because he's accountable for our performance. In the team environment of the Aussie side, I don't think these roles are a problem. However, when someone from within the team set-up says stuff in the media in order to motivate us, I'm not sure it works. I'm not a big fan of the tactic, and unless the person speaks to you privately first, I'm disappointed if he uses it. Had John had a real crack at us in the rooms, and then come out in the media and said, 'I felt that the lads had a poor day and told them so,' that would have been okay. That would have been a more professional way to approach the issue. Instead, we read in the paper that John didn't think we played well.

Don't get me wrong: I have no problem with copping a serve in the media once in a while — it's good to receive the praise, and you have to accept that sometimes you'll get some criticism. If we play badly, we have to accept it. However, if you're copping it from someone within the team, you'd rather hear it straight from the horse's mouth first.

DURING THAT TEST, A FEW OF MY MATES DECIDED TO ORGANISE a get-together in North Adelaide over a few drinks to celebrate my wedding. The former Redback bowler Brad Wigney was one of them, and he arranged for a cardboard cut-out to be placed on the bar in case I couldn't make it to the pub because of my Test commitments. As part of the promotion for the upcoming VB Series, a few of the lads had had action shots taken of them to be placed on cartons of beer, so Brad had this photo of me handy.

As it all panned out, the get-together took place on the second night of the Test, and because I had some bowling to do the following day, I opted to have a quiet night off my feet rather than go to the pub, and the blokes understood. They more than made up for my absence by sinking a few coldies after what had been a particularly warm day. Adam Gilchrist actually made an appearance to fill in for me, and the substitution pleased the lads no end.

India were in top form and won the second Test match by four wickets. They had the shakes a bit as they were getting close to the target, but Dravid was still in, so they were always going to get there. He made 72 not out, to add to his double ton he'd achieved in the first innings. In this match, he ended up making more than 300 runs and batted for 10 hours — an unbelievable effort considering the weather conditions. It was hot for the whole match, and on each of the last two days the temperature was higher than 40 degrees — very testing, to say the least.

I was truly pleased with how I'd bowled in that Test in Adelaide. The figures of 1/106 and 1/22 mightn't sound fantastic, but I'd bowled a lot of overs and I was happy with how they'd come out. In the second dig, I'd hurt my groin because I'd stretched out a little too much. I'd gone fairly hard in my delivery stride, done my groin and gone straight off, which had been a big disappointment. The damage wasn't that serious, but I'd had to come off to prevent doing more. To make things worse, as a result of the injury I'd been forced to miss the third Test at the MCG, so I had to work hard to get myself right for the SCG, which was to be the last Test of Steve Waugh's career.

Fourth Test, at the SCG, 2–6 January 2004

Even though I couldn't play in the third Test at the MCG, I spent time in Melbourne having treatment from Errol to get myself right for the last Test, scheduled for Sydney. The groin came along fine, and I was glad to be selected for a Sydney Test match. I declared myself fit to play, and Steve Waugh was kind enough to say that if I said I was fit, that was good enough for him. Consequently, the onus was on me to make sure I was adequately fit, however, I'd done the work earlier in the summer and I had a good base.

Once the muscle had healed, I knew I'd be okay, and I ended up getting through pretty well. We had to bowl first on a pitch that was extremely good and to field on an outfield that was lightning fast. I managed to take four wickets for the match, which under the circumstances was a decent return.

Brett Lee copped a bit of a hiding from the Indians: in the first innings, he conceded 200 runs. The concession was a rare feat in Test cricket, as was the total of 7/705 that we conceded. Binga received a lot of criticism about his bowling, especially about the fact that he was sometimes bowling balls from a foot-and-a-half behind the popping crease. Left, right and centre, people were saying he'd lost his run-up and he needed to get some help from outside the team set-up. In this instance I'll step up and defend Brett. In reality, he had been having a spot of ankle trouble so had decided to bowl from well behind the line in order to avoid the deep footmarks that had been created. To uneducated observers, he would seem to be missing his mark and having all sorts of problems, but it was simply that he wanted to miss the footmarks. Ask any bowler who's hurt his ankle in a footmark and he'll tell you how painful the injury is. When you hit the edge of that foothole, it's like twisting an ankle every time you come in to bowl.

Geoff Lawson was commentating for the ABC, and at times he doesn't sound as if he knows a whole lot about the game. He was saying that Brett was having all sorts of issues with his run-up. I'll never forget the 2004 Sri Lankan tour and some of his TV commentary over in Sri Lanka. He had a real crack at me for bowling off a short run; however, what he had failed to take into account was that we needed to get through a number of overs and the day was extremely hot and humid. My rhythm wasn't particularly good at the time, and I thought it mightn't be a bad idea to bowl a four-over spell off a short run and thereby solve a few issues with my bowling. During Lawson's commentary, he had a go at me, saying it was a bad tactical move, that it wasn't working, that it was ridiculous and that my pace was down. When he said my pace was down, he failed to notice that it was actually a slower ball — a big off-spinner. Had he been watching the game properly, as a professional commentator should automatically do, he'd have noticed as much. I often wonder whether he really concentrates on what's going on out in the middle when he's commentating.

After India made their massive score, we needed a big effort with the bat if we were to save the Test and the series. When my turn came to go in, Simon Katich was batting well, and I had to put my head down and try to help him put together a partnership to get us somewhere near the follow-on mark. At the time, his spin on things out in the middle was that although it was hard to settle in, things became easier after the first 15 or 20 minutes. I just tried to play straight and follow his advice. When I was facing Anil Kumble, I tried to keep my pad out of the way because whenever he hits you on the leg, there's a fair chance you'll be out lbw. I had to make sure I kept hitting the ball and that if he spun a leg break, it would miss the bat and the stumps, so I'd survive. The way I'd try to score would be to either punch a few drives or work the odd short ball off my hip for runs. It was pretty basic stuff really; during our partnership, we'd try to achieve a target of 10 runs at a time. Once we'd achieved that, we'd try to get another 10, and go on from there. I only had to support Simon, and thankfully our approach paid off: we took the score from 7/350 to 8/467 — a reasonable effort. Simon was ecstatic to make his first Test ton, and shrieked, 'Yes!' when he made it to the three figures. It was a special moment for him, and I was pleased for him.

For the second Test in a row, I had a chance to make 50, but was stumped off Kumble for 47. Although India bowled us out before we reached the follow-on, they decided to bat again in order to give their bowlers a rest. They ended up setting us 443 to win with little more than a day left to play.

On the final day, a bit of rain caused us to lose a few overs and forgo any chance of winning. However, it was going to be hard work for us anyway although the outfield was lightning fast. We couldn't really get a big partnership going, and when you're chasing such a tough target, everything has to go right for you to make the runs.

Tugga's final Test innings

When Steve came in for his final Test innings, he went for his shots straight away. More than 25,000 people were there to watch him, and they got their money's worth. He played exceptionally well, and the crowd madly cheered every run. However, he batted too well, got a little carried away and holed out on the boundary for 80, so put us in danger of losing the match. Maybe he thought we could still chase down the runs or perhaps he became caught up in the moment. The next day, it was interesting to read in the paper that a few words from the little Indian wicketkeeper Parthiv Patel might have had something to do with the dismissal. He'd been saying to Steve that he should try to get a hundred in his final innings, suggesting it would be wonderful if he finished his career with a ton and that he should keep playing his shots. Tugga had kept playing his shots alright, eventually being caught on the boundary, and reckons he might have been suckered in by the little Indian keeper.

On balance, his dismissal reads quite well: 'Caught Tendulkar; bowled Kumble'. He was caught by probably India's greatest ever batsman, and the bowler was one of India's best ever spinners.

For Steve's final Test match, we had a special guest in the rooms: Barry 'Nugget' Rees, who'd flown in from Adelaide for it. I'd decided Nugget should be there because he was a huge fan of

Tugga, and Steve would like to see him, given it was going to be Steve's last game. Steve had once described Nugget as the nicest person he'd ever met — and that is a fair description, because Nugget is a lovely character, has a wonderful nature and would never say a bad word about anyone. He stayed in Sydney with me and Anna — a good arrangement, because I'd organised with Cricket Australia to have a two-bedroom apartment instead of the usual one-bedroom.

Over the years, Nugget has been known to be a particularly early riser. Most days, he gets up at the crack of dawn, and for that reason, I had to set down some ground rules for his stay in our apartment. I told him he wasn't allowed to move till 7 a.m. because I needed to sleep in. I remember getting up for a toilet break at about six one morning and thinking I'd look in on Nugget to see whether he was awake. Sure enough, there he was: lying still in bed, staring at the alarm clock and waiting for it to tick over to seven so he could get up. As soon as it ticked over, he was up and away — that's how literally he takes you. He's a real beauty is Nugget, and in the final session of the match, he had the honour of taking out the drinks wearing his whites and baggy green.

It was the great Norm O'Neill who had actually presented Nugget with his 1961 tour of England cap, and this is what Nugget wore when he was sitting with us in the rooms during Tests in Adelaide. Poor Norm has been struggling in recent times and quietly requested the cap back so he could raise some money to help him in his retirement. The former Aussie wicketkeeper Barry Jarman spoke to Nugget, explaining the situation, and he was only too happy to send the cap back. To Jars's credit, he was kind enough to give Nugget his cap in return — a generous gesture.

WE MANAGED TO DRAW THE TEST. I'D HAD TO GO IN AND BAT out the last few overs with Simon Katich. The series finished 1–all, which was a reasonably fair indication of how the two teams had played.

Some memorable scenes took place after the match. Steve Waugh did a lap of honour to acknowledge the fans who were there to see his finale. A fantastic photo was taken of him in his whites walking on the ground with his wife, Lynette, after the commotion of the final day. Steve showed how much he thought of Nugget by going out on the pitch with him and having a look at it.

Vale, Hookesy

THE ONE-DAY SERIES FOLLOWED, AND IT WAS DURING THAT PERIOD that something devastating happened that sent shockwaves through the worldwide cricketing community: the former Australian cricketer David Hookes died outside a Melbourne hotel. He'd been coaching Victoria, and that day the team had been playing South Australia in an ING Cup match at the MCG. Players from both teams were having a few beers in a St Kilda pub. Without going into detail, I can only say that a great night out turned into a tragedy.

I was in Sydney when I heard the news, at a sponsors' function, and was gobsmacked to hear it. I couldn't and didn't want to believe it. I tried to get in touch with Darren Lehmann and Wayne 'Flipper' Phillips, who had been there in their roles as South Australia's skipper and coach. I couldn't get in touch with them and found myself extremely upset. In shock, I ended up having maybe a couple too many sherbets. I didn't feel too good the next day. My feelings of disbelief about what had happened were shared by the other Aussie guys there.

David had been going great guns in Melbourne, having moved over there in the mid 1990s after finishing his cricket career with South Australia. At the time of his death, he wasn't only coaching Victoria; he was flat out with media commitments with Radio 3AW and Fox Sports. On top of that he was writing various columns for the newspapers and going on most Australian overseas tours as a TV commentator.

Hookesy was a natural media talent. He'd started doing radio work with the legendary K. G. Cunningham on Adelaide radio station FiveAA, and he was doing the drive sports show at that station before the bright lights of Melbourne beckoned. David always said what he thought, and that's why he was such a popular personality. He always had a theory about something, and was terrific company over a meal or a beer.

I knew Hookesy reasonably well, but wasn't as close to him as Darren and Wayne, who'd played a stack of cricket with him and been close mates with him. It was tremendously difficult for someone such as me to deal with his death, and it's hard to imagine how Darren and Wayne dealt with it.

David's funeral was held at the Adelaide Oval, and at least 10,000 people were there to send him off. We'd played at the ground the day before, and we were all there to pay our respects to one of South Australia's favourite sons. It was a highly emotional time for a great many people. What a waste of a valuable life.

For me, one result of David Hookes's death was that I took more care whenever I went out to have a few beers. I know that Boof and Flipper are also a lot more careful these days because of what happened that night. After a game, I love to have a beer and a chat with teammates and opponents, but the main thing now is to make sure everyone gets home safely and without any trouble. Whether it takes a few phone calls or text messages, I know that the senior guys make sure everyone who goes out after a game is accounted for.

I've never been someone who stays out till all hours, even though I've always liked to go out and have a few beers. Generally there'll be a few people who come up and want to say 'gidday' and shake my hand. Ninety-nine per cent of the time, they're pretty harmless and they mean well. They sometimes offer to buy me a beer, but I always say I'm in a round already and politely decline. I'm not being disrespectful; it's simply the way I like to handle the situation.

It's terribly sad that it took the tragedy of David's death to make us all realise we should take extra care when we're out socialising and having a few drinks. What a wake-up call.

The Sri Lanka tour and a series at home, 2004

We arrived in Sri Lanka and, as modern tours go, were straight into a five-match one-day series after a few days of practising in the nets. We were without Glenn McGrath because of an injury and lost Brett Lee to an ankle problem during the early stages of the tour, so our fast-bowling reserves were tested.

When Brett went home, Shaun Tait was called up to join the tour party. He was young and raw but had plenty of pace. During the 2003–04 season, he'd taken 8/43 in an ING Cup match, and the selectors had been impressed with his speed and ability to trouble top-order batsmen with a good outswinger.

Shaun's nickname had always been 'Taity', on this tour he received another one: 'Sloon'. He'd been checking into one of the hotels in Sri Lanka, and the guy at reception had asked him his name. The guy couldn't find it in the register because it had been recorded as 'Sloon' rather than 'Shaun' Tait. The error caused mirth all round for the team, so after that, Shaun was known as Sloon.

Dambulla was an interesting place to stay because it's in the middle of nowhere. It's located in a densely bushy jungle area, and the hotel is surrounded by jungle. Consequently there were heaps of monkeys around the place. Even though the monkeys were only small, you never knew whether they were riddled with disease, or would bite you; they were offputting, to say the least. My preference was to keep plenty of distance between them and me. Being freaked out by monkeys became second nature to me.

After two games in Dambulla, we moved to Colombo. In the third game I was named Man of the Match and in the fourth we wrapped up the series, courtesy of Michael Kasprowicz, who took 5/45. All the bowlers were well prepared, and during the tour match leading into the first Test, most of our batsmen made hundreds so were put in good stead for the opening of the series in Galle.

Many people consider the Galle International Stadium to be one of the world's most beautiful Test venues. It's located in the heart of the city and overlooked by a 15th-century Dutch fort. Plenty of people watch the game from the fort rather than pay the admission price to go into the ground. The ground has a nice atmosphere in that a band plays music while the match is going on. It's not quite as noisy a scene as in the West Indies, but the locals get the trumpets and drums going to add to the ambience.

First Test against Sri Lanka, Galle, 8–12 March 2004, and Warnie's 500th wicket

It was Warnie's first game back from suspension, and he looked really fresh; it's altogether possible that having an enforced rest for 12 months was probably the best thing that could have happened for him. During his break, he'd taken stock of things and maybe even come back a better bowler. He seemed to be a new man, having done some commentating and spent time with his family. He was more relaxed, and if you wanted to put a positive spin on the absence, you'd say that without the time off, he might well have decided to retire long before he did. In each innings, he took five wickets and reached his 500th — a remarkable achievement — in what turned out to be a memorable game of Test cricket.

Simon Katich was unlucky to be omitted for the Test, having played very well against the Indians in Sydney. Andrew Symonds had done well in the one-dayers, and although it's not the best way for the selectors to pick the Test team, they believed that it resulted in the handy option of having a fifth bowler. For that match, we elected to go with two seamers and two spinners, and obviously felt that with Symmo in the team, we could use him to bowl some mediums as well as a bit of off spin. If you threw in his hard hitting as a batsman along with his exceptional fielding ability, you'd see we had a terrific cricketer. I think you can have one of those jack-of-all-trades type of players in your team. Looking back on the history of that series, it's clear that the tactic didn't quite work. I agreed with the selectors, and although it was unlucky for Simon, given his dazzling form against India, it was a gamble worth taking.

Again it was an occasion on which we had to overcome Muttiah Muralitharan if we were to win in Sri Lanka. He bowls half the overs and is a more difficult proposition on his home tracks. He's a real challenge over there because of the tremendous amount of turn he gets. In team meetings before the Test series, we had a lot of discussion about how we should play him, because we felt that if we could deal with him to some extent, we'd be on our way to winning. The former Australian one-day all-rounder Ian Harvey once told me it's best to keep your tactics as simple as possible. His theory was that if Murali bowls wide outside off, the ball will spin and that if he attacks the stumps, it won't.

In the first innings, we didn't go so well against him: he bowled us out for 220 and got six wickets. Darren Lehmann played him beautifully: he made 63 and in that knock showed what a superb player of spin he is. Boof always tries to score and stay attacking, and the tactic works in his favour because he puts the bowlers under pressure and they know they don't have much margin for error. As a result, they tend to bowl rather negatively to him because they don't want to go for the runs they know he's capable of scoring. He's not afraid to take guard 2 feet outside leg stump or to cut balls aimed at middle stump. He has such a sharp eye and constantly challenges the bowlers; he likes to try to upset their rhythm.

SRI LANKA MADE THE MOST OF THE GOOD BATTING CONDITIONS and got a lead of 161, and gaining it was vital to their chances of winning the match. In the second innings, we needed a few guys to stand up and make big scores if we were to stay in the game. Fortunately, three guys did, and each had a different way of playing the Sri Lankan bowlers.

Boof, Marto and Matty: three winning styles

DARREN FOLLOWED UP HIS 63 FROM THE FIRST INNINGS WITH 129 in the second. He produced a sterling display, using pretty much the method I've described. He and Damien Martyn put on more than 200 for the fourth wicket and really set things up for our eventual victory.

Boofer had a look up to the sky in remembrance of his mate David Hookes, who'd died only a few months earlier. No doubt he had a tear or two in his eyes, because he's a pretty emotional sort of guy. In fact Boof will cry at the drop of a hat, sometimes even when watching a kids' movie.

The way he handled himself both publicly and privately during the period after Hookesy's death is an indication of the man's calibre. In each innings of this match, he ended up getting three wickets, so in all aspects it was a memorable Test for him.

Marto plays the spinners a bit differently because he likes to play off the back foot a fair bit. In these innings, he liked to bat deep in his crease. If he went back, he went right back, and if he went forward, he made sure he got a good stride in to smother the spin. He seemed to be reading the bowlers off the pitch really well, and adjusted to any turn off the pitch. Helpfully, he also picked them out of the hand. To that point, he hadn't been that renowned for his batting against the slow bowlers; however, he'd now formulated a plan and it worked extremely well for him.

At the top of the innings, Matty Hayden made a nifty hundred and attacked the opposition's spinners by using his feet, especially if the ball was well tossed up. If any ball was above his eye line, he could get right down to it on the half volley or full toss and whack it back over the opponents' heads. As he'd done in India in 2001, he used the sweep shot to good effect. He's another batsman who uses his crease well, but he leaves it reasonably often to get down the track. So, the three guys who made a hundred each had highly effective but contrasting styles that all had the same result.

WE SET THE SRI LANKANS 352 TO WIN IN SLIGHTLY LONGER than a day, and unlike in the first innings, were all over their top order. Our plan was to dry up the singles and keep the one guy on strike for as long as we could. We had them 5/56 and eventually skittled them out for 154, and had a memorable 197-run victory. To come back from such a large first-innings deficit was a remarkable effort, and little did we know we'd also win the next two Tests after trailing in the first innings.

Our plan in the field was to bowl really tight lines and not give the Sri Lankans any width. What we wanted to do was make them hit the ball. In Australian conditions, we tend to bowl a bit outside off, to encourage the opposition to nick behind, whereas on the subcontinental wickets, we need to use different tactics. We had to bowl straight, and I know that in the past we'd tried to bowl 'Australian style' on their tracks and the tactic just hadn't worked. The best way to bowl is at the stumps, because lbw and bowled are brought more into play. We bowled at the stumps throughout the Sri Lankan series, and if you look at those scorecards, you'll notice a high proportion of that type of dismissal. There were a few caught behinds but hardly any catches in the slips off the pacemen. I took 10 wickets in the series, and with the exception of one dismissal, they were all bowled, leg before or caught behind by Gilly.

This game plan was different from our past game plans, and we set slightly more defensive fields. We were happy to put a bloke on the deep square-leg fence from ball one, a tactic that was a bit unusual. We had a theory that although subcontinental players live in hot and humid conditions, they don't necessarily like them, so if they can avoid doing much running between the wickets, they will. It's much easier for them to sit back and hit boundaries, but if we block that avenue of scoring and they get only a one instead of a four, that can sap their energy a bit. Our thinking was to make them run every run: get them tired by running twos and threes rather than let them get boundaries easily. So, we set a few defensive fields because we wanted to challenge our opponents' fitness levels. We managed to dismiss a few of them because of the tiredness factor.

Stuie's bar

It was during that tour that Stuart MacGill did a pretty funny thing in a nightclub after a Test win. Our celebrations were in full swing when Stuie headed over to the bar and bought an armload of drinks, including a bottle of spirits, and various cans of beer and soft drink. Much to our amusement, he somehow found some glasses and a bucket of ice, and proceeded to set up his own bar in a corner of the nightclub. Because he was an Australian cricketer, the locals were keen to buy from his bar rather than the established one. Stuie would have made a financial loss on the project. However, from that point on, after we'd won a Test, he set up his own little bar in the change rooms. He found a bit of towel to use as a bar mat and set everything up to cater for the demanding thirst that follows a Test victory.

Second Test, Kandy, 16–20 March 2004

After our big come-from-behind win in Galle, we headed for Kandy, where the pitch was more to the liking of the pacemen. After day one, though, it lost its pace and became a bit on the dusty side. It was still helpful for us because we were able to get the ball to reverse swing.

We made an appalling start to the match: we got bowled out for only 120 on the opening day. Murali picked up his 500th wicket, and the milestone was a big deal. A little 'wicket count' scoreboard was set up in the crowd, so everyone knew he'd reached the milestone. Some of our supporters set one up for Warnie, just to let the locals know that his wicket tally was right up there as well.

We had quite a few overs to bowl and managed to have the Sri Lankans 7/92 at stumps, so were brought right back into the game. The next day, though, their tail wagged and they ended up with 211; even Murali hit 3 sixes and made 43 — a real nuisance.

In the second innings, we started badly till Adam Gilchrist went in at number three, blasted 144 and changed the game. If he'd kept wicket for a day-and-a-half, it's highly unlikely the turnaround would have happened. We bowled the Sri Lankans out in 63 overs, so changing the line-up was worth a go. The tactic was something a bit different; it did come off and had a lot to do with our winning that Test. We caught them on the hop, so it was an effective strategy. Some teams simply see the batting order, have their plan and prepare to implement it. A spanner can be thrown in the works if there's a line-up change. In Test cricket, teams don't often change their line-up. Every now and then, they can use it to throw the opposition, and on this occasion we definitely did.

Damien Martyn played brilliantly for the second Test in a row: he made 161, and added exactly 200 with Gilly. We set the Sri Lankans 352 to win and knew we'd have to work hard to bowl them out.

Sanath Jayasuriya was going well, and it seemed they'd pull things off. I eventually had him caught behind, with a reverse swinger from around the wicket. I knew the ball must have been reversing a heap if I could get him caught behind, because I used to bowl wide of the crease, and to get the ball to swing from that angle, I must have well and truly got it going.

Over the years, I've found bowling at Sanath an extremely difficult proposition. Bowling at the stumps can sometimes work, but when he gets set, he has that flick over or through square leg that flies to the boundary. He's such a strong off-side player, and when he gets going, there aren't many places you can bowl to him to keep him tied down. He's one of the subcontinental players who's supremely fit. However, he was one guy for whom we weren't afraid to put blokes out on the fence in order to make him run two for shots he would normally get boundaries for. We tried to frustrate him and test his fitness by using this tactic, and who knows whether it worked in the second innings of that Test? He made only 131 from 145 balls, and we were glad to get rid of him, because another hour of his batting and Sri Lanka was in the box seat to chase down the runs.

When the last day started, the Sri Lankans needed 51 to win and had three wickets in hand. A big crowd turned up, hoping to see their countrymen level the series. Chaminda Vaas was dropped by Andrew Symonds, of all people, but was taken in the deep by Justin Langer off Warnie shortly afterwards when 33 were needed. Straight after that, we managed to knock over the last two wickets and win the Test by 27 runs. Shane had picked up another 10-wicket haul and was named Man of the Match after another superb performance.

Third Test, Colombo, 24–28 March 2004

Colombo was the scene of another brilliant Test match. Both sides made 400 in the first innings and Darren Lehmann made a superb 153 for us. It was another big moment for Boofer, being his second hundred in the series.

Early on the third day, I got two wickets in two balls, having Mahela Jayawardene caught behind and Tillekeratne Dilshan out bowled for a duck. The Dilshan dismissal was one of the best balls I've ever bowled in a Test. I was pumped because the ball came out exactly as I wanted it to. It pitched on about off-stump, straightened a bit, and clipped the top of off-stump as Dilshan played defensively off the back foot. He played all around it and made it look as though it was a better ball than it was. However, we needed the wickets, and by getting two of them on the opening session of the third morning, we got right back into the match.

Simon Katich came in to replace Andy Symonds for the Test, and in the second innings played superbly in a long partnership with Justin Langer. We were in all sorts of trouble when Katto joined Alfie with the score at 5/98. They added 218 to save us and then put us in a position to win the match. Katto had missed the first two Tests and was now making the most of his return: he played a significant innings of 86.

In that game, Brad Williams played and didn't get a wicket bowling his fast stuff. In the nets, he'd been bowling some off spin, and having faced it, I was surprised he didn't give it a whirl during the game. He could have had a go at the Sri Lankans, because in the nets he was landing the balls so well. Perhaps he felt he'd go to water if he tried the tactic in a game. None of the quicks were doing much on that pitch, and I thought it would have been worth the experiment. Warnie and Boofer were spinning the ball away from the right-handers, So Willo would have been worth a try, even for only two or three overs to see how he went. Maybe that's why I haven't captained too many teams: my tactics are too radical!

Having set our opponents 370 to win, we were struggling to get them out. At tea, they were only four down, and looking like they'd save the match and prevent us from getting a clean sweep. Warnie worked his magic, getting four wickets, and Kasper got the last wicket in the last over of the match. We clinched the series 3–nil.

In that game, I think everyone struggled with the weather. The humidity and heat were tough yakka, but you have no choice but to keep going and make sure you maintain your fluid intake. That's Sri Lanka for you; it's always hot and sticky, and the cricket grounds tend to be dry. All in all, the conditions are demanding. But it's well worth rising to the challenges because Sri Lanka's a lovely country.

After a day's play in the heat on a dusty wicket, we had the restaurants at the Colombo Hilton to look forward to in the evenings. There was a Japanese place we found to be absolutely brilliant, and an Italian restaurant that was also very good. The lads were happy to rotate between the two eateries.

Each night in Colombo, before we'd have a feed, we made our way up the street in a *tuk-tuk* to a place called the Galle Face Hotel. There you could sit outside and look at the ocean, watch the sun set and slip down a few Lion lagers which we called 'King Browns'. It was a beauty of a spot. Our accommodation in Galle was also sensational. We stayed right on the water in one of the most stunning places I've ever been to. Tragically, not long after we'd stayed there, Galle was devastated by the Indian Ocean Tsunami of December 2004, the deadliest in recorded history. It was a shock to view footage of Galle taken soon after the tsunami ripped through. Where we'd stayed had been washed away completely. I found the whole thing terribly sad. I'd like to think that the people are getting back on their feet.

Overall, Sri Lanka is beautiful. It's still a Third World country, as you notice when you take the rugged trip from the airport to the main part of Colombo. The road is terrible, and the hour-long trip from the airport to the hotel isn't exactly enjoyable. You're in a bus that doesn't have airconditioning, and after you've flown in, it's quite an uncomfortable trip. However, I'm really splitting hairs here, because overall Sri Lanka is a nice place to play cricket in.

Sri Lanka is very much like India in that the streets are always busy. Although it's rather polluted, what makes it such a good place to visit is that the people are so friendly.

Who's the better bowler?

The exciting thing about the series was that Murali and Warnie were pitted head to head, because both were going to have to bowl a stack of overs. Both ended up with outstanding numbers: Murali took 28 wickets at 23, Shane 26 at 20. If you used strike rate as the basis for deciding who was the better bowler in the series, Warne would win because he got his wickets at 39 balls per wicket compared with Murali's 45. The question of who is the better bowler always comes up. Some people would argue that because Shane bowled leggies, he applied the harder craft and is the better bowler. However, if you look at the overall figures, Murali's stack up very well. Some people would argue that Warne should get the nod because of the doubts over Murali's action. When you look at Murali's performances in International cricket, it's unfortunate that in some quarters the action goes against him.

A couple of Test matches up north, 1–3 and 9–13 July

After our trip to Sri Lanka, we had to host the Sri Lankans just four months later for a couple of Test matches in Darwin and Cairns. Matthew Elliott played his first Test for a long time; he came in for Ricky Ponting, who was unavailable. Poor old Herbie was on a hiding to nothing: he made only 1 and 0 in the match, which we won fairly easily. The wicket was a drop-in track and wasn't too flash to bat on. Also, we had to start at 9.30 a.m. each day, so batting wasn't made any easier.

Drop-in wickets have been one of my cricketing gripes over the years along with some practice facilities, when there's only half a pitch. The bowlers have to run in and bowl on grass rather than a hard, rolled-turf surface. It just goes to show what a batsmen's game cricket can be sometimes.

The Test was our first opportunity to have a close look at paceman Lasith Malinga, who used a particularly strange bowling action in the game. He charged and let the ball go with his arm almost parallel to the ground, rather than high up and from a vertical position. Therefore, when he let the ball go, it came out of the umpire's shirt, which meant he was difficult to pick up. It was truly a unique action. At one point our batsmen asked the umpires to remove their black ties so the batsmen's vision wouldn't be impaired as a result of Malinga's low arm action. The sight screen had to be placed directly behind the umpire, and the batsmen all found Malinga to be an absolute handful. He picked up 2/50 and 4/42, and has since gone on to be a tremendously handy bowler for Sri Lanka. Our batsmen had to re-train themselves to watch the ball out of the hand, so he's tough to face.

Malinga has an advantage because he lets the ball go in the line of stump to stump. He gets a high percentage of his wickets bowled and lbw. If he hits a batsman on the pad, it almost has to be out every time, because he lets the ball go from the line of middle stump.

After the Sri Lankans bowled us out for 207 in our first innings, we managed to have them 3/43 by stumps, and I snared my 200th Test wicket, that of Kumar Sangakkara. Not many Australian bowlers have reached that milestone, so it was nice to keep the ball from that innings. I must have been pretty lucky, because normally Shane Warne would have wanted it for some reason or another.

In the second innings, Michael Kasprowicz picked up seven wickets and helped us wrap up the match fairly comfortably inside three days.

We were straight off to play at Cairns for the next Test, and Murali wasn't playing, which meant Warnie was a chance to equal or break his record. The Sri Lankans were blocking out time to save the game, and it was too dark to keep going. However, we played on with spinners from both ends. Finally, on the last day, Warnie took four wickets and equalled Murali's record. We set our opponents 355 to win in 80-odd overs, and in the end, they were nowhere near making the runs: they finished on 8/183.

WE'D WON FOUR OUT OF THE FIVE TESTS AGAINST SRI LANKA IN the space of only a few months. We'd beaten them on their own soil and then backed up the victory with a series win at home. The next challenge we faced was a massive one: to beat India on their soil. We'd been hurt badly after losing the 2001 series there. Now, a four-Test series was looming in October, so we had a chance to make up for the disappointment.

Our 2004 tour of India

After the successful Sri Lanka series, we had a few months off from cricket before our departure for India, scheduled for October. Having lost the 2001 series, we were conscious that we'd have to change our tactics when we were bowling to their batsmen.

Prior to the series, we had a team meeting and agreed that we needed to bowl straighter, much like we'd bowled in Sri Lanka when we were there in March that year. In the two previous series against India, we'd persisted with bowling about a foot outside the off-stump. I was never a big fan of the tactic, even though I could see why we were using it. We wanted to make them hit through the off side, because they tended to flick anything on the stumps easily to leg. We'd lost in 2001 and drawn in 2003–04, so thought we had to come up with a better plan. We sat down to nut it out and decided we'd put fielders in place to dry up the runs from those shots. Then, we felt, if we attacked closer to off-stump and the Indians happened to miss, we'd have more chance of getting them out.

It'd been a big advantage playing in Sri Lanka before the series, because it was there that we first tried those tactics. The tour had almost been a dress rehearsal for the Indian trip, and we'd been quite successful. We'd have an extra person or two on the leg side, and that tactic had worked quite well on the pitches in Sri Lanka. The pitches there are slightly lower and slower, and we'd achieved some reverse swing as well.

First Test against India, Bangalore, 6–10 October 2004

Michael 'Pup' Clarke made his debut in Bangalore, and although many media reports thought it was slightly overdue, I didn't necessarily share that view. Over the years many players have waited much longer than Pup did to get their opportunity. Mike Hussey is a good example, and look how well he started in Test cricket.

Pup is a special player and he wasted no time in showing why everyone was keen for him to get into the Test side. His innings of 151 was brilliant: he went out and batted without any fear, and the way he used his feet to the spinners was exceptional. He played like a veteran, and some of his shots against the quality spinners, Anil Kumble and Harbhajan Singh, were superb. To make a hundred on your debut, in those conditions, against that attack, was something genuinely classy.

As Mike approached his hundred, he called to the rooms to change from his helmet to his cap. The request came as no surprise, because to bring up the ton wearing your baggy green makes the event somehow more memorable. I recall that's how it was in the old days before helmets, and Justin Langer once put the cap on when he was bringing up his 200. It's something of an old-fashioned and symbolic gesture but adds a nice touch of tradition, and I think that's a good thing.

When our turn came to bowl, the quicks picked up eight of the 10 wickets in the first innings, although the pitch wasn't exactly in our favour. The ball was scuffing up rapidly so we knew we were a chance to get some reverse swing. All the bowlers could get the ball to reverse. Michael Kasprowicz tended to sling it slightly and squeezed a lot of reverse into the right-hander, Glenn reversed it a bit both ways, and I could reverse swing as well. Kasper couldn't get any to go away, but he did get the vicious in-duckers going, so was hard to play. I don't think the Indian balls had much to do with the situation, even though they had a slightly bigger seam. They were made in the same factory as the ones we use in Australia, but given they were roughing up quicker, it did help us to get some reverse.

Sachin Tendulkar was notable for his absence from the Indian team, because he had a tennis elbow injury. We were quite pleased he was out because he'd made thousands of runs against us in the past. Ricky Ponting had a broken thumb, so was out of our team. Consequently, Simon Katich got an opportunity to play, and batted at number three. He made the most of his chance: in that game, he made 81 and 39.

We set the Indians 457 to win, and they were in trouble at 4/19. We were set on our way in the form of a couple of lucky lbws. We ended up winning by 217 runs, just after lunch on the last day. It was a great effort by all the bowlers.

Second Test, Chennai, 14–18 October 2004

Although we used our tactic of bowling more at the stumps in Chennai, Virender Sehwag made a stunning 155 in the Test. He likes width, so from that point of view the tactic worked, because he uses minimal foot movement and likes to thrash the ball through the off side. We aimed at the top of off-stump, and Glenn McGrath started the innings bowling with four men on the fence. He had a long leg, deep square leg, deep point and third man, all on the fence to try to restrict our opponents' scoring. The theory was the same as in Sri Lanka: restrict the boundaries and make your opponents run between the wickets a lot in the heat, because they don't like it.

It might have been the 'non-Australian' way to bowl and set the field, but we tried it and it was ultimately helpful in our winning the series. It could be viewed as being a defensive ploy, but we felt it would cause them to change their style of game because the boundaries would dry up. Our plans were highly effective against VVS Laxman, who'd made a heap of runs in the past two series against us.

In the first innings of the Test, a good numberof catches were put down. Most of them were behind the wicket, and even though it was quite hot during the Test, I wouldn't say the temperature had anything to do with having the chances put down. The problem was that because the pitches in India don't bounce as much as those in other countries, the keeper and slip fielders have to stand up as close as possible to make sure the ball carries to them. As a result, the reaction time is less, and even though I've never fielded in the slips that much, I consider India the hardest place to have to field in.

The ball still doesn't always carry, so you get occasions when it bounces just in front of you. The guys in there cop them on the body because the ball has the same pace, and on the bumpy field, players can get a nasty bounce. The ball can kick up, and you can get hit on the head or be whacked in the mouth from it. Fielding behind the wicket is a big challenge, and it's every bit as difficult for keepers. Gilly always says it's tough because there is less time to react.

LATE ON THE THIRD DAY, I HAD TO GO IN AS NIGHTWATCHMAN. We were only four runs ahead with six wickets in hand, so I had a sizeable job in front of me. I managed to get through the day, and the next day had to come back out with Damien Martyn to try to build a lead and give us something to bowl to in the last innings.

Chennai is a tough place to play in, not only because of the extreme heat but because of the stench emanating from the Buckingham Canal located near the ground. The canal smells like an open sewer, and hot winds bring a stink over the ground. The heat was terrible in that game, which was one of the only times I've seen Glenn McGrath say he couldn't bowl; he'd just had enough, and he went off the ground, put on an ice vest and jumped into an ice bath. He was cooked. I bowled a five-over spell and was also physically gone. I went off and put a cold towel around my head, then came on and bowled another over. The sole reason I didn't hop in the ice bath myself was that I didn't have the energy to take my clothes off — I was that buggered.

The batting in the match called for incredible mental toughness, which was the reason I was so phenomenally tired. Physically, though, it wasn't too bad because I was only blocking the hell out of the Indians, so I got through okay. During my four hours at the crease, the only time I had to run was when Marto scored runs. Batting isn't as taxing as bowling, but you are stuffed mentally. Also, you're under a helmet, so you sweat even more. I was sweating profusely because I was wearing a thigh pad, an inner-thigh guard and a chest protector. I changed my gloves frequently. When you took all that into consideration, it was quite an uncomfortable way to earn a living!

As a bowler, you lock in what you want to do, and it's automatic: you simply run in and aim at a spot on the pitch. As a batsman, you very much react to what that bowler's going to do, so you need to be totally switched on for every ball. Batsmen say that one of the keys to batting is to switch your concentration off and on between deliveries. Well-performed batsmen can do that; otherwise, they burn themselves out.

DURING OUR LONG PARTNERSHIP OF 139, MARTO AND I DIDN'T really talk a hell of a lot between overs. It was a case of, 'Keep going, mate.' 'Keep working hard.' 'Keep gutsing it out.' 'Just stay out here.' We managed to do these things for a while and not give the Indians an opportunity. From 4/150 — nine ahead — at the start of play, we managed to add 80 in the first session — I made only 15 — and then very nearly made it through to tea. Marto brought up his ton with a six and was then dismissed next ball, caught at slip for 104. We were only 144 ahead when I was out, so were still a long way from being in a strong position. Michael Clarke and Darren Lehmann added a few, and we managed to get to a lead of 228 before being all out shortly before stumps for 369. India had three overs to bat that night, and were 0/19.

At no stage was I thinking that batting was becoming any easier at that point in my Test career, despite the fact I was putting together a few decent scores. My approach was still that of purely surviving, and if I scored any runs along the way, it was a bonus. My only specific plan was to stay there, defend my wicket and be involved in a partnership. If I could push one into a gap in the off side or work off my pads, it would be all well and good. If I'd been in for a while, the odd shot might come out. Basically, though, my only game plan was to watch the ball and play as straight as I could.

The last day was washed out, and I was sure we didn't quite have enough runs to win the match. Having said that, if we'd played that final day and managed to get some early wickets, we could have put the Indians under immense pressure. Although we wanted to head out there and have a bowl, we thought we might have got away with it as well. In the first innings, we didn't quite bat or bowl well enough to put ourselves in a better position, so it's fair to say we might have got out of gaol in that game.

THERE WAS AN EIGHT-DAY GAP BETWEEN THE SECOND AND third Tests, a welcome chance to recharge. Some of the lads opted to have a breather from India. Marto and Michael Clarke headed off to Singapore. I think a few of the lads went away with their families to Goa and Mumbai (formerly Bombay). My choice of desination was Mumbai, where I spent about four days resting and chilling out around the pool. After the break, we all assembled in Nagpur for the third Test.

'Green wicket-itis' in Nagpur for the third Test, 26–29 October 2004

ON OUR ARRIVAL IN NAGPUR WE WERE ASTONISHED TO FIND that the pitch had some grass on it. On the morning of the match, it was quite amazing that nothing had changed, and even more odd that Sourav Ganguly and Harbhajan Singh were late withdrawals from the Indian team. To this day, we remain convinced they were suffering from a little-known disease called 'green wicket–itis'. They might argue differently, but it appeared to us that they both pulled out because the pitch wasn't what they'd hoped it would be.

Harbhajan apparently had the runs, which we felt was no excuse, because you can take a heap of Imodium to solve that problem. From our side of the fence, we couldn't quite follow that thinking. Gilly came back from the toss and asked stand-in skipper Rahul Dravid why Sourav wasn't playing, to which he replied, 'Stuffed if I know.' He'd summed up the feelings in the Indian camp: they weren't happy that Sourav had pulled out of the match because the wicket was a tad green.

A rumour began circulating that the reason the pitch was on the grassy side was that the groundsman had had a run-in with the Indian Cricket Board. He'd decided to prepare the wicket the way he wanted rather than the way the board wanted. I think his argument of preparing the best wicket was right: it had some pace and bounce early in the game, and flattened out and was helpful for the slow bowlers as the match wore on. Preparing the wicket in a way that suits the home team isn't unique to India; there's always that element to it. Most countries like to set up things in their favour. For example, in Sri Lanka, where they have Murali, the pitches usually turn from the word go, and we've come to expect that.

Things are no different in domestic cricket; the home team tries to do that extra bit to get an advantage. During my stint with Yorkshire in 2006, I figured out that whenever we went to an away dressing room, it'd be smaller than the home side's, just so we'd be ever so slightly uncomfortable.

In Nagpur, Darren Lehmann blazed 70, Michael Clarke made 91, Marto made his second hundred in a row, and we made 398 in our first innings. I managed to take five wickets in the Indians' first innings as we shot them out for 185. I swung the ball and had some help from the pitch. The best part about getting a little movement from the track is you don't know which way it'll go. If you put the ball in the right areas and it goes away, the slips come into play, if it jags back, lbw and bowled are right in the mix.

In the second innings, Simon Katich made 99, and we were all disappointed he couldn't make that one extra run. As I've mentioned, he always seemed to end up being a fall guy in the team, that is, someone who makes way for someone else. He played very well, as did Marto yet again; Marto finished with 97, narrowly missing out on his second hundred in the match.

We set the Indians 543 to win in five sessions. At tea, they were done and dusted at 5/84. During the last session, I was that close to getting my 10th wicket in the match; to that point, it'd proved to be elusive. When the Indians were 8/122, I had one more wicket to get to the 10, and Gilly told me that he was quite happy to keep me on till I'd reached the milestone. I kept bowling, trying to get one of the last two wickets, but couldn't get the breakthrough. In the end, I was spent from a long spell and said to Gilly, 'All I want is to win the game and get off the ground; I'm not that worried about the ten-for.'

WARNIE TOOK THE LAST WICKET AND SCENES OF JUBILATION followed. Gilly had done a wonderful job as skipper, and was quite rightly excited and emotional about the result. The celebrations were rather large at the ground and back at the hotel, seeing as we were the first Aussie team since 1969–70 to win a Test series in India. We all went berserk but at the same time were stuffed because the Test had taken so much out of us.

Fourth Test, Mumbai, 3–5 November 2004

WE HAD ONLY A THREE-DAY BREAK BEFORE THE FINAL TEST. The pitch in Mumbai was completely different from the one in Nagpur and turned out to be a raging turner from the start. There was hardly any play on day one because of heavy monsoonal rain, and when we started on day two, we bowled the Indians out before lunch for only 104. We were all out ourselves before stumps for 203. So, on the second day, 18 wickets had fallen, and nine of our 10 had gone to the spinners, Anil Kumble and Murali Kartik.

After play that day, because I'd picked up four wickets, I had a press conference. I was asked for my thoughts about the state of the pitch, and I replied that I couldn't really comment on it. However, I admitted that I'd spoken by phone to my mate, Jono, in Adelaide, where he was watching the Test on TV, and he'd been of the opinion

NEWSPIX

Blowing a kiss to my daughter, Sapphire, during the second Ashes Test in Adelaide in 2002–03. I took four wickets in the first innings, and it was as good as I've ever bowled.

NEWSPIX

Taking the prize wicket of Sachin Tendulkar during the first Test at the Gabba in December 2003. Sachin was a bit unlucky as the ball looked to be going over the stumps.

NEWSPIX

Dismissing Sri Lanka's Hashan Tillakaratne during the third Test in March 2004 in Colombo. It was a brilliant match in a series we won 3–nil, in spite of trailing after the first innings in all three Tests.

Kumar Sangakkara was my 200th Test victim in the match against Sri Lanka in Darwin in July 2004. It was nice to keep the ball from that innings.

NEWSPIX

NEWSPIX

I send Zaheer Khan's stumps flying in the third Test against India in Nagpur in October 2004. I couldn't quite manage my first 10-wicket Test haul, but I was happy with nine, especially as we clinched the series 2–nil: Australia's first series win in India since 1969–70.

The FBC (Fast Bowling Cartel) with Aussie fast-bowling legend Dennis Lillee in Perth in 2004–05. From left: Glenn McGrath, Brett Lee, Dennis Lillee, Michael Kasprowicz and me.

Looking fairly pleased after scoring my first Test half-century against New Zealand in November 2004. A few years earlier, I'd told some mates at the Adelaide Cricket Club that if I ever got a Test 50, I'd celebrate with this Happy Gilmore routine.

FAIRFAX

We managed to wrap up the Third Test against New Zealand in 2005 in four days, so Pigeon and I enjoyed the rare day off with a leisurely boat ride. Well, it was leisurely for him at least.

The 2005 Ashes series was a huge disappointment, both for me and the team, and I was dropped from the side after the third Test. Here's a happier moment, dismissing Andrew Flintoff during the second Test.

NEWSPIX

AAP

Raising my bat after reaching my double century against Bangladesh in 2005. I thought I had a chance to get 50, but never in my wildest dreams did I look any further than that.

I had a lump in my throat when I saw Anna come down the 'aisle' on our wedding day. Anna looked more beautiful than ever.

NEWSPIX

A perfect, intimate wedding. From left to right: Cherida Palmer, Wendy Fleming, Sue Carmichael, Anna, me, Damien Fleming and Greg McEvoy.

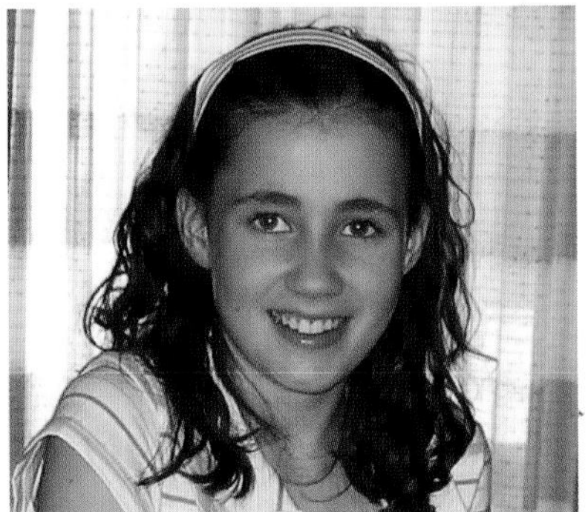

Left: My parents, Neil and Vicki, have always supported and encouraged me, particularly in the early years. Right: My beautiful children: Jackson, aged 17 months, and Sapphire, aged 12.

A family celebration after my brother Luke's graduation. Clockwise from top: Dad, Mum, my brothers, Rob and Luke, and me.

it was an absolute disgrace — not a bad way of getting around a tricky question!

The wicket had been blatantly prepared to help the spinners; it'd been crumbling virtually from ball one. Whether that was because Warnie had gone home because of a thumb injury, I don't know. What I do know was that Warnie couldn't leave India quickly enough: as soon as he knew he was injured, he was booked on a Qantas flight and was out of there.

NATHAN HAURITZ CAME IN FOR WARNIE TO MAKE HIS DEBUT. The wicket did have a bit in it for the quicks early on, and happily I managed to capitalise on the fact. Then, however, it started to turn square and it became almost impossible to bat on.

India went back in and managed to get 205, setting us 107 to win. They were going well at 4/182 till part-time spinner Michael Clarke came on and took 6/9. It was quite amazing, how that all came about. Pup speared them in and was turning the ball a long way, and was therefore extremely difficult to play. He was superb and knew exactly what he was doing. Some he turned; some he didn't, and he ended up with some amazing figures.

I was batting at the end of the run chase and felt quite comfortable. Unfortunately, no one else could hang around and we lost the match by 13 runs. The pitch by that stage probably suited the lower-order batsmen, because the upper-order guys were good enough to nick some of the unplayable deliveries whereas the tail-enders would play and miss at them.

WHEN I LOOK BACK ON THAT SERIES, I'M ALWAYS AS PLEASED AS punch that I took 20 wickets at 16 on those pitches; with the exception of Nagpur, the pitches weren't exactly helpful. Some people might say I was rather unlucky not to be named Man of the

Series, but Damien Martyn played consistently well: he made 444 runs at 55.55, including two hundreds and a 97. He batted gallantly in India, and had done in Sri Lanka earlier in the year, and he showed people he could play the spinners as well as he could play pace bowling. He'd been brought up on the bouncy wickets in Perth but demonstrated that he could adjust his game to turning pitches.

It's always a tough assignment playing cricket in India, but you just have to get through. We were used in reasonably short spells and had good recovery sessions each night under our physical-performance manager, Jock Campbell. He made sure we kept our fluids up, had our ice bath and ate well at night so we'd be ready for the following day. Because of that regimen, I found I didn't suffer any significant weight loss.

Both on and off the field, everyone in our outfit pulled his weight on the tour, so it was a success. I did feel slightly sorry for Ricky, because he'd missed the first three Tests, and when he'd come back, we lost in Mumbai — somewhat disappointing for him. At the end of the day, to be a member of the first Aussie team to win in India since 1969–70 was pretty special.

Against New Zealand and Pakistan, 2004–05

There was hardly any time between drinks in 2004. The first Test against New Zealand, to be played at the Gabba, was scheduled to start 11 days after we'd completed the Indian tour, so we had to try to recover quickly from what had been a taxing series.

On the Kiwis' previous tour, in 2001–02, they'd drawn the series, but now were without paceman Shane Bond, who'd been injured.

First Test against New Zealand, Brisbane, 18–21 November 2004

In the first Test, the Kiwis' big all-rounder Jacob Oram batted really well in making a hundred and showed us straight away what a tremendously good cricketer he is. His bowling had also come along at about that time, and he took another step up. Since then, he's suffered the odd injury. However, I still consider him to be a highly talented cricketer.

For me, the most memorable aspect of that match was that Glenn and I had our big partnership — we each made a half century. Whenever I've batted with him, we've had plenty of fun; batting with your bowling mates is always a hoot. As lower-order players, we always felt we didn't have a huge deal to lose because not much was expected from us. On this occasion, however, our combined effort of a hundred-plus completely put the Kiwis out of the game.

That day in Brisbane, we thought we'd just bat and make as many runs as we could, because the wicket was flat and the bowlers were tired. The ball was old and there wasn't a whole lot to making runs. Glenn came out and tried to play every shot in the book, and I started to worry that he was getting a long way across to the off side and making himself susceptible to a full ball on the stumps. He loves his pull and hook shots; I think they're two of the few shots he can play. Fortunately, the Kiwis didn't bowl that full to him, so he got away with that approach.

As for me, I continued with my normal way of batting: playing straight and trying to hang around. It was almost like batting with a top-order player, because Glenn was playing all these big expansive shots, and I was just pushing a few ones and twos as usual. Our partnership developed, and after a while I kept saying to him, 'Keep going,' because neither of us would ever have a better opportunity to make a 50 each. I'd made a few 40s the previous summer and was keen to get there.

Once Pigeon reached 30, I think his mind began to focus on getting to 50; when he'd reached the 40s, he was definitely starting to think about it. However, he didn't seem nervous at all, because we were having so much fun batting out there.

Early on in the partnership, the Kiwis were going through the motions, expecting one of us to get out. After a while, though, they changed their tune when they realised that neither of us was going to move and that we had no intention of declaring.

When Glenn reached his 50, it was a classic moment, and all the lads in the viewing area went berserk. They were enjoying the moment and all absolutely thrilled he'd reached the milestone because he'd taken so long to achieve it.

The interesting thing about Glenn's highest score of 61 is that it's slightly shy of nine times his career average of seven. If you equate it to Ricky Ponting's average of about 60, it would be the equivalent of his making a best score of 540. In my view, then, Glenn's feat has been underrated. Statistically, having a highest score nine times your average isn't too sluggish an effort.

At the end of the day's play, Glenn was on 54 and I was on 44. I'll never forget Glenn cheekily asking me what it was like to make a Test 50. Before I could answer, he said, 'Oh, that's right: you haven't made one.' He was quite pumped and was having a bit of fun at my expense.

HEADING INTO THE NEXT DAY, I WASN'T THAT NERVOUS; I needed six for my 50. Over the years, I've felt that for top-order players, making a 50 is a tad overrated. When Ricky Ponting makes a 50, he hasn't even reached his Test average of nearly 60. Plenty of guys average more than 50, and these days I think it's different from the old days, when they played on uncovered wickets.

The legendary Victor Trumper, who in the 1890s and 1900s averaged 39.04, made his runs during the early days of Test cricket, when I'm sure making a half century meant a lot more. They used to play on some dodgy tracks back then, so making a 50 let alone a hundred was more of a big deal. The tracks nowadays are better and the bats have improved, so I just wonder whether a 50 carries the same weight as it did in days gone by.

When I reached my maiden 50 on the fourth day of that Test, I have to confess that the unique way I celebrated the milestone wasn't spur of the moment. The inspiration for it came some years earlier, from the movie *Happy Gilmore*, starring Adam Sandler. In it, after he'd played a good shot, 'Happy' had pretended to ride his club, which amused me no end. One day, around that time, I was at the Adelaide Cricket Club chatting away with my club mates Paul Amato, Erin Bernhardt and our A-grade team manager, Lyle Wheeler, and for some reason I told them if I ever reached 50, I'd celebrate by riding my bat, copying Happy. I just thought it'd be a fun way to go rather than doing the usual old thing of raising the bat.

I was facing Jacob Oram, and he bowled one that decked back into me. I inside edged it past the keeper and reached my 50. Not the most glamorous way to bring up your maiden half century, but it was worth four in the scorebook and I had the 50. True to my word, I rode my bat down the wicket to celebrate, and the other Aussie lads got in on the act.

New Zealand were demoralised, and we bowled them out for only 76, so had an innings victory inside four days. During that last day, Craig McMillan and Adam Gilchrist had a verbal stoush. McMillan had inside edged a ball off me to Gilly and been given not out by Steve Bucknor. Earlier in the game, Matthew Sinclair had edged a ball from me to Ricky Ponting in third slip and wouldn't walk when Ricky said he'd caught it. It didn't matter, because when the TV replay was called for, it was clearly shown that Sinclair was out.

McMillan and Gilly sorted it out on the boundary edge at the end of the game, and everything was fine. Again, it was highlighted in the television coverage and probably looked a lot worse than it was.

Second Test, Adelaide, 26–30 November 2004

For the second Test, in Adelaide, we decided not to make the Kiwis follow on, after leading by 324 in the first innings. I think the follow-on can be overrated and that you should enforce it only if you've bowled the opposition out particularly quickly. It took us a whole day to get them out, and in this day and age, with so much cricket, you need to give your bowlers a break.

Some former-players-turned-commentators, such as Ian Chappell, reckon we should enforce it more. However, they don't understand that the bowlers have a bigger workload and appreciate having a little time off in between innings. During Ian's time, they also had a rest day, which we'd find more than welcome. I agree with Ian in a way, though, in that you do send a strong message to the other team by making them follow on. The fact remains that because more games are being crammed in, you need to give the bowlers a chance to put their feet up. They feel massively better after having those few hours off the field, and if there's enough time left in the match, you should win anyway.

After we'd again flogged the Kiwis in Adelaide, their captain Stephen Fleming came out and likened the Australian pace attack to having three Richard Hadlees. Given Hadlee's standing in the game as a bowler, this was generous praise to receive from a visiting Test skipper. I believe that in the cricket world, Fleming is highly respected for the way he conducts himself, the way he plays and the fact he can get the most out of his team. Having played against him, I know he's a tough competitor and that he always finds his best for matches against Australia. As bowlers, we were really chuffed by his remarks.

There's a great photo of the Adelaide Oval scoreboard at the end of the match in which all five of the bowlers have two wickets against their name: McGrath, Gillespie, Kasprowicz, Warne and Lehmann all with 'two-fors'. It's a photo I'd like to get hold of. I have a photo of the scoreboard from the 1999 Trinidad Test in which we were bowling out the West Indies in the second innings for only 51. It's special to me because my last wicket partnership of 66 with Glenn was more than the Windies made in their whole innings.

After the match, Darren Lehmann and Mark Richardson had their famous 100 metre running race on the oval to decide who was the slower runner. Normally you'd call the race a sprint, but it was hardly that. Richardson hit the tape first, and it turned out to be the last time we saw him play on an International field. About a week after the Test, he announced he was retiring from all forms of the game. During the series, he made only 19, 4, 9 and 16 in the four innings, so maybe his timing was right. He's now part of the commentary team for Sky Sports Cricket in New Zealand.

Interestingly, Darren Lehmann played only two more Tests, as he was dropped from the team after the Boxing Day Test against Pakistan.

Test series against Pakistan, December 2004–January 2005

For the second part of the summer, the Pakistan team were in Australia. The first Test was to be played in Perth, so it was going to be interesting to see how Shoaib Akhtar would go bowling on the pacy WACA pitch. It didn't take long to find out, because we were 5/78, and Shoaib took three of the five. He bowled bloody quick, and it took a tremendous knock of 191 from Justin Langer to get us out of trouble. I made 24 and faced Shoaib for a while late on the first day, and I can tell you first hand he was getting them through pretty smartly.

The Pakistanis were completely ordinary with the bat, and in the second innings, we skittled them for only 72, so had us a massive win. We'd bowled them out for 59 and 53 in a Test in Sharjah a year or two earlier, and if you couple that fact with all the stuff that's gone on in world cricket, you sometimes wonder whether the Pakistanis are fair dinkum.

In the second innings, Glenn McGrath picked up his best figures: 8/24. Kasper got the other two, and I couldn't get one in 12 overs. I didn't bowl well, but I probably could have snuck one or two in.

I followed up my half century in Brisbane, managing another one in the second Test, in Melbourne. It was a memorable milestone because I hit Mohammad Sami into the stand for a six. I also played a front-foot pull shot off the bowling of Shoaib that went for four, and even though it was a slower ball, I was happy to take it. I bowled quite well in that Test and took five wickets as well.

After a poor run of form, Darren Lehmann was dropped from the side for the Sydney Test, to make way for Shane Watson to make his debut. It was terribly sad to see Darren out of the team after his brilliant efforts in Sri Lanka earlier that year.

In the Sydney Test, we bowled first and I had two catches dropped in my opening over. Off my third ball, I had Yasir Hameed put down by Shane Warne at slip, and off the next delivery, Adam Gilchrist grassed a chance behind the stumps. At the time, my rhythm was perfect; I was feeling good and bowling effectively. After those chances, I didn't look like getting a wicket for the rest of the game, till the second innings when I dismissed Asim Kamal, which was the last wicket we captured in the match.

I was really annoyed that those catches went down, because I finished the series with only seven wickets at 36.85, so my figures could have been a whole lot better. If those chances had been taken, I could have had a crack at Younis Khan in the second over of the first innings. I would have fancied my chances of knocking him over with the new cherry and their middle order with him. Dropped catches can really affect your day's bowling, and although I know that blokes don't try to drop them, it was bad timing for me personally and I was shattered. I felt deflated, my bowling was affected for the rest of the game.

In that match, Ricky Ponting made 200 and Adam Gilchrist blasted a brilliant hundred, hitting 5 sixes. His onslaught during the middle session of the third day was something to see. He made 96 from only 86 balls and smashed the Pakistan bowlers to all parts of the SCG.

MUCH MILEAGE IS MADE OUT OF HOW MUCH SOME PLAYERS 'love' to bat. Justin Langer and Phil Jaques are a couple of blokes who really get a kick out of practising. The truth of the matter is that Ricky isn't all that different from them; in fact, he applies himself to the task every bit as well as anyone does. He wouldn't have the record he has if he hadn't worked diligently and consistently on his game. The perception exists that because some of the blokes are seen having an extra net or throw down, they love batting more than others do. That sort of comment doesn't sit well with me, because all Test cricketers put enormous effort into honing and polishing their game.

If there's one bugbear I do have with professional sport it's that some guys manage to do their 'extra' work in front of the cameras, to build the perception that they put in more than other guys do. This ploy can reflect on other blokes in the team in that it's suggestive that they don't work as hard. I've always done my training to get ready; I don't need to do it in front of the media reps or TV cameras.

Across the Tasman

After the one-day series, I was off to New Zealand for the first time for a series of One Day Internationals and three Tests. I really like the place, apart from the fact that the crowds really get stuck into us. I don't know what it is — maybe small brother versus big brother or a bit of small-man syndrome. One thing I did notice off the field was that on TV and in the papers, there are always stories about Australia — a lot of our TV shows are aired, and there's always stuff about Australia in the papers.

In Australia, we never read or hear about much to do with New Zealand unless it's a major story. The Kiwis almost see themselves as part of Australia, whereas we don't look at it that way at all; this is just how you perceive things when you're in NZ.

We started the New Zealand tour by playing a Twenty20 game at Eden Park, in Auckland on 17 February 2005. The Kiwis went with a 'retro' outfit and got into the spirit of the game. It would have been nice if our team had embraced it slightly more; that really didn't happen as we took it quite seriously. Twenty20 was still in its early stages, and despite the fact the game was far from serious Cricket Australia had important sponsors that needed to be recognised.

From a bowler's point of view, I think 20-over cricket will be helpful for getting the bowlers to focus on their skills more, because the margin for error is more unforgiving than the 50-over game. Bowlers need to be able to produce more yorkers and slower balls, otherwise they'll get carted.

The matches will always be played on good batting tracks, because the fans want to see the teams score runs. They're looking for plenty of boundaries and for balls going into the crowd. It will be a sad day if the selectors consider dropping a guy from other forms of the game because of his performances in 20-over games. I don't think they ever will, because Twenty20 should always exist to entertain the fans and should be challenging for the bowlers.

Having said that, I'm not that convinced about having a World Cup for Twenty20 cricket, even though the fans love and demand the concept. At present there's not a lot of it, which is perhaps why so many people are coming along to have a look at it. In the case of a World Cup, I wonder what the level of interest will be when heaps of games are played in a short space of time. I remain unconvinced that the public will embrace the concept quite as much after a while. It's a cheaper form of cricket for spectators in terms of both money and time. It has a bit going for it at the moment and will certainly hang around.

The Twenty20 form seems to work best in County cricket in England, because you drive from ground to ground rather than fly, which you have to do in Australia. Driving for 30 minutes or an hour on the motorway isn't a big deal, whereas in Australia, you're looking at a minimum of three hours by the time you've taken into account driving to the airport and then checking into your hotel. At the moment, thanks to the big crowds, Cricket Australia can justify flying the New South Wales team to Perth, and vice versa.

In the one-day series before the Test series, we whitewashed the Kiwis 5–nil. In each match after the first, which we won by only 10 runs, we beat them quite comfortably.

First Test against New Zealand, Christchurch, 10–13 March 2005

In the first innings of that Test at Jade Stadium, New Zealand batted impressively and made 433. There was nothing in the wicket, and most of their batsmen made runs, especially Hamish

Marshall, who made his debut hundred. The Kiwis managed to block us early and punished the loose ones later in the day.

The sad part of that game was that hardly anyone attended it. There were small pockets of fans and probably not even as many as a thousand people at the venue. After getting good crowds for the one-dayers, we found the turnout disappointing. However, that's how it is in NZ: the fans go for the shorter form of the game and can't be bothered attending the five-day games.

Looking on the positive side, however, in your spare time you were free to wander around at night and unlike at home, you could have a meal and not get hassled by anyone. It was possible to fully relax away from the game, which was a pleasant change.

After the Kiwis made their big score, we struggled for a while, and when I'd been dismissed batting as a nightwatchman, we were 6/201, still short of the follow-on. From there, both Simon Katich and Adam Gilchrist made superb hundreds: they added more than 200 for the seventh wicket and got us back into it. Kat played in his usual way, and Gilly was particularly aggressive in hitting 6 sixes, one of them off Daniel Vettori that pitched in the rough and was smashed out of the ground. After Daniel had bowled that ball, you could see him shaking his head thinking, *I bowled a good ball there, and I'm still getting hit for six.* Daniel is a tremendously good finger spinner, probably the second best after Muralitharan. He's also a well-performed batsman, and everyone respects him.

In the first innings of that Test I didn't manage to get a wicket. However, in the second dig, I snared three and helped us to our nine-wicket win. I was bowling okay and felt quite good. The thing about my bowling is I know when my action isn't quite right. The signs are when I get in the 'danger' area of the pitch or I'm not following through properly. Once or twice during the series, umpire Rudi Koertzen told me I was getting dangerously close to the 'no go' zone on the pitch and to be careful; I was creeping up a bit on the front line as well.

Second Test, Wellington, 18–22 March 2005

FROM CHRISTCHURCH, WE HEADED NORTH TO WELLINGTON FOR the second Test. Wellington thoroughly deserves to be nicknamed the Windy City: it's the gustiest place I've ever been to. When we were there, it was surprisingly cold and we were quite uncomfortable. There was a fair bit of rain about, and the match ended in a draw. The ground itself, Basin Reserve, is picturesque, but when we were there it was much too windy to be able to take all that in. For most of the game, I had to bowl into the wind and struggled to reach the crease. Hitting the track was hard, but all I could do was keep running in and bowling.

Gilly again went on the rampage in that Test: he made 162, which included another 5 sixes. One of the balls smashed a window in the upper deck of the RA Vance Stand, so it was a fairly decent hit.

Third Test, Auckland, 26–29 March 2005

AFTER THE RAIN HAD CAUSED A MESS-UP IN WELLINGTON, WE headed further north to Auckland for the last Test, at Eden Park. I picked up three wickets in our win there and felt the bowling was the best I'd done on the tour. In the first innings, I bowled Lou Vincent with one he didn't offer a shot to, and in the second, I took the best caught and bowled of my life: a one-handed reflex catch to dismiss Stephen Fleming. He drove it back at me, I stuck my hand out, and the chance stuck.

Eden Park is a weird-shaped ground: it's used for Rugby, so has spots at which the boundary is quite short. The New Zealand grounds don't excite you too much; the country reminds you a bit of what Tasmania was like 10 years ago in that it's a bit behind the times. I don't mean that in a condescending way, but that's how it is over there. It's a nice place, just a bit off the pace in some areas.

One of the really upmarket spots we went to in Auckland was Viaduct Harbour, the city waterfront area developed for the America's Cup challenge of 2000. Packed with pubs and restaurants, it's phenomenal. We went to an all-you-can-eat Argentinean grill, where the food was fantastic. They brought out skewer after skewer of meat; it was a great dining experience. Glenn McGrath and Kasper both had a huge feast; they tried to see how much meat they could eat in the one sitting.

We wrapped things up in that third Test in four days and took the Test series 2–nil, having won the one-dayers 5–nil. It'd been a comprehensive effort by the team over the summer: if you include the Indian tour, we'd won nine out of 12 Tests, drawn two through rain, and lost only the one, on a raging turner in Mumbai, by 13 runs.

The 2005 Ashes, and the winds of change

Before I headed to England for the 2005 Ashes, I grabbed the opportunity to get away from cricket and unwind for a month in April. The pitches were still up at the Adelaide Oval, so a couple of times a week I popped in there to bowl for about 20 minutes at a time, just to keep things ticking over. I didn't want to do too much, because I knew I'd have a lot of bowling to do in England.

When we arrived in England, we encountered plenty of excitement because the Poms had been building up the series to be one of the biggest ever. England had been playing well, especially away, having won the Test series in the West Indies and South Africa over the previous two years.

Against England, a Twenty20 International, 13 June 2005

The tour started at Southampton, where we played England in a Twenty20 International. We treated it as something of a warm-up game whereas England came out hard and took the whole thing much more seriously. They played well and absolutely killed us. I came on to bowl after Glenn and Brett's opening spell and had the umpire tell me that we were three overs behind time, so ended up bowling off a short run to help us get through. I was trying to work myself into it, and ended up getting smashed for 49 runs from my four overs.

Early in the tour, I made a decision not to show the England batsmen my change-ups; I thought I'd save them for later on, closer to the Tests. I was trying to bowl full and straight, and when I erred slightly I was getting belted. England won the game from a psychological point of view and took something from it.

NatWest Series

Our first game in the NatWest One Day Series was against Bangladesh, in Cardiff, Wales, on 18 June 2005. That game sticks out in my memory because Andrew Symonds turned up suffering the ill effects of a late night. The day before it had been Shane Watson's birthday, so there'd been some celebrating. Symmo had hooked up with Shane and a few of the guys who'd been told they weren't in the 12. After a few drinks, most of the lads got in at about midnight — nothing unusual there — but despite knowing he was supposed to play, Symmo chose to kick on into the small hours. Evidently he managed a bit of sleep, because when it was time to leave, Michael Clarke went into his room and threw water on him to get him going.

During the warm-ups at the ground, Symmo kept his leg on the fence for rather long while doing a stretch. Plus he was chatting away quite loudly, but I think the final giveaway that he was under the weather was when he took a baseball glove to take some throws and he dropped about two out of every three balls. At that point, Ricky Ponting and John Buchanan seemed to cotton on to the fact that Andrew wasn't fit to play, and they dropped him like a hot brick. Now when you look back, you can see the hilarious side of the incident, but at the time it was a serious breach.

Andrew, to his credit, took full responsibility for what he'd done, offered no excuses and admitted his actions were unacceptable. He copped the dressing down. Seemingly it turned out to be a turning point in his cricket. Since then, I believe he's become one of our better one-day cricketers, and hopefully he'll remain that way for some time.

We batted first against Bangladesh and made 249, which in hindsight probably wasn't enough. The Bangladeshis started slowly and at one stage were 3/72, but Mohammad Ashraful got a hundred and they beat us with four balls to spare.

I was on right at the death: I bowled a slowish ball that went for six, and they won the match.

You have to hand it to the Bangladeshis, they'd improved out of sight. They continued to play quite well in the series. Over four or five days of a Test match they tend to get found out, but in a 50-over game they can putty over some of the holes in their side. Full credit to them for the win. We had our best attack, so we had no excuses.

The day after our defeat at the hands of the Bangladeshis, we had to face England, in Bristol. It was the second time we'd come up against their new gun batsman, Kevin Pietersen. We'd seen some footage of him, and we knew he'd done well playing in South Africa a few months earlier. We were aware that he could give them a bit of a whack, and he was one of the guys I didn't want to show my slower ball to, not till later in the tournament.

In my first over, I started with four wides and a no-ball. Then, when I was bowling to Marcus Trescothick, we took the second slip out and put him at short cover. Sure enough, I found the edge of his bat and it went right between the keeper and the floating slip at catchable height. From then on, I sensed that it wasn't going to be my day. Later I got hit for a few sixes by Pietersen, and the Poms won the game after being in all sorts of bother.

Final of the NatWest Series, against England, 2 July 2005

After that disastrous weekend in the NatWest Series, we started to put some wins together and made it to the Final, which was played at Lord's, against England. We batted first and were 50 without loss but collapsed to be 5/93. Then Michael Hussey rescued us by making 62 not out, and we managed to scrape up 196.

The conditions were favourable to the bowlers, and we had the opposition 5/33. Next thing we knew, Paul Collingwood and Geraint Jones added 116 to put the Poms back in the match. They then lost some wickets, and when they had an over to go, they needed 10 to win. It was a chaotic end: there was a no-ball and a run-out and finally, with three needed off the last ball, Giles and Harmison scrambled two leg byes to tie the match. The game ebbed and flowed, and perhaps a tie was the only fair result.

I bowled my 10 overs for 42 and didn't get belted. I didn't get a wicket, though, and that is what cost me my spot in England in 2005, when I hadn't taken many wickets and in a few games had gone for a run per ball.

While I was bowling during most of those one-day matches, I kept saying to myself, *Stick to your plan of no change-ups; keep the ball full and straight.* Looking back on that tactic, I think it probably cost me my spot in the One Day International team.

Things were starting to fall into place in that game: my opening spell was eight overs for 2/20, but when I came back to bowl my last two, Pietersen was going well and that was when he hit me for that six. I bowled this really good bumper, or so I thought, and Kevin smashed it over long on, with a kind of tennis shot. I just thought, *If he's 'arsey' enough to hit that over the fence, good luck to him!* Then and there, I realised the game was on the line and it was time for a slower ball. Sure enough, I bowled a slower one, Pietersen didn't pick it, and he was bowled; it was to be my last wicket in a One Day International.

In hindsight, I probably left my run too late and should have bowled more of that sort of stuff earlier. I had it in my head to save the full repertoire for the big games. I was reluctant to bowl my slower ball to players such as Pietersen and Flintoff.

In the end, the selectors decided that because I'm not such a hot fielder and I don't slog with the bat that well, it was time to make way for someone else. I wasn't exactly thrilled, but when I look back on my one-day figures, I realise they weren't too good, so I guess the decision was fair enough. Nevertheless, it still grates on me that I got 3/44 in my last game and haven't played since.

BEFORE THE TEST SERIES, WE HAD A TOUR MATCH AT LEICESTER from 15 to 17 July, during which I came unstuck with my rhythm. I changed ends, things felt better and the ball came out well. West Aussie Chris Rogers played for them and I had him out off a no-ball. Chris, to his credit, played well and could go on to have a big Test career and open for Australia.

First Test against England, Lord's, 21–24 July 2005

THE OPENING OF THE TEST SERIES AT LORD'S CAME UPON US quickly and there was plenty of hype. After we won the toss, we opted to bat.

The match got off to a dramatic start when, in the opening over, Justin Langer got hit on the arm by Steve Harmison. In fact, most of our batsmen copped some sort of hit during that first innings. Matty Hayden, in trying to hook, got one on the grille. Ricky Ponting copped the worst: a blow to his right cheekbone that drew blood.

England bowled solidly on a helpful pitch, and having been 5/87, we did well to get to 190.

England had a few overs to bat before tea and managed to get through. However, immediately after the break, Glenn McGrath had Marcus Trescothick caught in the slips and bagged his 500th Test wicket. It was a wonderful moment for Glenn, savoured in front of a packed Lord's and with all his family there. After he'd reached the 500 mark, he demolished the opposition's top order. England collapsed to be 5/21, and Glenn had the lot.

Kevin Pietersen managed to ride out the McGrath spell, and played confidently and well in his Test debut. He wasn't frightened to take on the bowlers. Early on the second day, he actually drove Glenn into the Pavilion for six. Thankfully, Damien Martyn took a blinder of a catch on the boundary to dismiss him for 57, and England were all out for 155, 35 behind.

In the second innings, we were battling before Marto and Michael Clarke had a brilliant fourth-wicket partnership of 155. Thanks to their effort, the game started to turn in our favour. Pup was going so well he looked set for a ton, but then he played an extravagant drive at Matthew Hoggard and got bowled. The game had been really heading our way, and the shot wasn't quite on in that situation; Pup practically gave it away with that shot.

It's interesting when some guys get out like that and the argument is *That's the way he plays.* To be blunt, I don't buy that. We had it in the case of Kevin Pietersen sometimes, and I think it's a real cop-out; it's just an easy excuse for not being careful enough. With the advent of Twenty20 cricket, blokes sometimes forget they don't need to smack a four off every ball. Sometimes I think batsmen need to be more patient in the four- or five-day game.

Simon Katich was on a winning streak, and we ended up on 384, so England had to get 420 to win. They were never going to get them on that wicket, and on the fourth day we rolled them for 180, so that put us 1–nil up. The game ended at about five o'clock, and we stayed at the ground celebrating till about midnight. Stuart MacGill set up his quirky bar in the change rooms, and all the families came in to help us savour what was a phenomenal win. We actually sang the team song in the England dressing room; of course they'd left by that stage!

I bowled only 14 overs in that game and wasn't needed that much because we got the Poms out fairly cheaply in both innings. I felt that the ball was coming out okay, even though I wasn't setting the world on fire. Leading into the game, I had a few back injections, but my back was now fine. Mind you, bowling only 14 overs, you can't really impose yourself on the game.

We outplayed England at Lord's, and Glenn, Brett and Shane all bowled particularly well. After the match, Glenn said we'd beat them 5–nil again. He meant what he said, but at no stage did he or any of us get carried away with the situation.

Second Test, Birmingham, 4–8 August 2005

During the next Test, at Edgbaston in Birmingham, Glenn trod on the ball and was out with a buggered ankle. Ricky won the toss and decided to bowl, and I was extremely surprised that he did so. A mini-cyclone had gone through the area and dumped a lot of rain, but the pitch had recovered well and looked flat, so it seemed odd to bowl first, especially as Glenn had gone down injured. I remember coming in after the warm-ups, hearing we'd sent England in and thinking the decision was quite strange. It's rare to win the toss and decide to bowl on a pitch that looks that good. Ricky had his reasons, and I suppose he wanted to take advantage of any moisture in the wicket. To this day, I've never discussed the decision with him, so I don't know his exact reason for inserting the opposition.

England smacked us around and at lunch were 1/132 from 27 overs. However, the score should have been better in the wickets column for us because Warnie dropped Andrew Strauss in the slips off me when he was only 4. It would have been interesting to have an early crack at Vaughan, but England's openers added 112 and he didn't come in till soon before lunch.

They simply got stuck into us after that, and with the aid of short boundaries, they played skilfully enough to make 407. I thought I bowled pretty well, having 2/91 from 22 overs, in comparison with our other paceman, Brett Lee, who had 1/111 off 17, and Kasper, who took 3/80 from 15. England got away with a few shots on a good deck, and that's why I was surprised when we were to bowl.

It's interesting to think back as to why England suddenly became positive about their batting after the poor effort they'd put in at Lord's. I suspect they figured they had nothing to lose: they came out, had a crack, and it came off, so good luck to them.

In the second dig, I bowled only eight overs and started to get the feeling I wasn't in favour with the skipper. I felt there were stages at which I should have been thrown the ball more. We'd lost Glenn, and although I was the next-most experienced Test fast bowler, I wasn't getting the ball. To be honest, I wasn't sure why. I dropped a few hints by warming my shoulders up in the field, but Ricky kept throwing the ball to other players, and I found it a tad disheartening.

In the end, we lost the Test by two runs. If we'd won it, I'm sure we would have kept the Ashes. The last wicket to fall was Kasper, caught behind. According to the video of Kasper's dismissal, he wasn't out, so the outcome also included an element of plain old bad luck. On top of that, we had Simon Jones plumb lbw in England's second innings. Then again, they had a few go against them, too, so we couldn't complain too much.

Our batting let us down. We had to get 282 to win, and the tail should never have been put in the position of our needing 107 for the last two wickets. However, I guess our bowling wasn't that good in the first innings. We simply didn't play that well, and we still lost by only two runs.

It would have been nice to knock England over; it was disappointing to get so close.

Third Test, Manchester, 11–15 August 2005

Heading into the third Test, to be played in Manchester; at Old Trafford, I had no real concerns I wouldn't be picked even though I'd had only two wickets in the first two Tests. Before the game, I spoke to Merv Hughes, who was the selector on the tour. We didn't have a bowling coach with us, so he was the next-best person to talk to about a few things.

We lost the toss, and England batted. Both Glenn and Brett had come up fit after being in major doubt heading into the game. Glenn had recovered quickly from the ankle injury he'd incurred in Birmingham, and Brett had come good after suffering from an infected knee. They opened the bowling, and after a while it was time for me to bowl my opening spell.

After my first over, I had a feeling it wasn't going to be my day. I wanted a third-man fielder for Michael Vaughan but was overruled by our skipper, Ricky. In the past, Vaughan had said he liked it when no fielder was there because he could let the ball come on to the face of the bat and play it down there for easy runs. Darren Lehmann, who'd played with Vaughan at Yorkshire, had confirmed the preference as well. I bowled my first over, and Vaughan scored 10 runs, all down near third man. A couple of fours and a two could have been much less if I'd had a fielder there, and unfortunately I didn't recover. At one stage, Glenn had Vaughan bowled off a no-ball — unhelpful — and Vaughen went on to make a brilliant 166.

After tea, I didn't bowl particularly well: I had a spell of four overs 0/42 and finished the day with 0/89 off 15 overs; England made 5/341. In that opening over, the balls were coming out nicely; I was getting them to shape away, and Vaughan edged a few. However, things deteriorated after that. My thoughts became negative. It was up to me to change them, but I didn't get it out of my mind I was going to have a bad day. It wasn't that I couldn't change them; I just didn't.

In the second innings, I bowled only four overs out of the 61 and knew I was going to get dropped. It was as plain as the nose on your face: I was in trouble.

My weak performance ultimately cost me my Test spot and my career. Looking back on it, I think two things stand out as turning points. First, in the case of my one-day bowling early in the summer, I was too set in my ways, so I wouldn't show my slower balls to some blokes. Later, when I did show them and the tactic worked, I realised I should have showed them earlier in the tour. What an idiot I was.

The second turning point was in the Manchester Test, when I went for those 10 runs in my opening over. I should have insisted on the field placing I wanted but I didn't stand my ground, and that is clearly my fault.

We managed to get out of that Test without embarrassing ourselves, mostly because Punter batted all day to make 156. He got out with a few overs to go, which meant Glenn had to bat out the remaining overs with Brett Lee. In the last over, Glenn decided to bat out of his crease in order to reduce the threat of being lbw. He was facing Steve Harmison, and let one go and forgot to go back in his crease. England's keeper, Geraint Jones, didn't notice and actually threw the ball to the short leg, who also didn't notice and threw the ball back to the bowler. The Test match could have ended in tatters there and then. In the rooms, we all noticed and sent Stuart MacGill out with a message to tell Glenn to make sure he got back into his crease. It's comical to think about it now, but the Test could have ended in tears because of Glenn wandering around outside of his crease.

When Glenn came in, he said that if we'd had a few more overs we'd have gotten the runs — we were 52 short, so I'm not so sure about that. In the second innings, I made a duck, given out lbw to Hoggard by Steve Bucknor when I was well forward of my crease. In my career, I was lbw about 25 per cent of the time; I got hit on the pads a lot.

Towards the end of the match, I was writing on the back of a used envelope to count the balls remaining. I crossed the last 90 balls down, and after we'd saved the game, I got Glenn and Brett to sign the envelope. I just thought we needed to do a countdown; Simon Katich had tried it with runs to go in Birmingham, and Darren Webber had done one when South Australia saved the 1995–96 Shield Final.

Sure enough, I was dropped for the Trent Bridge Test; my instincts had proved correct. It was chairman of selectors Trevor Hohns who delivered the news. We chatted for a while, and Ricky came over and asked, 'Has Trevor spoken to you yet?' I indicated that he had. With that, Ricky just said, 'Okay,' and walked off. There was no 'Bad luck, mate,' or pat on the shoulder, which confirmed for me that I no longer had the support of my captain. All through the tour, I'd had this niggling feeling that I'd fallen from favour, and at that moment was 100 per cent sure Ricky didn't want me in the side. Why he didn't have some sort of chat with me, I don't know. It's bewildering. Then again, I'm sure he had other things on his mind. It seemed slightly odd, but I can't say I was shattered.

From that moment onwards, however, I felt left out. Yes, and probably let down, too. After all I'd done playing Test cricket for Australia, I felt I deserved better than that.

The upside of being dropped was that Shaun Tait got to debut in my place. I was mighty chuffed for big Sloon, and wished I could be there on the field with him to share the moment. I thought he handled himself quite well.

Fourth Test, Nottingham, 25–28 August 2005

What I will say about that fourth Test, played at Trent Bridge in Nottingham, was that I could see how the pressure was really starting to weigh the lads down.

On the second day, when Matthew Hayden was dismissed lbw to Matthew Hoggard, he came off and was yelling obscenities in the rooms. Obviously it was all getting to Matty, which was a concern to us all. Matty got beaten because of a good plan, and his outburst said to me that he was becoming seriously rattled.

England were playing incredibly well and had a real sniff at that point that they could really get the Ashes back.

The substitute fielder issue came to a head in the second innings when Ricky Ponting was run out. Damien Martyn pushed one to cover and ran, and Garry Pratt was fielding at cover and threw Ricky out. Ricky was fuming as he was coming off. Apparently, he saw that England's coach, Duncan Fletcher, had a bit of a grin on his face, and yelled a few things at him.

England flouted the use of the twelfth man in that series. Bowlers were always coming off after spells for a couple of overs, and we believed they shouldn't be. The Poms brought in a specialist sub-fielder. These days, we use a local player in that role, so the official twelfth man can go and play domestic cricket and at least stay in some sort of form. Over the years, someone such as Andy Bichel would be twelfth man a bit, and because he had to hang around and perform the duties, he missed out on match bowling. Then, when a tour team was picked, he missed out and was told that another bowler had been picked ahead of him because that individual was doing well in domestic cricket. Andy suggested that because he'd been in the best 12, he should be in. He got told that he missed out because he hadn't had a lot of cricket. That's all changed now in Australian cricket in order to allow the twelfth man to play back with his state.

It was out of order, however, for England to pick Pratt as a sub-fielder. They also used their fielding coach, Trevor Penney, a former Warwickshire player, who was a gun fielder. That goes beyond stretching the laws; it's plain cheating. They were replacing, for example, a Steve Harmison, who lumbers around in the field, with a slick athletic fielder such as Pratt, who can throw down the stumps. Fletcher said they were acting within the laws of the game, and technically he was correct, but you can't tell me they were acting in the spirit of cricket, especially as the ICC and Cricket Australia are pushing the 'spirit of cricket' aspect pretty hard.

After the loss at Trent Bridge we were 2–1 down. However, never did we think we couldn't win at the Oval and square the series, thereby keeping the Ashes. We knew we could win there but were conscious that the conditions weren't helpful.

In some quarters, we were criticised for not batting on in bad light on days two and three, when we were going well. Looking back, I think it's easy to say the batsmen should have kept batting, but I believe they made the right decision at the time because they were finding it hard to see the ball. The sight screen at the Pavilion end of the Oval is terrible.

DURING THAT OVAL TEST, WE HAD AN INTERESTING VISITOR AT the rooms: the actor–director Ron Howard, who starred as Richie Cunningham in the TV show 'Happy Days'. Ron is busy making movies these days, and the reason he was at the Test was that he was associated with our physio, Errol Alcott. Errol had fixed Russell Crowe's shoulder before the making of *Cinderella Man* and had got to know Ron, who was the director on that film. Ron was now in London making *The Da Vinci Code* and had a day off, so Errol had invited him along. Ron's assistant director, Bill Connor, also came along.

I'd been a huge fan of 'Happy Days', so spending some time with Ron and having a photo taken with him were real highlights. He is a big baseball fan, a game I enjoy as well, although I don't know the intricacies of it.

Ron likes his cricket but isn't completely *au fait* with how the game is played, so for a session while the lads were in the field, Ron, Bill, Kasper, Stuart MacGill and I explained it. I asked Ron a lot of questions about baseball, and likewise he and Bill asked about cricket while the game was going on. It was quite interesting having to explain some of the basics to them. It was enjoyable to have a chat to them to pass the time and forget I wasn't in the team. I was a bit down. Ron and Bill said I reminded them of the pitcher Randy Johnson, who'd won a World Series with the Arizona Diamondbacks. Both of us have the long hair, and Ron thought we looked quite similar.

While I'm on meeting famous people during that series, the Aussie actor Hugh Jackman came into the rooms during the Lord's Test. I went up to him and introduced myself. I could tell he was pretty chuffed to be in the rooms. He was a really nice bloke. He's a bit of a cricket nut and was probably as excited to be there as we would be if we were on the set of one of his movies.

I've met Her Majesty the Queen a couple of times. As I've already mentioned, at Lord's back in 2001, the Queen had commented to Colin Miller about his interesting pink hairstyle. Near the lunch room at Lord's, there's a painting of us meeting her on that day, so not only am I on the visitors' honour board for my bowling efforts, there's a painting of me and a few of the lads meeting Her Majesty.

She reminds you of your grandmother a bit. The conversation was quite brief, and I didn't say anything out of the ordinary — unlike Dennis Lillee, who in 1972 said 'G'day' to the Queen and the Duke, or Barry 'Nugget' Rees, who asked her how the corgis were going.

I met the Duke of Edinburgh at the Oval in 2005, and we all said, 'Hi.' He seemed nice enough as well.

I've also met Prime Minister John Howard a few times and found him to be a pleasant fellow. He's passionate about his cricket, and he loves kicking back and watching the game.

AT THE END OF THE TOUR, I WAS WEIGHTED DOWN WITH disappointment. Even though I hadn't played in the last two Tests, losing the Ashes was shattering.

In hindsight, I feel I mightn't have taken enough notice of the warning signs in New Zealand: maybe things hadn't been as good as I thought they were and I should have done more remedial work before I went to England. After the tour, I worked out that I hadn't been following through enough, and that I'd been stopping myself from getting that little extra zip and shape at the end of my deliveries. That wasn't picked up from any of our support staff in England, and it wasn't till I caught up with former Redbacks coach and friend Jeff Hammond that I identified the problem.

Bomber came down to the nets and worked it all out in about two balls. As soon as he picked that I wasn't finishing my follow-through properly I started to focus on that aspect and *bang!* I was done. I ended up having a fantastic season with South Australia in 2005–06. I got the ball to swing and continued to do so in my stint with Yorkshire in 2006. I've always had my 'checkpoints', but I hadn't been picking up on the follow-through. Peter Muggleton, our bowling coach at the Redbacks, keeps an eye on me now, and when he notices I'm not following through, he brings it to my attention straight away.

Jubilation

On the personal side, it was early in the tour that I found out Anna was expecting our first child. The team had just arrived in Brighton, in the south of England. After the long trip, we were all weary and took the afternoon off. Because I was feeling jaded, I thought I'd sneak in a nap. Anna rang me from Adelaide and we chatted for quite a while. Towards the end of the call, she casually announced, 'By the way, I'm pregnant.' I was gobsmacked by the news and was jumping for joy. After that, I had no chance of getting any sort of nap. After a few days went by, I just had to share my news with someone, so I went for a feed with Glenn McGrath and told him. My former Redback teammate and good mate Paul Wilson was next; he was in Brighton as well, playing for Brighton and Hove Cricket Club.

Someone once told me, I'm sure, that news like that can be a turning point in your career: that's certainly how it was for me. As soon as I knew that this baby was on the way, no longer did I feel that cricket was the most important thing in the world for me. It *had* been to that point, but now, even though it's still my career and I love playing, my family is much more important.

My feelings about becoming a father again were hugely different from the first time, 10 years earlier. When Jackie was pregnant with Sapphire, I had been at the start of my career, I was very young, I wasn't married, and I had no intention of marrying. This time around, I was married and much more settled. I had a clearer focus; I had achieved several of my life goals; I owned a nice house that had a pool and a tennis court. More importantly, because I had already brought a beautiful daughter, Sapphire, into the world, I knew about the love this baby would bring, and I was more than ready.

Maybe subconsciously I took my foot off the pedal at that point. Realising that I had achieved many of my goals, and because Anna was about to have our baby, perhaps a change in my life was triggered. It's hard to know.

I wouldn't change a thing, though: it's all part of your life experience. I still don't think I've played my last Test — but having said that, it wouldn't kill me if I didn't play again.

17 Last blast in Bangladesh, and a double ton for the road

When I returned from the Ashes series, there was to be the Johnnie Walker Super Series against the Rest of the World, comprising three one-dayers in Melbourne and a Super Test in Sydney. It cut me to the quick that I wasn't to be selected, because the team was supposed to be picked on the basis of performances over the four years up to the present, and during that time I'd been a big part of the team in both forms of the game. The selectors just said, 'You're not playing,' and I was pretty gutted.

I felt let down at not being given the opportunity to play. I was dropped for having a bad game, and there was no intention to reinstate me. It was almost as though I'd been totally forgotten, as though I'd fallen off the face of the earth. I just felt that having been a part of that team, played so much and been one of the highest wicket takers ever produced in this country, I would have liked to have been given another opportunity. In only a few months I'd gone from being in the side to being out of favour.

Over the years, I've got on fairly well with the selectors, having spoken with them every now and then. It has never been my style to phone them to ask why I hadn't been picked; most of the time you know why you're in or out of the team.

Perhaps part of my problem has been that I'm too honest. At one time, I mentioned to chairman Trevor Hohns that if I were the selectors I wouldn't pick me for the one-dayers. That was at the start of 2005–06 and I was having trouble with my shoulder when I was throwing from the outfield, even though it was okay when I was bowling.

I worked out that the shoulder problems had arisen because I was doing bench presses at training. It still irks me that I allowed the issue to go on for so long. The thinking was that strength work was the way to go when it was clearly having an adverse effect on my body. If only I'd said, 'No, this isn't working,' and stopped doing it. The older you get, the more you know what you need to do to get yourself right to play. With all due respect to some fitness instructors, they don't always know what the correct training for bowlers is; they don't know what it's like to bowl heaps of overs. We were lucky to have Jock Campbell as our fitness adviser in the Australian set-up for a while, because he had been a bowler at First Grade level in Sydney and knew what it was like to bowl 20 or so overs in a day. Although he was only a medium pacer, he had a better grasp of how to assist a bowler than most fitness people did.

Setting my sights on performing well with the South Australia XI

HEADING INTO THE 2005–06 SEASON, I FOCUSED ON PLAYING for South Australia and on getting as many wickets as I could in order to give the national selectors a reason to pick me again.

Anna was by now in the later stages of her pregnancy, and we were both on cloud nine. That happiness was compensation for the disappointment I felt at not being in the Australian team. Anna was having a reasonably comfortable pregnancy and she had the healthy glow which showed that everything was going well.

WITH THE SOUTH AUSTRALIAN TEAM, I HAD AN EARLY SETBACK when we played our first game, against New South Wales in a one-dayer at Bankstown. Brett Lee hit me in the right side of the ribs, and missed my chest guard. My lung was bruised and I had to miss the four-day game scheduled for a few days later. I was frustrated and wanted to play, but the doctor couldn't guarantee I'd be okay.

Once I recovered from the injury, I bowled fairly well in the early part of the season for South Australia and very much enjoyed playing state cricket. We had a good bunch of lads who were playing extremely well, and at Christmas we were leading the Pura Cup competition. I managed to pick up seven wickets in an innings against Victoria, at the Junction Oval in Melbourne, so the selectors came to know I was still around and good enough. Unfortunately, there was no place for me in the Australian team.

Oh, boy!

THE BIRTH OF MY SON, JACKSON, ON THE MORNING OF THE first of February 2006, was one of the greatest days of my life. Anna and I were at home for about 3½ hours counting the minutes between contractions, then about 4.30 a.m. she told me it was time to go to the hospital. The labour was progressing reasonably quickly but Jackson showed no movement for a little too long and they decided that he needed to come out very quickly with the aid of the ventouse. Everything worked out fine, and once Jackson was delivered at about 9 a.m., I excitedly texted and phoned everyone to convey the happy news that my son, Jackson Anderson Gillespie, was born weighing in at 8 pounds 14½ ounces.

I MANAGED TO KEEP MY FORM GOING WITH THE REDBACKS. I finished the season with 40 wickets at 21.27, and in the final innings of our win against New South Wales, in Adelaide, picked up 5/56. Before the season had ended, an opportunity came up for me to play with Yorkshire in County cricket for the 2006 English summer, which I gladly accepted. However, immediately after the end of the Australian summer, something else happened out of the blue: I was needed to play for Australia again.

Cricket Australia CEO Michael Brown rang me and said I needed to get on the plane to go to Bangladesh. Anna and I were full steam ahead with preparations for England but I had no hesitation in quickly changing my plans. Although I was slightly apprehensive about it all, it was an honour to be selected again and I went gladly. I knew I'd been picked only because there were a few injuries, but to my credit, I'd always bowled well in previous tours of the subcontinent. I think that down the track, I still might be a chance to be selected for future tours there, given my record.

TO MY WAY OF THINKING, ANYONE PLAYING FIRST CLASS CRICKET in Australia is never that far away from getting to play for his country; after all, there are only six teams, and if you can put together some good performances in a row, you can get picked. The English set-up is different in that there are 18 teams, and if a batsman makes a few hundreds in a row, often no one will look twice at him. If it happens here, you get noticed straight away, because our four-dayers and one-dayers are the hardest and most challenging competitions in the cricketing world. There are only 66 players going at the one time, and chances often present themselves. If you're doing the right things at the right times, you can get a run.

First Test against Bangladesh, Dhaka, 9–13 April 2006

In Bangladesh, I was stoked with the way the ball was coming out. I was hitting the right areas as well as experimenting with a shorter run-up. I used the tactic to rush the batsmen a bit, and was enjoying the challenge and fun of being part of the action at Test level again.

In the first Test, I was pleased to get a wicket in my first over. The Bangladeshis batted very well and made 427 in their first innings. I picked up two wickets, and Stuart MacGill took the other eight. Amazingly, Shane Warne got a touch-up; he conceded 112 runs without getting a wicket in 20 overs.

We were in trouble in the first innings, and it was only due to an innings of 144 from Adam Gilchrist that we were able to pass the follow-on. There weren't too many demons in the wicket, and I ended up making 26 in about two hours, so I found it hard to work out why everyone else had been getting out. I used my simple plan of blocking straight balls, and played an aggressive positive shot if the ball wasn't on the stumps. The only time I deviated from the game plan was if the ball was short and I thought I could play the pull shot. However, after being bowled by Mohammad Rafique when I was trying that tactic, I vowed that if I got another chance to bat in the series, I'd put that shot away. I didn't do it again, and it's fair to say that it worked for me in the next Test!

To our relief, we won that match by three wickets. The Bangladeshis set us just over 300, and thanks to Ricky Ponting's unbeaten hundred, we narrowly got there. Losing would have been an upset bigger than our loss to the Bangladeshis in Cardiff in 2005.

Mercifully we avoided the embarrassment of losing a Test to them after the disaster of our loss in that one-dayer the year before.

During that series, I really enjoyed my cricket. Each night after play, a few of us would head out for a nice meal and a few beers. It was good to be back in the mix, play my cricket and enjoy the time after stumps. I didn't have any late nights, just a few wines with dinner and a great time.

That historic second Test against Bangladesh, Chittagong, 16–20 April 2006

THINGS WERE FEELING MORE COMFORTABLE IN THE SECOND TEST when we fired the opposition out for 197. In my first over, I managed to get first Test centurion Shahriar Nafees out on the way to an opening spell of 3/11 from five overs. My fellow Redback Dan Cullen made his Test debut and took his first wicket in that match.

Late on the opening day, I was asked to put the pads on as nightwatchman. It came as a surprise to me. However, especially given that the wicket was an absolute 'road' of a pitch, I jumped at the chance. I'd have been mad not to. Sure enough, Matthew Hayden was dismissed just short of stumps, and in I went at number three.

Although I was confident there were runs out there, it didn't enter my head that I could get a double ton! I thought I was a chance to get a 50, but never in my wildest dreams did I look any further than that. With so much time left in the Test, it was a fantastic opportunity. When I reached 80 or so, I was starting to think, *Jeez, I can get a hundred here*. There were no real demons in the wicket or the attack, the field was out, and I simply thought, *I'm on here*. I just kept on batting. I stuck to my game plan of blocking the straight stuff and waiting for the loose stuff off the stumps to score from; it was as simple as that. Another reason why I wanted to stay out there is because I didn't really want to face Ricky in the change rooms after our mix-up that resulted in him being run out. I defended a delivery that went to backward point and being in my own bubble I wasn't even contemplating a run. I looked up and Ricky was halfway down the wicket and a direct hit from Abdur Razzaq from backward point ended Ricky's innings. It was his call and I was basically in the wrong. He was clearly annoyed because he knew that there were plenty of runs out there for him.

The Pakistani left-arm spinners Mohammad Rafique and Abdur Razzaq were bowling mainly around the wicket. However, they weren't getting much turn from the pitch, because there were no footmarks for them to aim at. The straighter delivery was the only danger, so I opened up my stance a bit more to make sure I didn't get hit on the pad. If the delivery was full or wide, I tried to play a positive shot.

I HAVE A MENTAL PICTURE OF MYSELF MAKING IT INTO THE 90S, which is when I grasped it — I was in uncharted territory; it was the highest score I'd ever made. In trying to get those last 10 runs, I thought *If I've gotten 90 sticking to my game plan, why rush? Just keep batting as you have been and the runs will come*. I brought up my ton off a cover drive, and it was a bizarre feeling because I'd never gotten to a hundred in any form of cricket.

Michael Hussey, who was batting with me, came up and congratulated me. He said there was no need to 'throw it away', because there were plenty of runs left in the pitch for me, if I wanted them.

THAT NIGHT I FACED THE MEDIA REPS, WHO ASKED ME ALL SORTS of stuff about being a nightwatchman and what a fairytale it all was. For one thing, I never thought I'd ever be at a press conference discussing my batting, so it was all strange.

It was in the rooms after play, when I was getting a massage from Lucy Frostick, that the phrase 'double ton' popped up. Lucy suggested how good it would be if I went on and got a double ton the next day. In no uncertain terms, I responded there was no way known I could get a double. If somehow I did, I added, I'd run around the ground nude. We all had a laugh at that.

When I arrived back at the team's hotel, in Chittagong, I went to the bar. Up to that point, no alcohol had ever been served from it. Bangladesh is a predominantly Muslim country and alcohol is prohibited. Adding to the record-breaking nature of the day, I celebrated reaching my maiden ton by drinking the 'maiden' bottle of Foster's there. Later that night, I enjoyed a nice dinner and a few bottles of wine with our manager, Steve Bernard, security officer, Reg Dickison, and selector, Merv Hughes. The celebration capped off a magical day.

An unexpected maiden ton becomes a history-making double ton

THE NEXT DAY, I TOLD MYSELF, *YOU HAVE TO GO OUT AND BAT again, so you might as well make the most of it.* I stuck with my game plan, and it continued to work pretty well. Early on, I wasn't all that worried because I had nothing to lose: I already had a hundred under my belt, something I never thought I'd have. I started to play a few sweep shots, and my score continued to grow. The bowlers were getting tired and a few fielders were on the fence, so there were plenty of singles out there for the taking. I reached 150. Only when I got to the 170s did I start to think that 200 was a possibility. During that period, I played a silly shot, and straight away Michael Hussey came down to tell me off. He urged me not to throw it away and reminded me I'd never get another opportunity to make a Test double ton. He was dead right, so after that rush of blood, I put my head down and pushed on.

I made it to 197 and brought up the 200 with a tuck around the corner off Rafique that went to the fence. To see all the lads clapping and laughing up in the stands was fantastic. There were a few Aussie fans there, and they were cheering too, as were the waving-the-flag crew, led by Luke Sparrow; they were beside themselves.

Later, I was pretty pumped to receive notes and letters from people congratulating me on making the 200. One came from former SACA CEO Barry Gibbs, who was back home in Adelaide battling cancer. Sadly, he passed away not long after. He'd helped me during my early days playing for South Australia, so it was especially good to know he was pleased about my success.

Obviously it was a great feeling to get to 200. However, when we declared straight away, the one downer was that I had to go back out into the field immediately. I bowled four overs with the new ball, and had a catch dropped by Warnie. If I'd had a wicket, that would have really topped off the day.

Overall, it was a surreal feeling to get a double century. Unbeknown to me at the time, while I was batting that day, Matty Hayden came out with the statement that if I made it to 200, he'd do a nude lap of the Chittagong ground. Just as well, though, Steve Bernard knocked that idea on the head — not that it probably would have happened anyway. We knew we were in a Muslim country and that something like that wouldn't go down too well.

For the second day in a row, I found myself speaking to the journalists about my batting — a truly bizarre experience. It was one aspect of a wonderful personal highlight and a great time of my career.

After we'd bowled Bangladesh out on the final day, the celebrations got under way. On the roof of the team hotel, I got to lead the team song that night. It was a fantastic honour, and it was almost as if most of the blokes knew it would be my last time playing for Australia. Even though I was named Man of the Match and Man of the Series, deep down I felt that this could be it, so I made the most of it.

The fact that it coincided with Dan Cullen's first Test was terrific, because he was not only a teammate at the Redbacks; he was also a teammate at Adelaide Cricket Club. What a phenomenal trip, and what a magic time. I enjoyed the country and the people there immensely.

I THOUGHT I MIGHT HAVE BEEN A CHANCE TO PLAY IN THE three one-dayers, because of my efforts with the bat and ball in the Test series. However, I wasn't throwing too well from the outfield at the time, and coach John Buchanan didn't like the fact I was underarming the balls in from the fence rather than tossing them in overarm.

Anyway, I have nothing but brilliant memories of Bangladesh, and if it was the last time I was to represent my country, it would be hard to beat as a way to go out.

Player profiles

Over the years, I've had the good fortune to play in 71 Test matches for Australia, so I've played alongside some interesting lads. I thought it'd be appropriate to give some insights into the guys, so in alphabetical order, here goes.

Michael Bevan

I get along well with Bevo but people often find him introverted. Once you get to know him, you find he has his own beliefs and sticks to them. I roomed with Bevo frequently, and one or two of his personal habits could be a bit annoying. First, he had a lot of trouble sleeping at night: he always seemed to have a cold, and as a result was on all sorts of tablets to stop getting the flu. Second, because of that problem, he was sensitive to noise and particularly hated anyone who snored, which I didn't. Everything had to be silent for him to get any sleep. I think there were times when he got a lot more sleep than he thought he did. He must have had insomnia. I think he had a lot to do with the decision by Cricket Australia to change us from shared rooms to single accommodation.

Bevo was extremely hard to bowl at and was always a challenge to get out. He was a quality player and very inventive, especially in one-day cricket. In four-day cricket, you could get him if you were disciplined. He was patient, but then his instincts would take over and occasionally he tried to manufacture something that would cause him to be dismissed.

Andy Bichel

Bic is a fantastic team man — he always puts the side first. He's passionate and proud and gives 150 per cent when he plays. He also enjoys a beer, especially after a win. Although a superbly fit guy, over the years Bic has often been the one who's made way for someone else, unfortunately. Had he played at another time in cricketing history he'd have played a lot more than his 19 Tests for Australia. His First Class record is absolutely phenomenal: more than 700 wickets at about 26 apiece. He could have played more; he was unlucky.

Fast bowlers tend to ease themselves into training, but not Andy. He was always flat out from the first ball because he's so fit and strong. I always thought he had the best of actions: a straight run-up, and a straight and simple action. Watching him in action with his easy style, I was reminded to keep nice, straight and tall when I bowled. When Bic's playing days are over, he'll make an excellent coach, because he's a real thinker about the game and he has fantastic communication skills. After games, he loves to tell stories among the lads; the trouble is that most of the stories don't have a point. It's quite funny: he just rambles on and gets so into his story, he forgets what he's telling you.

Greg Blewett

Blewy is a good friend of mine, and we played a lot of Tests and matches at South Australia together. He has been one of the few guys from South Australia to play for Australia at the same time as me. With Boof, Taity and Dan Cullen, it's a special little club. He's an absolute quality bloke and an outstanding cricketer. It's an accident of history that, for Australia, Blewy always had to open or bat at six, and the situation mightn't have suited him. No other spots were available because the Waughs had a mortgage on the middle order for so long. Blewy batted a bit at three, but there were no other options. But because he could bat in the top six and could also bowl well, he was a handy man to have in the team. His bowling skill meant we were able to play two pacemen, two spinners, and Blewy as a third seamer, which was often invaluable.

I was lucky enough to play in the Test in South Africa in which he scored his 200; he and Steve Waugh batted the full day at the Wanderers. It was one of my favourite days of Test cricket, because I could put my feet up, have a cup of tea and watch them make a heap of runs.

A story not many people would be aware of is that during the 1997 Ashes series Blewy received a letter from a homosexual man. In the letter, the fellow mentioned he liked Blewy's looks at short leg and let him know there were a lot of gay men in England who enjoyed watching him crouching down at short leg. From that point on, Blewy was quite wary of fielding in England. The lads gave him a bit of stick for it, and it was very amusing for a while.

Nathan Bracken

I ROOMED WITH BRACKS IN 2001, ON THE WAY TO ENGLAND VIA Gallipoli. I haven't had a heap to do with him over the years, but he can be a very gifted bowler when he gets it right. Bracks battles with his action, but when he's 100 per cent right, he's hard to face. He needs to swing the ball if he's to trouble top batsmen around the world. Although he's struggled to get into the Test side, he's become an automatic starter in the one-day team and he has a fantastic record in that form of the game.

Early on, there were a few question marks over both his personality and his lack of hardness as a bowler. I think he's improved tremendously over the years. He's toughened up a bit, and he's a better player now. I fully expect him to take a lot of wickets in his career, especially in One Day Internationals for Australia.

Stuart Clark

STUART IS ANOTHER PLAYER I HAVEN'T HAD A HEAP TO DO WITH, because he came on the scene late in my career. He's a talented bowler and has done extremely well to date, and he's had to really earn his stripes at First Class level. He's worked hard on his game, he manages to hit good areas all the time, and he's very patient. He nibbles away on a good length, and does it enough to test your skills. He had a terrific 2006–07 Ashes Series for Australia. He's had a wonderful start to his career, and it'll be interesting to see how long he goes for. He's in his early thirties and living the moment, as he should.

Michael Clarke

I REGARD PUP AS A SOLID PLAYER, BUT WHEN THE AUSTRALIAN selectors put him up to number four after the Ashes series, it seemed premature. Even though it failed, it might be something the selectors try again after Michael has played a few more Tests.

He was identified quite young as a future Aussie skipper, which is big wraps for a young guy and can be hard to live up to. Undoubtedly he has the capacity and personality to pull it off. For a young man, his comments in the press are quite mature. He says what he thinks, which won't hurt him if ever he is made captain.

He's an exciting player, and you want that type of bloke to succeed. At the moment, I only want to see him play, establish himself fully — just bat and not put too much pressure on himself. If he gains that experience now, when a few of the blokes make their way into retirement, he'll be ready to take on more responsibility. Talent-wise, he stood out as a junior but didn't stamp his authority on First Class cricket as much as he should have early on. Over time, however, I think he'll show what a good player he is.

Dan Cullen

I remember first playing a Grade game at Adelaide with Dan when he was 15 or 16. Although he was very young, he looked to be a good prospect. The things I love about Dan are his aggressiveness and his positivity. He's your genuine fiery redhead, that's for sure. He gets right in a batsman's face, and although that's a useful tactic, he sometimes goes over the top. Once, during a Grade semi-final for Adelaide against Sturt, Dan went a bit overboard. Down the track, he'll learn to hold himself back.

As a spinner, Dan has a lot to offer and could turn out to be a more than useful batsman in First Class cricket. His work ethic is as good as any I have seen. He puts in a solid effort with his fielding, always does his bowling drills, and is highly focused. If anything, sometimes he needs to chill out a bit; he's a kid in a hurry. I'm looking forward to seeing him play a big part for Australia in the future. If he sticks to playing and enjoying himself, Dan could have a wonderful career.

Matthew Elliott

HERB AND I STARTED OUR TEST CAREERS AT ABOUT THE SAME TIME. In 1996 he did his knee in his second Test at Sydney against the West Indies, which was my debut Test match. When we toured South Africa and England together in 1997, I discovered what a ripper sense of humour he has. Matty is a phenomenal player. In the early part of his career he had a 'purple patch' but then struggled in the West Indies in 1999 and lost his place.

Herb has always been a driven sort of bloke, but he's been hampered by his knee troubles. He's always worked hard, but he finds it difficult to deal with the fact his body can't keep up. Since coming across to South Australia, he's loved telling hilarious stories about his former teammate from Victoria, Jason Arnberger. The Redback boys lap up all that sort of stuff.

After our 1997 Ashes series win at Trent Bridge, someone took a photograph of the two of us with beers in one hand and screaming at the camera. That photo is a prize possession. It's always good to be around Matthew Elliott.

Damien Fleming

DAMIEN IS ONE OF MY BEST CRICKET MATES. IN MY EARLY Test cricketing days, I roomed with him quite often and he worked on my taste in music. Flem loves his hard-rock music with a passion. He's also one of the great storytellers. Both of us love our AFL — he follows Hawthorn, and I support the Western Bulldogs.

In India in 1996 and 2001, we had a lot of fun with his home-movie camera. We walked around the streets with it and asked locals questions such as,'Who will win out of Collingwood and

St Kilda this Friday night at the MCG?' We replayed the footage for the boys, and they got some humour out of it. In Delhi on that same tour, we were so bored that Flem, Michael Kasprowicz and I found a nine-hole putt-putt course near the hotel pool and invented a sport, Slam Putt Mania, which combined 'professional' wrestling with putt-putt golf. We gave ourselves names: Flem was Triple F, or F***-Face Fleming; I was Goofball Gillespie; and Kasper was the Blue Vein Hooligan. Flem filmed the 'match'. It was a hoot.

On one of the greatest pub crawls I've been on around Adelaide, Flem and I made up a dice game. We'd approach a pub and spin the die. If it came up evens, we went in; if odd, we moved on to the next hotel. Once we were in a pub, we'd have six options for each spin: one might mean a cocktail, two a shot, three a beer, four a water, five a wine and six a spirit. We carried on like that for a few hours, and ended up having one of the best nights ever. Flem came to Anna's and my wedding.

Adam Gilchrist

ADAM IS A GENUINELY DECENT BLOKE. HE'S ANOTHER ONE MY close mates in the Aussie Test set-up, someone I like to chat with about life in general over a beer. Gilly has always worked hard at his game but he knows how to relax, too. He loves a beer and likes to celebrate a Test victory. He treats every win as if it'll be the last one he has. That's one thing I like about him. He reminds me a lot of Ian Healy — it must be something about wicketkeepers; they have the toughest job ever. I remember when he came in as the back-up keeper because Heals was still there; they worked very hard together.

I found out early in my career what a challenge he is to bowl to. He made 189 not out in the 1995–96 Sheffield Shield Final in Adelaide and hit me for a massive six to bring up his hundred. He took it from the top of off-stump and smashed it over deep mid-wicket — not a bad shot.

Gilly is another guy you really want in your team. He makes new players feel at ease. He loves wearing his baggy green cap for hours after a game.

Nathan Hauritz

NATHAN IS AN OFF-SPINNER WHO PLAYED IN ONE TEST, IN Mumbai in 2004, because Warnie had pulled out with a broken thumb. Nathan managed to bowl very well and took five wickets. Not that long afterwards, he lost his place in the Queensland team and moved to New South Wales. Hopefully for him, the move will be the best thing for his cricket. He was under-utilised in Queensland. Heading south means a fresh start for him and I'd like to think it will improve his chances of getting a recall at some point

Matthew Hayden

MATTY IS THE FIRST AUSTRALIAN TEST CRICKETER TO WRITE A book about cooking. He was kind enough to give me a mention in his book, for bangers and mash, but reckons the only reason he put me in there was to shut me up. I also told him he should write about how to peel a prawn properly. He agreed, but due to space restrictions was vetoed by his editor, so Matt tells me! Matty's a towering figure in Australian cricket; since 2000 he's been one of the most important players in the team. When he's at the crease, he likes to dominate, as per his personality. He's one of the best catchers I've seen in the slips or the gully; he's taken some blinders in there over the years.

In relation to off-field matters, such as dealings with Cricket Australia and the Australian Cricketers' Association, he's a real leader, always one to tackle any issue head on. If he disagrees with anything that's thrown up in those situations, he's the first to say so, and he was like that even before he'd notched up lots of games for

Australia. Matty's another guy whose stories can ramble all over the place, much as he enjoys telling them.

Like his good mate, Andrew Symonds, Matty loves the outdoors, fishing and cooking. He's very close to his wife and children.

Ian Healy

I ENJOY THE COMPANY OF HEALS. LIKE MOST QUEENSLANDERS, he loves to tell stories. Compared with Andy Bichel, he's much better at telling them. These days, he's doing a brilliant job commentating with Channel Nine. When he got the gig, he explained to me how he was going to approach commentating slightly differently from the way everyone else does. And I think he has given viewers something different.

The amount of work Heals did to prepare himself for a game was world-class. He always gave 100 per cent on the field. At times, he played when injured whereas he perhaps shouldn't have. I suppose he was a bit of an old-style player in that he wasn't afraid to have a few beers after play.

On tours, he always worked with the second keeper. That method really stood out for me, and throughout my career I've tried to emulate his work ethic as best I could.

Brad Hogg

BRAD IS ONE OF THOSE BLOKES WHO SIMPLY CAN'T STAND STILL. He's another player you wouldn't want to room with because, being a postie, he's an early riser: if you like your sleep, that habit would prove difficult to deal with. Hoggy tends to cop grief because he's from the country, and a few of the other lads in the team think he's a bit simple. However, once you become his mate, you're his mate for life.

As well as being a nice guy, Hoggy's a good all-round player. He's evolved and improved his game enough to play Test cricket, and that achievement is a testament to his character.

More than anyone else I know, Hoggy loves to practise. In Sri Lanka in 1996, our coach was Geoff 'Swampy' Marsh, and he and Hoggy got on brilliantly because they both loved training for ages. One boiling hot day, we were all sitting on a bus after a long training session. The bus had no air-con; it was very uncomfortable, and we were waiting to go back to the hotel. We spotted Hoggy bowling at a hanky in a net. On that occasion, even Swampy had had enough.

Mike Hussey

I FIRST MET UP WITH HUSS WHEN WE WERE TOURING INDIA together with the Australian Under-19s. He has sensitive skin, and this is how I found out. One day, as we were about to head out into the field, I asked him whether I could use some of his sunscreen. Not knowing it was a special type of cream, I lathered it all over my arms and face. Poor Huss was shattered because that bottle was supposed to last him the whole trip! He couldn't use any other type because of his skin problem. It was the last time he ever let me near his sunscreen.

Huss has had a wonderful start to his Test career, and he should go on to make plenty of runs in both Test cricket and one-dayers.

Phil Jaques

PHIL IS A TEST-QUALITY PLAYER AND HE'S BEEN UNLUCKY NOT to have had more of a go by now. He should have a long career as an Australian cricketer; he's too good a player not to. He loves batting and practising even more than Justin Langer does, if that's possible. His nickname is The Pro because he practises, and practises, and practises. Someone said to me recently that if Phil could find someone to throw balls at him for six hours, he'd be happy to bat them for six hours.

Michael Kasprowicz

Kasper is a completely team-oriented player. He's one of the few fellows who've had a near-death experience, on a cricket field in Cochin in 1998. I wasn't there but I saw on TV that he had heat exhaustion.

He's also hilarious; his sense of humour is much the same as Andy Bichel's and Damien Fleming's. Kasper is very similar to Andy Bichel, and that's why they're close mates. He was a key member of the Slam Putt Mania trio.

I've roomed with him a couple of times, and I can honestly say that as soon as Kasper gets to the room, he doesn't worry about unloading his clothes: his first priority is to get his music set up. He's big on his music.

Our two families hit it off well. Anna and me and Kasper and his wife, Lindsay, had a wonderful holiday together in the Maldives. They brought their daughter, Greta, who at the time was only eight weeks old. We relaxed and snorkelled, swam and drank beer. They're lovely people, and we had a great time together.

Simon Katich

One of my favourite moments playing Test cricket was in 2003–04 when I was batting with Simon and he brought up his maiden Test ton in Sydney against India. He hit Anil Kumble through the covers for four to reach his ton. In his excitement he screamed out an almighty *Yes!* and raised the bat. Knowing what he'd gone through, being in and out of the team so much, I was really pleased for him.

Oddly enough, he was dropped for the next two Tests in Sri Lanka. A good indication of his temperament was that when he was brought in for the last Test, he made a superb 86 and helped us win that game. Simon was in and out of the side more than he should have been. Luckily, he's a very resilient guy. He's a mellow sort of person who's always excellent company.

Justin Langer

ALFIE IS A PERSON WITH STRONG PRINCIPLES. HE'S A DEDICATED family man who is passionate about everything he does in life, not only his cricket. Whether he's in the middle, in the nets or facing a bowling machine, he loves having a bat in his hand. Over the years, he's been hit on the helmet many times, and not just when batting, either. But he always bounces back fast. JL, as he's also known, is the hardest little nut I've come across over the years and at times he can be intense.

He has written a few books, including *The Passion to Play*, for which he was that keen he wrote about 25,000 words too many.

In his home gym, JL has a VersaClimber. One day I went over to check it out and noticed that he has a special wall in the gym, so that if he thinks of something, he writes it there. The gym is the place he goes to get away from it all. In the morning of a day off at home, he loves nothing better than to do a workout in his gym, followed by a swim in his pool, which has an outdoor shower; then he goes to his patio and bar area, where he has a coffee machine. He's mates with Matty Hayden, and when they're together they love getting to a coffee shop for their lattes and cappuccinos.

Brett Lee

AS WELL AS BEING AN AMAZING CRICKETING TALENT, BINGA IS enthusiastic about everything in life, and he tries to please everyone all the time. Much like Brad Hogg, he's full of energy and can't sit still for too long, whereas I can sit down all day and relax, watch TV and just chill out. Binga has heaps of sponsors, and partly because of that, is the busiest man going around. His view is that the sponsors have treated him well, and he does his utmost to repay them. He always has a packed diary.

Because we are good mates, I once stayed with Binga for a week in Sydney. His routine was insane: 8.00: breakfast with sponsor; 9.00: meeting with sponsors; 10.15: in car to next meeting; 10.30: meeting with another sponsor; 11.30: home for an hour's power nap; 12.30: lunch … His life is pretty full-on.

Although he's amazingly busy, Binga can fall asleep at the drop of a hat, which he does if he has an hour to spare. On tour one time, he slept from 10 p.m., then woke up at 6 p.m. the next night, got up, had a meal, went back to sleep a few hours later, and woke up again the following morning. He's like a sloth; incredibly busy when he's up and about, but at times he needs to have a long recharge.

Binga is another tremendous fellow; he'd do anything for you. He's close to his family and one of the few guys I know who speaks to his mother every day. Before he got married, he reckoned he'd have five kids. Now he has a son, so he's on his way to achieving his goal.

Darren Lehmann

I've been lucky enough to play a lot of cricket with Boof. We made our One Day International debuts together, in Sri Lanka. I was one of the few people to see him make both his triple tons in First Class cricket. He's been such a wonderful player and made so many runs over the years.

Darren's friendliness is his best quality. He treats everyone the same, no matter what sort of company he's in. He talks to the prime minister the same way he'd talk to some bloke off the street. That's why he has so many mates from all walks of life. Also, he's big on making everyone feel included: if he's in a room full of people, he'll make a point of trying to speak to them all. He made me feel very welcome when I first started playing for South Australia, and I'm grateful to him for his friendship.

Over the years our families have become very close. Andrea Lehman and Anna are very good friends, as are Darren's daughter, Tori, and my daughter, Sapphire. Ethan and Amy (the Lehman's twins) both dote over Jackson.

Boof could end up doing anything he sets his mind to when his First Class career ends. For sure, though, as soon as he gives it away, he'll want to spend some quality time at home with his family. He hates being away from his wife and children for any length of time. If he's still president of the Australian Cricketers' Association, he'll put in some work there. He's capable of being a fantastic commentator; he could coach, no worries at all; and he'd make a very good selector. I was disappointed he didn't get a job as an Aussie selector while he was still playing; the chance to appoint him came along. Cricket Australia missed a great opportunity there.

Martin Love

Martin is unlucky not to have played more Tests for Australia, another victim of Australia's particularly long stretch of success. He's been a big accumulator of runs for Queensland, and he's one of the many reasons for their strong performance in First Class cricket since 1994–95, when they broke their Sheffield Shield drought. He's one of those lovely, relaxed blokes. His favourite drink is Bundaberg rum with Coke.

Stuart MacGill

Over the years, Stuie's been known to be intense. That's the general perception, but if you actually sit down with him over dinner or a few drinks, he's one of the most interesting people you could meet. He's knowledgeable on a wide range of topics. I've got a nice little wine collection, and he's taught me stuff about looking at a wine and telling how old it is; I've got to thank him for that skill. As cricketers, we tend to fall back on talking about the game most of the time, but not Stuie. However, when he is thinking and talking cricket, he always gives good advice, and he will take people under his wing.

Stuie's one of the more competitive blokes around. Over the years, this has led to a few blow-ups, but that's just the way things are. I think he's getting tired of playing Club cricket, and that might have had been a factor when he 'blew up' in a Club game early in the 2006–07 season.

Glenn McGrath

I'VE ALWAYS HAD A LOT OF TIME FOR GLENN. IN HIS EARLY DAYS, he could be a real pest in the dressing room but he's more mellow these days. He's a lovely bloke. Over the past few years, he's been through a lot because of his wife Jane's illness, but the ordeal doesn't affect him outwardly; he keeps those sorts of thing close to his chest. In the team set-up, one of the few blokes he confided in was Errol Alcott.

As a player, I felt privileged to open the bowling with Glenn so many times in Test cricket. The fact that he kept it so tight at the other end was lucky for me. Perhaps the reason the batsmen felt they had to slog me was that they couldn't score at his end, and that's why I got a few of them out. Statistically, Glenn and I are the best opening bowlers to have played for Australia, so that's one thing I can tell my grandkids: I opened the bowling with that bloke McGrath who took more than 500 Test wickets. I'll be very happy with that memory.

Pigeon is another teammate who's keen on hunting and shooting. One of my great memories is of a wonderful visit to his property at Wancobra, in the outback of northwestern New South Wales. It's literally the back o' Bourke, about 130 kilometres from that town. Glenn's brother and sister-in-law — Dale and his wife, Sandy — live and work on the property with their children. It's as dry as anything. A bunch of us went there for three or four days: myself, Brett Lee, Glenn and a mate of mine, Mark. We did all sorts of stuff, including pig shooting. We paid a visit to the 'neighbours', about 50 kilometres away, and had a midnight spa with them — something a bit different. I've got to know Pigeon's dad and mum as well as his sister, Donna, who also came on the Wancobra trip.

Apart from the hunting and shooting, Glenn loves outdoor stuff such as fishing and playing golf. Over the years, he's claimed he can play off a 10 handicap, but I think he's overrating himself a bit. Although he can strike the ball well, he's kidding himself if he thinks he's a 10 handicapper; that's for sure.

Damien Martyn

Marto is easily the best timer of a cricket ball I've ever seen. He was a good teammate and a fine player, because he always put in and got the job done. He had a wonderful tour to India in 2004, and we had a very long partnership in Chennai there, where he made an outstanding hundred.

Away from the cricket, Marto always liked to keep a low profile. When it came to doing interviews or other press stuff, he preferred to slip under the radar. Official functions, especially functions for Cricket Australia, weren't his favourite activity; he met only the minimum requirement in that area. If we had to be at an official function till 7.00, he was gone by 7.01 at the latest — he never did any overtime, that's for sure.

In the squad, Damien used to stick close to a couple of people and rarely ventured far from them. He was a member of the 'coffee club', along with the likes of Matthew Hayden, Justin

Langer and Ricky Ponting. Although he enjoyed the social aspects of being in the team, it's fair to say that over the years, not a lot of his other teammates got to know him that well, and I admit I'm one of them.

Colin Miller

THE FIRST TIME I CROSSED PATHS WITH COLIN WAS IN THE 1995–96 season, when South Australia played Tasmania in Hobart. Colin was batting and we were expecting a declaration to open the game up and to try to set up a chance for an outright result. Our skipper Jamie Siddons was starting to get cranky as the closure was taking longer than expected, so he instructed me to bowl off my full run to Colin and let him have a few bouncers. I bowled one to him which jagged back about a metre from outside off and it hit him in the head, breaking his cheekbone. It wasn't until later that I learned that Colin had to get a plate inserted to help the injury heal; in fact, it is still there to this day! The first time I got to know Funky was in 1998, on the Australia A tour to the United Kingdom. Subsequently we went on a few tours together and he became one of my really good mates from my time playing for Australia. He was introduced to people as 'Cutback Col the Pro Surfer' at a party one night by my Redbacks teammate, Shane Deitz. He had that nickname for a while but 'Funky' was always his main nickname. During his early Club cricket career he was known as 'Zulu' but has yet to explain fully to me why. Someone once called him 'Swiller, Driller, Killer, Chiller, Thriller Miller', which I thought was hilarious.

Funky transformed himself from a medium pacer to a spin bowler and became a Test cricketer as a result. That took a lot of 'balls' because he never would have done as well in his career if he hadn't taken on spin bowling. Deciding to leave Tassie and head back to Melbourne probably cost him a year of First Class cricket, but he wanted to go home, and that was fair enough.

I've especially always loved the story of his getting 43 against the West Indies in Antigua and hitting Curtly Ambrose for two sixes. In the casino there after play, Allan Border walked past, and Funky yelled out and asked him whether he'd ever hit Ambrose for two sixes. AB's reaction was spot on; he was as pleased as me that Colin was enjoying a great moment in his Test career.

Colin is also well known for going with the blue hair for the 2001 fifth Test versus the West Indies. Because it was the hundredth anniversary of Federation, he decided he'd go with the 'Federation blue' look. The hair colouring had started during the 1998 tour to the UK, when the pair of us bleached our hair in Scotland. At first, Dene Hills and I had a bet, which was along the lines of, *If Hillsy gets an earring, I'll bleach my head of hair*. After Dene got an earring, I had to go and get my hair done. Funky came along to watch and decided he'd do likewise. He loved the result, and that's how it all started. Colin is a great man, and we still catch up a fair bit.

Ricky Ponting

I FIRST CAME ACROSS RICKY IN ABOUT 1993, WHEN SOUTH Australia was playing Tasmania in the national Under-19s. He'd already played some State cricket, so it was a pretty big thing for me to be playing against a First Class cricketer at that stage of my career. He was smashing us all around the park in Melbourne and got to about 70, so I decided to change the field and bowl to him with a 9–nil off-side field. I ended up bowling about 2 feet outside off-stump to try to contain Punter. After a while he became frustrated, hit a cut shot and was caught in the gully. That really pissed him off: he knocked over his stumps in disgust and as a result was suspended from the next game!

Over the years, Ricky has been an ace batsman and easily one of the best players I've played with. His batting in the 2006–07 Ashes Series was superb.

We have some common ground in that Ricky is a fellow World Wrestling Federation 'tragic'. Few people would know that about Ricky. One of his favourite wrestlers used to be this guy called The Undertaker, so that became Ricky's nickname for some time. At one point, I gave him a poster of The Undertaker. I was injured at the time, and when the boys were in Adelaide, I called by the team hotel to drop off the poster. I put it in an envelope and left it for Punter at the hotel reception. He had it in his cricket bag when he made a hundred during a one-dayer, and kept it there for a while because it'd brought him some good luck. It might still be there, for all I know.

Paul Reiffel

Pistol, the former Victorian and Australian seam bowler, is the last person I'd ever have thought would become an umpire. He's progressed to First Class level fairly quickly, so clearly he knows what he's doing out there.

Paul was always a very determined cricketer. He was a talented bowler, and it's quite common to hear blokes say he was one of the best bowlers they faced in State cricket. Many guys who've faced him reckon he was one of the most accurate going around.

Pistol enjoys a joke, is fantastic company and loves a night out as much as anybody. Overall, I found him to be a fairly reserved, quiet sort of bloke. When he was playing and we'd go out after a Test win, he was always the last to leave wherever we were celebrating. Inevitably, by the stage you'd be looking around to see whether any of the lads remained, Pistol would still be there, sitting or standing quietly in the corner with a beer in his hand and a smile on his face.

Yet another of the legendary sleepers, Pistol was obsessive about keeping the bedroom absolutely dark. He was such a fan of the Batcave theory that he would even put towels up on the windows in his efforts to get as much shut-eye as he could. When training finished, he used to put his feet up and order a club sandwich from room service for lunch. Then he'd close the blinds, darken the room and have an afternoon of dozing. He just rested up and got his body relaxed and ready for the hard grind of the next day's play.

Michael Slater

Slats is one of the greatest characters I've had anything to do with in my years of involvement in the Australian team. He's always worn his heart on his sleeve, and that quality was strongly evident when he was dropped for the 2001 Oval Test. I really felt sorry for him at that time. He felt he'd been dealt a harsh blow on that tour. I'll never forget it, and I felt bad for Slats because he never played for his country again. Off the field, he had a few issues and that sort of experience is never easy.

Slats was always a good guy to have around. He was never frightened to play his shots, and on most occasions that worked in his favour. He's well remembered for his batting in the opening over of the 1994–95 series as well as for his knock in the first innings of the first Test in the 2001 Ashes series, at Edgbaston.

These days, Slats is strongly making his mark as a TV personality, notably as a presenter on 'What's Good for You'. I think he has a huge future in the TV caper, and I genuinely hope it works out for him.

Andrew Symonds

Symmo is one of the great strikers of the cricket ball as well as being a brilliant fielder. He's also one of the funniest guys going around. He does the best Geoff Boycott impersonation I've ever heard — absolutely brilliant. We used to get him on the microphone of the team bus to do 'Boycs', and he never failed to crack us all up. Symmo enjoys his hunting and fishing, and is one of the Aussie team's biggest characters. He loves a few beers, and that penchant showed up in Cardiff during the 2005 Ashes trip, when he got himself into a bit of trouble. One especially likeable thing about him is that he isn't afraid to come out and admit it when he's stuffed up. When he got pissed before the game against Bangladesh, at no stage did he shy away from owning up and saying he'd done the wrong thing; he took the consequences on the chin.

Although he's usually hilarious, he can also say some downright silly things. Michael Kasprowicz has quite a few Symmo stories and reckons he could fill a whole book with them. One example of how silly Andrew can be was when his Queensland teammate Adam Dale was organising a party and getting the food and beer sorted out. He came up with a figure of something like six beers for each person, and everyone was happy with that. However, it had to be reconfirmed, so Adam asked, 'So, everyone's happy with half a dozen, then?' Symmo piped up and asked, 'Adam, is it six or half a dozen? Make up your mind!' At times he can be a bit vague. However, he doesn't care if he does or says something stupid; he shrugs and laughs and gets on with it, and that's what we love about him.

Mark Taylor

Tubby was extremely welcoming to me in 1996, when he was skipper and I was joining the World Cup squad. I was called up to replace an injured Craig McDermott. Mark and coach Bob Simpson were the first people I met when I got there, and I remember being surprised at what normal blokes they were. I was very young at the time, and Tubby well and truly put me at ease. He's certainly one of the best communicators I've had anything to do with, and he was a great captain to play under. Mark is one of the best slip catchers I've ever played with or against. His personal demeanour was never under question when he was struggling with the bat in 1996–97 and during the early part of the 1997 Ashes tour. The way he handled himself under all that pressure was extremely impressive.

He passed on some extremely good wisdom to me early in my career, when we were travelling on the subcontinent. His advice for warding off the tummy bugs was to make sure you had a few beers every night, the theory being that alcohol kills all the nasties. I've successfully followed that recommendation whenever I've toured that part of the world.

Shane Warne

SHANE'S CRICKET RECORD SPEAKS FOR ITSELF. WARNIE IS A REALLY outgoing character who has always been extremely loyal to his mates. It's funny how he's attracted a reputation for being an old-fashioned — that is, smoking and beer drinking — Aussie cricketer. Well, he does have a smoke, but he's never been much of a beer drinker. However, in 2004 he tried to make out he was when we were playing the Kiwis at the Gabba. Shane is a big St Kilda AFL fan, and one day after play, a few of the Brisbane Lions boys, including Martin Pike, dropped into the rooms to see him. Straight after stumps, Warnie got wind of the Lions guys' impending arrival. He decided to grab a beer out of the fridge, sit in his corner, put an ice pack on his knee and have the fags nearby. Maybe he wanted to portray a bit of an 'old school' image to the Brisbane lads. The rest of us all looked at each other and thought to ourselves, *What's going on here? Warnie with a beer?* We were all having a bit of a giggle, and in came the Lions lads to say, 'Hi.'

Nothing was really said till Glenn McGrath walked in. He sat down, noticed Warnie with a frostie and asked, 'What the hell are you doing with a beer?' Warnie replied, 'Bowling day, mate — just finishing the day with a beer.' Glenn responded, 'Mate, I've never, ever seen you with a beer.' Warnie came back with, 'Oh, hang on, mate: I always have a beer at the end of a bowling day.' We all pissed ourselves laughing, because none of us had ever seen him have a beer after a bowling day.

For the rest of that summer, Darren Lehmann, Gilly and I took it upon ourselves to make sure that at the end of each bowling day, Shane had a beer in his spot in the rooms. We chortled away, thinking we were the funniest blokes in the world. Warnie, of course, drank the frostie, albeit rather reluctantly.

After about six months, he said to me, 'Dizzy, enough is enough; you've made your point — well done.' We all burst out laughing and stopped the prank after that. Warnie loves a good joke, and took it all very well.

Shane Watson

WATTO IS A GIFTED CRICKETER WHO TRAINS VERY HARD — HE'S a real 'train-a-holic'. However, at times Watto is a bit like Dan Cullen in that he puts too much pressure on himself to perform. He gets down on himself if he has a bad day. Because he's something of an open book, you can always pick his frame of mind. He's trying to change and be more accepting of the ups and downs, and I'm convinced that's a good thing. He can be a class cricketer for Australia for many years; he's becoming stronger, and he works hard. I'd like to see him do more bowling at training in order to strengthen his body. It's good to do it in the gym, but he should do more work in the nets to make himself bowling fit. He's getting a bit older, and his body is filling out more, so that should be helpful for him. It would be good to see a hard worker such as Watto succeed in the years to come.

He and I will always be poles apart as far as dress sense is concerned, in that Watto has dress sense and I don't. He reckons I need to upgrade my wardrobe and a number of times has told me I'm allowed to 'dress my age'. He's a funny guy, and good company.

Mark Waugh

Junior was one of my roommates early on. In 1996, when I was a young pup at the World Cup, he took me under his wing and made a big effort in making me feel part of the team. Like Mark Taylor, he was particularly good to me on that trip and his support made a big difference to me.

It was on that trip that I discovered Junior enjoys tremendous popularity in India, where he is known as Mark Wog. It took a while for that knowledge to sink in, and while I was rooming with him, I seemed to be forever answering the phone. Some of the fans would ring him up and say, 'You are the best player ever,' and then just hang up!

One Indian fan used to ring him all the time to say hello and tell him what a wonderful player he was. On one occasion, the gentleman brought his family in to visit Mark and to present him with a birthday cake. The whole tribe turned up: the husband, wife, two kids and grandparents — all beaming away. 'Happy birthday, Mister Wog,' they said. 'You are our favourite cricketer.'

Mark is making his way as a commentator at the moment, and is doing a good job.

Steve Waugh

Undoubtedly, Tugga is one of the gutsiest cricketers I've ever played with; his achievement of twin tons at Old Trafford in 1997 despite sore hands is testimony to that assessment. Although he and Mark are twins — which explains why they're alike in so many ways — they've developed into two different individuals. You could see the differences in the way they played their cricket.

When there was no cricket on, Steve used to go off to see the sights; he was a real 'Tommy the Tourist', as people would know from reading his books *The Tour Diaries*. You got tired of him getting his camera out; he was like a Japanese tourist, and he wrote in his diary all the time. He squeezed in all sorts of things, and although I didn't venture out with him too many times, I could see that whenever he went for a look around, he loved checking out the sights and that he really embraced the tourist stuff.

Brad Williams

Early in his career, Brad had a few injuries. One day in 1995–96, when he was playing for Victoria, he bowled one of the fastest spells I've ever faced. It was in a Pura Cup game at the Adelaide Oval. Up to that point, he hadn't been bowling particularly well in the match and had figures of one for plenty. He must have had a top breakfast that morning, because he came out and bowled so fast he finished with six wickets. I'm more than happy to admit I was scared batting against him. It was one of those rare occasions when I'd have almost been glad to be dismissed.

Brad has always been a quiet sort of a bloke and seemed to be a bit on the periphery of the Australian set-up. He's another guy who kept to himself a fair bit. One of his few matches for Australia was in the third Test in Sri Lanka in 2004, and it was played on a track that didn't really suit his fast stuff. He could well have been used to bowl his off breaks, because they came out pretty well. We quicks weren't getting much out of the track, and his spinners would have been well and truly worth a go.

It was quite sad the way Brad's career with Western Australia ended. He spat the dummy at the Warriors officials over there for getting dropped, and there's no doubt he let himself down by succumbing to the urge.

My ancestry

The Kamilaroi connection

In January 2000, it came out in the newspapers that I'm of Aboriginal heritage. News Limited cricket writer Robert 'Crash' Craddock wrote a piece in which he said that I was the first player of Aboriginal ancestry to play Test cricket for Australia. I don't recall too much about what I'd said to him, but in the article he quoted me as saying, 'I accept that I have Aboriginal blood in me, though I don't go around preaching the word.' I'd mentioned I was proud of my heritage, but that it wasn't a big part of my life when I was growing up.

Up to that point, no one had asked me about my ancestry, so I hadn't told anyone that my great-grandfather was from the Kamilaroi clan. I'm very proud of the fact I have not only Aboriginal heritage but Greek and Irish.

After the article was published, the suggestion arose that I hadn't embraced my indigenous culture. I found that mind-boggling, because I'd always acknowledged my culture and been proud of it. I've known about my Aboriginal ancestry since I was seven or so, as have all my family members and friends. (At school I received the Abstudy Allowance, which was the indigenous version of the

Austudy Allowance the other kids received.) What did some people expect me to do once I started playing for Australia: have a press conference and announce, 'I'm Aboriginal'? It's not in my nature to do that.

There have been times I've been upset about things that have gone on in our country, when racism rears it ugly head. The Cronulla riots in December 2005 were an instance when I asked myself whether I could believe this sort of thing was really happening in my country; it was a very disappointing development. Why is there so much hatred around? Do people need to vent their anger in that way? Here in Australia we have a great place to live, and why would you question people's right to live here? Our country is not just made up of Aboriginal people or European settlers; people from all over the world have made Australia their home. I'm not saying these words as an Aboriginal and a fourth-generation Greek; I'm saying them as an Australian who loves his country. I've always been very proud to represent my country.

People ask me about my race and ethnic origin, but at the end of the day, I'm Australian born; it's as simple as that. My parents were born here.

People see a 'Middle Eastern' couple come here, have children and make a better life for themselves, but I think that once they're here and they get residency, they should be considered Australian, despite the fact that they were born elsewhere.

The line possibly becomes blurred when people who make their own way here tend to stick to their own little community and perhaps don't integrate as much as some people would like. Then again, what if the shoe is on the other foot? If people from Australia were in a similar position and they had to move to a foreign country, they'd probably react similarly: they'd look for an area in which Aussies lived, to make the transition easier.

I think it's vital we all integrate and appreciate the various aspects of each other's ancestry. Having said that, I think that, in general, people who come to our country should embrace the Australian way of life. Perhaps that's why the race tensions came to a head at Cronulla: a small percentage of people don't and won't fully accept our ideas and way of life. Whatever was behind it, I found that time very sad, and I hope there won't be a repeat of it.

Growing cricket in the wider Australian community

THINKING ABOUT WHY THERE HAVEN'T BEEN TOO MANY INDIGENOUS cricketers over the years, I can identify a few reasons. In my case, I was brought up in the city. Being in the urban setting is a big advantage. Opportunities are all around you; cricket nets and sporting fields are usually nearby; the infrastructure is highly developed in the form of the local club or school. It's difficult for kids in rural or remote Aboriginal communities to engage in any kind of organised social and sporting activities. Of course you'll always get that small group of diehard cricket fans no matter what; every sport has them, and it'll always be the case.

Cost is a huge barrier as far as indigenous kids are concerned. There are ongoing subscription fees and the like, and if you want to kit your child out properly (Grade cricketers have to have all their own gear to a minimum standard of quality) you're up for at least $1000. Footy is more attractively priced. All you need is a pair of boots and maybe some shorts and shin pads, because the balls are provided. Those things last you a season.

Another thing that lessens the appeal of cricket is that it takes a long time to play, and I think that the attention span of all kids — and not only Aboriginal children — isn't particularly long. Cricket involves a lot of sitting around waiting to bat or bowl plus standing around in the field. The gap might be bridged in Twenty20 cricket, but I don't think that form of the game will ever take off with indigenous communities. They like to watch and play it a bit, but as for taking it up more seriously, I don't see much changing in the immediate future. There is the Imparja Cup, which is important, but till Cricket Australia puts a bit more into developing cricket in Aboriginal communities, I don't think things will change much.

By comparison, you can see why Aussie Rules is so popular with Aboriginal kids. It involves hand–eye co-ordination and running skills. Another sport that in the future could attract the involvement of more indigenous kids is soccer — although I'm told we're supposed to call it football nowadays. With the addition of a little more structure in that sport for Aboriginal communities, there's every reason to expect that Aboriginal players will go far.

In other communities in Australia, however, I do think there are large untapped resources for cricket. Guys of Greek, Lebanese or Asian ancestry all have an interest in the game; there's real potential among them, and Cricket Australia are looking among their communities.

R-e-s-p-e-c-t!

Personally I was never racially abused at school. I do have a large nose, and my mates often called me 'Geppetto', after the Pinocchio character, or 'Spiros', because of my Greek background. At school, I never had any issues. Maybe I had my head in the clouds, but my mates and I all stuck together, and I can't remember feeling that my ancestry was ever a problem, whether in class, on the bus or in the schoolyard.

Likewise on the cricket field, I've never had any racism shown towards me. I'm lucky being a bowler, because I don't get sledged too much; instead, out on the ground, it's me doing the talking. The thing about it all is I've got pretty thick skin. Although I think political correctness is important, I don't get offended by anything much. Having said that, I do understand why people can get offended, and of course you have to allow for their feelings.

Where religion is concerned, the same principle applies. A few guys in the Redbacks team are strong in their particular faith, and at times you have to remember to be respectful of it. I make sure I don't offend them; and it's as simple as showing anyone respect for their beliefs.

Over the past year or two, there've been some instances of prejudice in Australia, and they've been regrettable. In other countries, though, I've never encountered a problem. In New Zealand and South Africa, they call Aussies sheep shaggers and one or two other things, and at one stage I might have copped a bit of flak for my 'mullet' haircut in those countries. In South Africa in 2002, some wags had a go at me about my big nose, in the form of a sign that bore the advice, 'Dizzy, don't be so nosey'. I thought that was a laugh. I was reminded of the old days at the MCG, when someone wrote on a white bedsheet the words, 'Bill Lawry's hanky'. If people are offended by things like that, they're a worry.

Happy to sign — off the field

THE ONLY OTHER BUGBEAR I HAVE IS GIVING AUTOGRAPHS. AT THE moment, the team members have a policy of not signing stuff while they're on the field of play. Steve Waugh instigated the policy when he was captain because he didn't want players to be distracted on the boundary if he wanted to signal them to move or get ready to bowl. In his view, there was nothing worse on the field than if he was standing there waving his arms wanting someone to move and that player's attention was being diverted by a fan with a pen in their hand. Cricket Australia has known about this policy for a long time but nail us if we don't give autographs. We've asked them to announce that this is our policy and that we're happy to sign when we're off the field, but to date, they haven't and won't.

It's not hard to see why: they sell merchandise — shirts, mini-bats and all kinds of stuff — that kids want to get signed. They are worried that if they let people know the players will sign only when off the ground, sales will decrease and the players will look bad. So it's all about Cricket Australia being able to sell a few extra shirts or mini-bats.

Life after cricket

I'D LIKE TO THINK I'LL BE ABLE TO FIND PLENTY OF THINGS TO do after I retire from the game. Some sort of media work would be up my alley, because for the time being I couldn't see myself being a full-time coach.

Dad and my brother both work in the area of Aboriginal legal rights, and although I admire and respect them for what they're doing, at this stage I can't see myself following in their footsteps. What they do is incredibly important, and from time to time I get the opportunity to make my contribution by coaching groups of kids from the Tiwi Islands on a Kanga cricket-coaching clinic, which I enjoy.

One day, I'd love to have my own fast-bowling academy with, say, four fast bowlers. My idea is to put them through all their weights, fitness training and bowling preparation. I'd train with them, oversee everything and help them to realise their dream of becoming a fast bowler. There mightn't be much scope for turning this vision into a reality unless I can attract a big sponsor. Nevertheless, I'd like to try, because I have good contacts in the fitness industry; I'd love to help the bowlers with their pre-season training; and I'd like to do it well.

I've always had my own ideas about fitness training, and it'd be good to put them into practice. One thing that's always puzzled me is why, in the case of pre-season cricket training, you get guys who do a lot of weights and running, and yet once the season starts, they stop and work only on their skills. So I have my own ideas, and one day, in some way, I'd like to bring them to reality.

Cricket has been very good to me and I feel very lucky to have played for so long. I have been a professional cricketer for my whole adult life and along the way I have played with and against some great people, and met some wonderful characters off the field as well. It has been an enormous privilege to wear the baggy green in representing my country and realise a childhood dream. At times it's been a wild ride, and the journey is still ongoing, but not for a moment would I change a thing.

Acknowledgments

DIZZY: THE JASON GILLESPIE STORY IS A TALE OF A VERY LUCKY man. Without the love and support of many people, I would not be where I am today. Firstly, thank you to my parents, Vicki and Neil, for your love and fantastic support, particularly in the early years. To my brothers, Rob and Luke, your love and support has been nothing short of awesome as well.

To my great friend Robert Crouch, thank you for your support, guidance and encouragement, particularly after the collision in Sri Lanka – it saved my career and was a major factor in helping me to get back to top shape and to International Cricket. To the long-time Aussie physio Errol 'Hooter' Alcott, thanks for helping me overcome various ailments while I was playing for my country, and for being a great sounding board for all sorts of other things, be it cricket or personal.

To Jeff and Pauline Hammond, you've been there for me at important stages of my life and cricket career and I'd like to say a heartfelt thank you for your love and support. Jeff, you have been one of the best men, managers and coaches I have been fortunate enough to know.

To the South Australian Cricket Association and Cricket Australia, thank you for giving me the chance to represent my state and country. I feel very fortunate to have worn the SACA and Australian caps on many occasions and have felt honoured each time I have stepped onto the field. To all the guys I have played with in District, First Class and Test level, thank you for a lot of wonderful times and memories that will stay with me forever. Through this I have made many lifelong friends. To the Adelaide Cricket Club, where it all started in South Australia, thanks for all the opportunities and for letting me be part of the club. It is truly an honour to be a life member. Also to Yorkshire, who I have played with for the last two seasons, thank you for making me so welcome. The Blue cap with the white rose is very special to me and to be a capped player for probably the most famous club in cricket is an absolute honour as well.

To my daughter, Sapphire, thank you for being so understanding at such a young age. I know that it has been very difficult for you at times without your Dad, especially when I have been away so often on tour. I really missed you whenever I was away playing the game. I love you.

To my young son, Jackson, you are such a special little man. You have given me so much joy. There will be lots of fun in the years ahead as you grow up in our loving household. With another child not far away, it will be a busy time at our place and I look forward to the fun times ahead.

To my beautiful wife, Anna, your love and support through good times and bad has been very special, and without you I would not have been able to get through some of the tougher times. We have exciting times ahead with our growing family and I am really looking forward to sharing them with you. I love you, babe.

Finally, thanks to my publishers, HarperCollins, for taking on this project, and to my mate and 'ghostwriter', Lawrie Colliver, for putting so much time and effort into this book. Thanks, Loz.

LAWRIE COLLIVER is a freelance journalist based in Adelaide. Since starting at Radio 5RPH in 1992, he has worked as a Sports Broadcaster for Radio 5DN, 5UV, ABC and is currently at Radio 5AA. He covered the momentous 2005 and 2006–07 Ashes series for Sky News Australia, where he works as a stringer, has worked for Cricinfo in various roles and writes a column for *The Independent Weekly* in Adelaide. Lawrie was also a contributor to the *Wisden Cricketers' Almanack Australia* that ran for eight editions.

Lawrie's main love has always been cricket, and he managed to play eight seasons with Tea Tree Gully in the Adelaide Grade competition. He has also worked with the Australian (2005) and South Australian (1998–2005) cricket teams as their video analyst. He currently lives in Adelaide with his partner, Sharyn.

Statistics

(All statistics current to 25 June 2007)

Jason Neil Gillespie

(Right hand batsman, right arm fast medium bowler)

FIRST CLASS CAREER

DEBUT

1994–95 South Australia v Queensland, Adelaide

BOWLING

Season	Country	M	Overs	Mdns	Runs	Wkts	Avrge	5i	10m	Best
1994–95	Australia	3	87.0	22	278	7	39.71	–	–	3–112
1995–96	Australia	11	366.3	93	1142	51	22.39	1	–	6–68
1996–97	Australia	5	135.0	38	340	9	37.78	1	–	5–64
1996–97	South Africa	6	177.3	56	534	32	16.69	2	–	7–34
1997	England	8	198.4	43	692	29	23.86	2	–	7–37
1997–98	Australia	2	37.0	14	83	1	83.00	–	–	1–61
1998–99	Scotland	1	7.0	1	20	2	10.00	–	–	2–20
1998–99	Ireland	1	24.0	3	89	4	22.25	–	–	3–49
1998–99	Australia	5	175.2	49	476	22	21.64	1	–	5–88
1998–99	West Indies	4	129.2	41	297	11	27.00	–	–	4–18
1999–00	Sri Lanka	1	12.0	2	43	–	–	–	–	–
1999–00	Australia	2	76.0	23	161	7	23.00	–	–	2–42
2000–01	Australia	5	175.0	51	463	22	21.05	2	–	6–40
2000–01	India	4	145.3	39	449	15	29.93	–	–	3–45
2001	England	8	228.0	54	801	29	27.62	2	–	5–37
2001–02	Australia	6	243.4	60	689	28	24.61	1	1	8–50
2001–02	South Africa	5	132.0	42	387	10	38.70	–	–	3–52
2002–03	Sri Lanka	1	35.3	10	117	3	39.00	–	–	2–62
2002–03	Australia	13	497.1	138	1289	57	22.61	1	–	5–54
2002–03	West Indies	5	186.4	58	382	19	20.11	1	–	5–39
2003–04	Sri Lanka	3	110.0	25	316	10	31.60	–	–	4–76
2003–04	Australia	2	81.4	18	210	7	30.00	–	–	3–116
2004–05	India	4	132.5	33	323	20	16.15	1	–	5–56
2004–05	Australia	5	165.2	45	439	15	29.27	–	–	3–37
2004–05	New Zealand	3	107.0	25	320	7	45.71	–	–	3–38
2005	England	5	110.0	16	445	7	63.57	–	–	2–40
2005–06	Australia	9	355.5	102	851	40	21.28	3	–	7–35
2005–06	Bangladesh	2	43.0	12	90	8	11.25	–	–	3–11
2006	England	14	434.3	103	1210	36	33.61	1	–	6–37
2006–07	Australia	11	345.1	76	891	32	27.84	2	1	5–41
2007	England	6	152.5	30	484	19	25.47	–	–	3–40
Total		160	5107.0	1322	14311	559	25.60	21	2	8–50

TEAMS

Team	M	Overs	Mdns	Runs	Wkts	Avrge	5i	10m	Best
Australia A	2	31.0	4	109	6	18.17	–	–	3–49
AUSTRALIA	71	2372.2	629	6770	259	26.14	8	–	7–37
Australian XI	18	410.5	101	1253	52	24.10	3	–	7–34
South Australia	49	1705.3	455	4485	187	23.98	9	2	8–50
Yorkshire	20	587.2	133	1694	55	30.80	1	–	6–37

MOST SUCCESSFUL OPPONENTS

Opponent	M	Overs	Mdns	Runs	Wkts	Avrge	5i	10m	Best
ENGLAND	18	536.5	123	1887	65	29.03	3	–	7/37
WEST INDIES	13	451.0	138	1056	50	21.12	3	–	6/40
Queensland	10	346.3	84	926	43	21.53	3	1	5/40
INDIA	10	398.3	105	1094	43	25.44	1	–	5/56
New South Wales	9	279.2	70	768	41	18.73	3	1	8/50
Western Australia	10	363.3	93	1029	40	25.73	2	–	6/68
Victoria	8	297.1	80	733	33	22.21	1	–	7/35
NEW ZEALAND	8	292.4	73	817	26	31.42	–	–	3/37
SOUTH AFRICA	7	229.4	76	654	24	27.25	1	–	5/54
Tasmania	8	279.0	77	705	20	35.25	–	–	4/89
BANGLADESH	4	104.4	26	260	19	13.68	–	–	4/38
Hampshire	5	146.0	38	428	19	22.53	1	–	5/33
SRI LANKA	6	203.4	45	569	17	33.47	–	–	4/76
Durham	3	89.2	15	284	14	20.29	1	–	6/37
Sussex	3	99.0	24	259	10	25.90	–	–	4/89
PAKISTAN	4	126.5	34	375	10	37.50	–	–	3/77

MOST SUCCESSFUL VENUES

Ground, Venue	M	Overs	Mdns	Runs	Wkts	Avrge	5i	10m	Best
Adelaide Oval, Adelaide	33	1214.1	347	3084	129	23.91	5	1	5–41
WACA Ground, Perth	11	360.4	76	1035	44	23.52	3	–	6–68
Headingley, Leeds	10	311.3	71	912	29	31.45	1	–	7–37
Gabba, Brisbane	8	253.2	63	749	28	26.75	1	–	5–40
SCG, Sydney	9	304.0	68	922	28	32.93	1	1	8–50
MCG, Melbourne	6	181.1	61	446	26	17.15	1	–	6–40
Bellerive Oval, Hobart	6	199.0	60	509	13	39.15	–	–	3–45
Riverside, Chester–le–Street	2	53.2	9	213	12	17.75	1	–	6–37
Cazley's Stadium, Cairns	2	93.2	22	250	12	20.83	–	–	4–38
VCA Ground, Nagpur	2	57.5	23	135	11	12.27	1	–	5–56
Edgbaston, Birmingham	4	109.1	17	404	11	36.73	–	–	3–52
Queen's Park Oval, Port–of–Spain	2	66.3	19	138	10	13.80	–	–	4–18

IN EACH COUNTRY

Country	M	Overs	Mdns	Runs	Wkts	Avrge	5i	10m	Best
Australia	79	2740.4	729	7312	298	24.54	12	2	8–50
Bangladesh	2	43.0	12	90	8	11.25	–	–	3–11
England	41	1124.0	246	3632	120	30.27	5	–	7–37
India	8	278.2	72	772	35	22.06	1	–	5–56
Ireland	1	24.0	3	89	4	22.25	–	–	3–49
New Zealand	3	107.0	25	320	7	45.71	–	–	3–38
Scotland	1	7.0	1	20	2	10.00	–	–	2–20
South Africa	11	309.3	98	921	42	21.93	2	–	7–34
Sri Lanka	5	157.3	37	476	13	36.62	–	–	4–76
West Indies	9	316.0	99	679	30	22.63	1	–	5–39

WICKETS TAKEN

How Out	Wickets	%
Caught Fieldsmen	180	32.20
ct RT Ponting	16	8.88
ct ME Waugh	13	7.22
ct SK Warne	13	7.22
ct ML Hayden	12	6.66
ct GS Blewett	10	5.55
Caught Wicketkeeper	152	27.19
ct AC Gilchrist	63	41.44
ct TJ Nielsen	24	15.79
ct GA Manou	23	15.13
ct IA Healy	15	9.87
ct SA Dietz	13	8.55
ct GL Brophy	11	7.23
Leg Before	125	22.37
Bowled	100	17.89
Hit Wicket	2	0.36

(*Note:* SA Dietz includes 3 catches, AC Gilchrist 1 catch as fieldsmen)

BATSMEN DISMISSED

Position	Wickets	%
Openers	152	27.19
Number 3	62	11.09
Number 4	50	8.94
Number 5	49	8.76
Number 6	61	10.91
Number 7	51	9.12
Number 8	36	6.44
Number 9	40	7.15
Number 10	39	6.97
Number 11	19	3.39
Number 1–6	**374**	**67.79**
Number 7–11	**185**	**33.10**

BATSMEN DISMISSED THE MOST

ME Trescothick	(England)	7
MA Butcher	(England)	6
A Chopra	(India)	6
JP Crawley	(England–Hampshire)	6
D Ganga	(West Indies)	6
N Hussain	(England)	6
JP Maher	(Queensland)	6
DS Smith	(West Indies)	6
SR Tendulkar	(India)	6

BEST BOWLING IN AN INNINGS

8–50 South Australia v New South Wales, Sydney, 2001–02

FIVE OR MORE WICKETS IN AN INNINGS

Wickets	Team	Opponent	Venue	Season
6–68	South Australia	Western Australia	Perth	1995–96
5–64	South Australia	Western Australia	Perth	1996–97
7–34	Australian XI	Border	East London	1996–97
5–54	AUSTRALIA	SOUTH AFRICA	Port Elizabeth	1996–97
5–33	Australian XI	Hampshire	Southampton	1997
7–37	AUSTRALIA	ENGLAND	Leeds	1997
5–88	AUSTRALIA	ENGLAND	Perth	1998–99
5–89	AUSTRALIA	WEST INDIES	Adelaide	2000–01
6–40	AUSTRALIA	WEST INDIES	Melbourne	2000–01
5–37	Australian XI	Essex	Chelmsford	2001
5–53	AUSTRALIA	ENGLAND	Lord's	2001
8–50	South Australia	New South Wales	Sydney	2001–02
5–39	AUSTRALIA	WEST INDIES	Georgetown	2002–03
5–54	South Australia	New South Wales	Adelaide	2003–04
5–56	AUSTRALIA	INDIA	Nagpur	2004–05
7–35	South Australia	Victoria	St Kilda	2005–06
5–40	South Australia	Queensland	Brisbane	2005–06
5–56	South Australia	New South Wales	Adelaide	2005–06
6–37	Yorkshire	Durham	Chester–le–Street	2006
5–41	South Australia	Queensland	Adelaide	2006–07
5–69	South Australia	Queensland	Adelaide	2006–07

BEST BOWLING IN A MATCH

10–110 (5–41 & 5–69) South Australia v Queensland, Adelaide, 2006–07

10–162 (8–50 & 2–112) South Australia v New South Wales, Sydney, 2001–02

BATTING

Team	M	Inn	NO	Runs	HS	0s	50	100	Avrge	Ct
Australia A	2	–	–	–	–	–	–	–	–	–
AUSTRALIA	71	93	28	1218	201*	13	2	1	18.74	27
Australian XI	18	17	6	269	57	–	2	–	24.45	5
South Australia	49	75	9	883	61	6	3	–	13.38	26
Yorkshire	20	27	9	552	123*	–	–	1	30.67	3

HIGHEST SCORE

201* AUSTRALIA v BANGLADESH, Chittagong, 2005–06

CENTURIES

100s	Team	Opponent	Venue	Season
201*	AUSTRALIA	BANGLADESH	Chittagong	2005–06
123*	Yorkshire	Surrey	The Oval	2007

TEST CRICKET

DEBUT

1996–97 Australia v West Indies, Sydney

BOWLING

Series	Opponent	Venue	M	Overs	Mdns	Runs	Wkts	Avrge	5i	10m	Best
1996–97	West Indies	Australia	2	33.0	9	94	2	47.00	–	–	2–62
1996–97	South Africa	South Africa	3	103.4	37	287	14	20.50	1	–	5–54
1997	England	England	4	91.4	20	332	16	20.75	1	–	7–37
1998–99	England	Australia	1	22.2	2	111	7	15.86	1	–	5–88
1998–99	West Indies	West Indies	3	108.2	36	241	11	21.91	–	–	4–18
1999–00	Sri Lanka	Sri Lanka	1	12.0	2	43	–	–	–	–	–
2000–01	West Indies	Australia	4	141.0	40	368	20	18.40	2	–	6–40
2000–01	India	India	3	126.3	31	394	13	30.31	–	–	3–45
2001	England	England	5	174.0	42	652	19	34.32	1	–	5–53
2001–02	New Zealand	Australia	3	111.4	27	316	11	28.73	–	–	3–45
2001–02	South Africa	Australia	1	34.0	11	80	2	40.00	–	–	2–23
2001–02	South Africa	South Africa	3	92.0	28	287	8	35.88	–	–	3–52
2002–03	Pakistan	Sri Lanka	1	35.3	10	117	3	39.00	–	–	2–62
2002–03	England	Australia	5	181.5	53	492	20	24.60	–	–	4–25
2002–03	West Indies	West Indies	4	168.4	53	353	17	20.76	1	–	5–39
2002–03	Bangladesh	Australia	2	61.4	14	170	11	15.45	–	–	4–38
2003–04	Zimbabwe	Australia	1	28.3	9	58	5	11.60	–	–	3–52
2003–04	India	Australia	3	139.1	41	377	10	37.70	–	–	4–65
2003–04	Sri Lanka	Sri Lanka	3	110.0	25	316	10	31.60	–	–	4–76
2003–04	Sri Lanka	Australia	2	81.4	18	210	7	30.00	–	–	3–116
2004–05	India	India	4	132.5	33	323	20	16.15	1	–	5–56
2004–05	New Zealand	Australia	2	74.0	21	181	8	22.63	–	–	3–37
2004–05	Pakistan	Australia	3	91.2	24	258	7	36.86	–	–	3–77
2004–05	New Zealand	New Zealand	3	107.0	25	320	7	45.71	–	–	3–38
2005	England	England	3	67.0	6	300	3	100.00	–	–	2–91
2005–06	Bangladesh	Bangladesh	2	43.0	12	90	8	11.25	–	–	3–11
Total			71	2372.2	629	6770	259	26.14	8	–	7–37

OPPONENTS

Opponent	M	Overs	Mdns	Runs	Wkts	Avrge	5i	10m	Best
BANGLADESH	4	104.4	26	260	19	13.68	–	–	4–38
ENGLAND	18	536.5	123	1887	65	29.03	3	–	7–37
INDIA	10	398.3	105	1094	43	25.44	1	–	5–56
NEW ZEALAND	8	292.4	73	817	26	31.42	–	–	3–37
PAKISTAN	4	126.5	34	375	10	37.50	–	–	3–77
SOUTH AFRICA	7	229.4	76	654	24	27.25	1	–	5–54
SRI LANKA	6	203.4	45	569	17	33.47	–	–	4–76
WEST INDIES	13	451.0	138	1056	50	21.12	3	–	6–40
ZIMBABWE	1	28.3	9	58	5	11.60	–	–	3–52
		Overs	**Mdns**	**Runs**	**Wkts**	**Avrge**	**5i**	**10m**	**Best**
First Innings		603.2	150	1848	72	25.67	3	–	7/37
Second Innings		844.2	241	2245	71	31.62	1	–	5/56
Third Innings		539.5	142	1565	66	23.71	3	–	5/39
Fourth Innings		384.5	96	1112	50	22.24	1	–	6/40

MOST SUCCESSFUL VENUES

Ground, Venue	M	Overs	Mdns	Runs	Wkts	Avrge	5i	10m	Best
WACA Ground, Perth	6	190.1	41	566	25	22.64	1	–	5–88
MCG, Melbourne	4	117.1	40	281	21	13.38	1	–	6–40
Adelaide Oval, Adelaide	5	204.0	58	515	19	27.11	1	–	5–89
Gabba, Brisbane	4	125.4	36	353	13	27.15	–	–	4–65
Cazley's, Cairns	2	93.2	22	250	12	20.83	–	–	4–38
Headingley, Leeds	2	84.4	19	272	11	24.73	1	–	7–37
SCG, Sydney	5	191.5	48	575	11	52.27	–	–	3–135
Queen's Park Oval, Port–of–Spain	2	66.3	19	138	10	13.80	–	–	4–18
Kensington Oval, Bridgetown	2	103.1	42	178	10	17.80	–	–	3–31

IN EACH COUNTRY

Country	M	Overs	Mdns	Runs	Wkts	Avrge	5i	10m	Best
Australia	29	1000.1	269	2715	110	24.68	3	–	6/40
Bangladesh	2	43.0	12	90	8	11.25	–	–	3/11
England	12	332.4	68	1284	38	33.79	2	–	7/37
India	7	259.2	64	717	33	21.73	1	–	5/56
New Zealand	3	107.0	25	320	7	45.71	–	–	3/38
South Africa	6	195.4	65	574	22	26.09	1	–	5/54
Sri Lanka	5	157.3	37	476	13	36.62	–	–	4/76
West Indies	7	277.0	89	594	28	21.21	1	–	5/39

WICKETS TAKEN

How Out	Wickets	%
Caught Fieldsmen	89	34.36
Caught Wicketkeeper	65	25.10
Leg Before	59	22.78
Bowled	45	17.37
Hit Wicket	1	0.39

BATSMEN DISMISSED

Position	Wickets	%
Openers	74	28.57
Number 3	23	8.88
Number 4	26	10.04
Number 5	19	7.33
Number 6	30	11.58
Number 7	25	9.65
Number 8	12	31.08
Number 9	17	6.56
Number 10	21	8.10
Number 11	12	4.63
Number 1–6	**172**	**66.41**
Number 7–11	**87**	**33.59**

BATSMEN DISMISSED THE MOST

ME Trescothick	(England)	7
A Chopra	(India)	6
D Ganga	(West Indies)	6
SR Tendulkar	(India)	6

MOST WICKETS FOR AUSTRALIA

Bowler	M	Balls	Mdns	Runs	Wkts	Avge	5i	10m	Best
SK Warne	145	40704	1761	17995	708	25.42	37	10	8–71
GD McGrath	124	29248	1471	12186	563	21.64	29	3	8–24
DK Lillee	70	18467	652	8493	355	23.92	23	7	7–83
CJ McDermott	71	16586	581	8332	291	28.63	14	2	8–97
JN Gillespie	71	14234	629	6770	259	26.14	8	–	7–37
R Benaud	63	19108	805	6704	248	27.03	16	1	7–72
GD McKenzie	61	17684	547	7328	246	29.79	16	3	8–71
B Lee	59	12279	410	7300	231	31.60	7	–	5–30
RR Lindwall	61	13650	419	5251	228	23.03	12	–	7–38
CV Grimmett	37	14513	736	5231	216	24.22	21	7	7–40

BATTING

Season	Opponent	Venue	M	Inn	NO	Runs	HS	0s	50	100	Avrge	Ct
1996–97	West Indies	Australia	2	3	2	22	16*	–	–	–	22.00	–
1996–97	South Africa	South Africa	3	4	3	7	6*	1	–	–	7.00	–
1997	England	England	4	7	2	57	28*	2	–	–	11.40	3
1998–99	England	Australia	1	1	–	11	11	–	–	–	11.00	–
1998–99	West Indies	West Indies	3	6	2	95	28*	–	–	–	23.75	1
1999–00	Sri Lanka	Sri Lanka	1	1	–	41	41	–	–	–	41.00	–
2000–01	West Indies	Australia	4	4	–	48	23	–	–	–	12.00	2
2000–01	India	India	3	5	–	54	46	2	–	–	10.80	–
2001	England	England	5	4	1	41	27*	1	–	–	13.67	2
2001–02	New Zealand	Australia	3	3	2	21	20*	1	–	–	21.00	1
2001–02	South Africa	Australia	1	1	–	3	3	–	–	–	3.00	–
2001–02	South Africa	South Africa	3	3	–	4	3	1	–	–	1.33	1
2002–03	Pakistan	Sri Lanka	1	2	–	1	1	1	–	–	0.50	–
2002–03	England	Australia	5	5	4	61	31*	–	–	–	61.00	–
2002–03	West Indies	West Indies	4	4	1	36	18*	–	–	–	12.00	–
2002–03	Bangladesh	Australia	2	1	1	16	16*	–	–	–	–	1
2003–04	Zimbabwe	Australia	1	–	–	–	–	–	–	–	–	–
2003–04	India	Australia	3	5	2	110	48*	–	–	–	36.67	2
2003–04	Sri Lanka	Sri Lanka	3	6	2	35	11*	1	–	–	8.75	1
2003–04	Sri Lanka	Australia	2	4	–	22	16	–	–	–	5.50	2
2004–05	India	India	4	7	2	66	26	–	–	–	13.20	–
2004–05	New Zealand	Australia	2	2	1	66	54*	–	1	–	66.00	1
2004–05	Pakistan	Australia	3	3	1	74	50*	1	1	–	37.00	3
2004–05	New Zealand	New Zealand	3	3	–	49	35	–	–	–	16.33	4
2005	England	England	3	6	–	47	26	2	–	–	7.83	1
2005–06	Bangladesh	Bangladesh	2	3	2	231	201*	–	–	1	231.00	2
Total			71	93	28	1218	201*	13	2	1	18.74	27

OPPONENTS

Opponent	M	Inn	NO	Runs	HS	0s	50	100	Avrge	Ct
BANGLADESH	4	4	3	247	201*	–	–	1	247.00	3
ENGLAND	18	23	7	217	31*	5	–	–	13.56	6
INDIA	10	17	4	230	48*	2	–	–	17.69	2
NEW ZEALAND	8	8	3	136	54*	1	1	–	27.20	6
PAKISTAN	4	5	1	75	50*	2	1	–	18.75	3
SOUTH AFRICA	7	8	3	14	6*	2	–	–	2.80	1
SRI LANKA	6	11	2	98	41	1	–	–	10.89	3
WEST INDIES	13	17	5	201	28*	–	–	–	16.75	3
ZIMBABWE	1	–	–	–	–	–	–	–	–	–

HIGHEST SCORE

201* Australia v Bangladesh, Chittagong, 2005–06

INTERNATIONAL LIMITED–OVERS

DEBUT

1996–97 Australia v Sri Lanka, Colombo

BOWLING

Season	Competition	Country	M	Overs	Mdns	Runs	Wkts	Avrge	5i	Best	RPO
1996–97	Singer World Series	SL	1	6.0	–	27	–	–	–	–	4.50
1996–97	Titan Cup	IND	3	29.0	1	158	2	79.00	–	1–44	5.45
1996–97	CUB Series	AUS	1	10.0	–	39	2	19.50	–	2–39	3.90
1996–97	SAf v Australia	SAf	6	55.0	4	247	8	30.88	–	2–39	4.49
1997	England v Australia	ENG	3	26.1	2	136	1	136.00	–	1–55	5.20
1999–00	Aiwa Cup	SL	4	32.0	2	119	10	11.90	–	4–26	3.72
2000–01	Australia v Sth Africa	AUS	2	20.0	1	79	3	26.33	–	3–40	3.95
2000–01	ICC Trophy	KYA	1	8.0	–	39	2	19.50	–	2–39	4.88
2001	NatWest Series	ENG	3	26.0	6	103	4	25.75	–	3–20	3.96
2001–02	VB Series	AUS	5	49.0	6	183	6	30.50	–	2–28	3.73
2001–02	Sth Africa v Australia	SAf	6	58.2	3	287	12	23.92	–	4–43	4.92
2001–02	Australia v Pakistan	AUS	2	19.0	1	77	1	77.00	–	1–43	4.05
2002–03	Triangular Series	KYA	4	38.0	6	165	15	11.00	2	5–22	4.34
2002–03	ICC Champions Trophy	SL	3	25.0	3	77	4	19.25	–	3–20	3.08
2002–03	VB Series	AUS	2	17.0	1	96	1	96.00	–	1–55	5.65
2002–03	World Cup	Africa	4	30.0	4	98	8	12.25	–	3–13	3.27
2002–03	West Indies v Australia	WI	5	46.0	4	180	6	30.00	–	2–30	3.91
2003–04	Australia v Bangladesh	AUS	2	20.0	9	39	4	9.75	–	3–23	1.95
2003–04	VB Series	AUS	8	77.0	4	343	10	34.30	–	2–21	4.45
2003–04	Sri Lanka v Australia	SL	4	31.0	5	106	5	21.20	–	3–36	3.42
2003–04	Zimbabwe v Australia	ZIM	3	28.0	6	90	7	12.86	1	5–32	3.21
2004–05	Triangular Series	NED	1	9.0	–	22	1	22.00	–	1–22	2.44
2004	Australia v Pakistan	ENG	1	8.0	2	26	2	13.00	–	2–26	3.25
2004	ICC Champions	ENG	3	23.0	2	93	6	15.50	–	4–15	4.04
2004–05	Chappell–Hadlee Trophy	AUS	1	10.0	1	41	2	20.50	–	2–41	4.10
2004–05	VB Series	AUS	6	53.5	2	233	8	29.13	–	3–62	4.33
2004–05	New Zealand v Australia	NZ	3	25.4	1	105	4	26.25	–	2–45	4.09
2005	Natwest Series	ENG	7	50.2	2	251	5	50.20	–	2–41	4.99
2005	Natwest Challenge	ENG	3	27.0	1	152	3	50.67	–	3–44	5.63
Total			97	857.2	79	3611	142	25.43	3	5–22	4.21

OPPONENTS

Opponent	M	Overs	Mdns	Runs	Wkts	Avrge	5i	Best	RPO
Bangladesh	6	51.2	11	166	11	15.09	–	3–20	3.23
England	14	116.1	10	580	10	58.00	–	3–20	4.99
India	12	113.0	6	497	19	26.16	–	4–26	4.40
Kenya	1	10.0	2	40	3	13.33	–	3–40	4.00
Netherlands	1	3.0	–	7	2	3.50	–	2–7	2.33
New Zealand	8	71.4	5	289	9	32.11	–	2–41	4.03
Pakistan	13	119.0	10	478	21	22.76	2	5–22	4.02
South Africa	18	172.2	13	779	29	26.86	–	4–43	4.52
Sri Lanka	8	60.0	7	224	9	24.89	–	3–26	3.73
United States of America	1	6.0	1	15	4	3.75	–	4–15	2.50
West Indies	9	79.5	5	335	13	25.77	–	3–62	4.20
Zimbabwe	6	55.0	9	201	12	16.75	1	5–32	3.65

	Overs	Mdns	Runs	Wkts	Avrge	5i	Best	RPO
First Innings	456.2	49	1868	70	26.69	1	5–22	4.09
Second Innings	401.0	30	1743	72	24.21	2	5–32	4.35

IN EACH COUNTRY

Country	M	Overs	Mdns	Runs	Wkts	Avrge	5i	Best	RPO
Australia	29	275.5	25	1130	37	30.54	–	3–23	4.10
England	20	160.3	15	761	21	36.24	–	4–15	4.74
India	3	29.0	1	158	2	79.00	–	1–44	5.45
Kenya	5	46.0	6	204	17	12.00	2	5–22	4.43
Netherlands	1	9.0	–	22	1	22.00	–	1–22	2.44
New Zealand	3	25.4	1	105	4	26.25	–	2–45	4.09
South Africa	15	134.2	10	582	26	22.38	–	4–43	4.33
Sri Lanka	12	94.0	10	329	19	17.32	–	4–26	3.50
West Indies	5	46.0	4	180	6	30.00	–	2–30	3.91
Zimbabwe	4	37.0	7	140	9	15.56	1	5–32	3.78

BEST BOWLING IN AN INNINGS

Wickets	Team	Opponent	Venue	Season
5–22	Australia	Pakistan	Nairobi	2002–03
5–32	Australia	Zimbabwe	Harare	2003–04
5–70	Australia	Pakistan	Nairobi	2002–03

LEADING WICKET TAKERS FOR AUSTRALIA

Bowler	M	Balls	Mdns	Runs	Wkts	Avge	5i	Best	RPO
GD McGrath	249	12928	279	8354	380	21.98	7	7–15	3.88
SK Warne	193	10600	109	7514	291	25.82	1	5–33	4.25
B Lee	150	7729	101	6048	267	22.65	6	5–22	4.70
CJ McDermott	138	7460	99	5020	203	24.73	1	5–44	4.04
SR Waugh	325	8883	54	6764	195	34.69	–	4–33	4.57
JN Gillespie	97	5144	80	3611	142	25.43	3	5–22	4.21
DW Fleming	88	4619	62	3402	134	25.39	1	5–36	4.42
GB Hogg	106	4814	29	3605	133	27.11	2	5–32	4.49
A Symonds	170	5588	29	4659	124	37.57	1	5–18	5.00
NW Bracken	67	3303	57	2392	112	21.36	1	5–67	4.35

BATTING

OPPONENTS

Opponent	M	Inn	NO	Runs	HS	0s	50	100	Avrge	Stk/Rt	Ct
Bangladesh	6	–	–	–	–	–	–	–	–	–	–
England	14	6	1	24	14	2	–	–	4.80	57.14	3
India	12	5	2	32	14	–	–	–	10.67	71.11	–
Kenya	1	–	–	–	–	–	–	–	–	–	–
Netherlands	1	–	–	–	–	–	–	–	–	–	–
New Zealand	8	2	1	28	15	–	–	–	28.00	62.22	1
Pakistan	13	6	2	22	9	2	–	–	5.50	57.89	3
South Africa	18	10	3	74	26	3	–	–	10.57	83.15	–
Sri Lanka	8	5	2	30	14	1	–	–	10.00	62.50	–
United States of America	1	–	–	–	–	–	–	–	–	–	–
West Indies	9	3	3	45	44*	–	–	–	–	135.95	1
Zimbabwe	6	2	2	34	33*	–	–	–	–	188.89	2
Total	97	39	16	289	44*	8	–	–	12.57	80.70	10

HIGHEST SCORE

44* Australia v West Indies, Adelaide, 2004–05

SHEFFIELD SHIELD

BOWLING

Season	M	Overs	Mdns	Runs	Wkts	Avrge	5i	10m	Best
1994–95	3	87.0	22	278	7	39.71	–	–	3–112
1995–96	10	329.3	84	1002	46	21.78	1	–	6–68
1996–97	1	30.0	8	64	5	12.80	1	–	5–64
1997–98	2	37.0	14	83	1	83.00	–	–	1–61
1998–99	3	111.0	28	289	13	22.23	–	–	4–42
1999–00	2	76.0	23	161	7	23.00	–	–	2–42
2000–01	1	34.0	11	95	2	47.50	–	–	2–95
2001–02	2	98.0	22	293	15	19.53	1	1	8–50
2002–03	–	–	–	–	–	–	–	–	–
2003–04	2	86.0	21	192	11	17.45	1	–	5–54
2004–05	–	–	–	–	–	–	–	–	–
2005–06	9	355.5	102	851	40	21.28	3	–	7–35
2006–07	10	321.1	69	853	30	28.43	2	1	5–41
Total	45	1563.5	404	4161	177	23.51	9	2	8–50

OPPONENTS

Opponent	M	Overs	Mdns	Runs	Wkts	Avrge	5i	10m	Best
New South Wales	9	279.2	70	768	41	18.73	3	1	8–50
Queensland	10	346.5	84	926	43	21.53	3	1	5–40
Tasmania	8	279.0	77	705	20	35.25	–	–	4–89
Victoria	8	297.1	80	733	33	22.21	1	–	7–35
Western Australia	10	363.3	93	1029	40	25.73	2	–	6–68

BEST BOWLING

8–50 South Australia v New South Wales, Sydney, 2001–02

BATTING

Season	M	Inn	NO	Runs	HS	0s	50	100	Avrge	Ct
1994–95	3	4	–	77	39	–	–	–	19.25	2
1995–96	10	18	2	113	35	2	–	–	7.06	3
1996–97	1	2	–	80	58	–	1	–	40.00	1
1997–98	2	4	–	43	25	–	–	–	10.75	–
1998–99	3	5	1	14	5*	1	–	–	3.50	–
1999–00	2	1	–	1	1	–	–	–	1.00	4
2000–01	1	1	–	51	51	–	1	–	51.00	1
2001–02	2	4	2	67	32*	–	–	–	33.50	–
2002–03	–	–	–	–	–	–	–	–	–	–
2003–04	2	4	1	58	32	–	–	–	19.33	2
2004–05	–	–	–	–	–	–	–	–	–	–
2005–06	9	11	1	135	33	–	–	–	13.50	7
2006–07	10	16	–	181	61	3	1	–	11.31	3
Total	45	70	7	820	61	6	3	–	13.02	23

OPPONENTS

Opponent	M	Inn	NO	Runs	HS	0s	50	100	Avrge	Ct
New South Wales	9	16	2	209	35	1	–	–	14.93	4
Queensland	10	16	2	123	39	2	–	–	8.79	7
Tasmania	8	9	1	94	33	1	–	–	11.75	5
Victoria	8	14	2	183	61	1	1	–	15.25	1
Western Australia	10	15	–	211	58	1	2	–	14.07	6

HIGHEST SCORE

61 South Australia v Victoria, Melbourne, 2006–07

DOMESTIC LIMITED–OVERS

BOWLING

Season	M	Overs	Mdns	Runs	Wkts	Avrge	5i	Best	RPO
1995–96	2	20.0	2	79	7	11.29	–	4–46	3.95
1996–97	1	10.0	3	27	2	13.50	–	2–27	2.70
1997–98	1	10.0	–	61	4	15.25	–	4–61	6.10
1998–99	5	49.0	6	174	4	43.50	–	1–25	3.55
1999–00	1	10.0	–	55	–	–	–	–	5.50
2000–01	5	46.0	3	215	10	21.50	–	3–27	4.67
2001–02	4	38.4	5	137	7	19.57	–	3–31	3.54
2002–03	3	30.0	4	100	3	33.33	–	1–28	3.33
2003–04	1	8.0	1	20	1	20.00	–	1–20	2.50
2004–05	1	10.0	–	46	1	46.00	–	1–46	4.60
2005–06	10	94.0	2	444	10	44.40	–	3–55	4.72
2006–07	9	85.4	7	296	9	32.89	–	2–26	3.46
Total	43	411.2	33	1654	58	28.52	–	4–46	4.02

OPPONENTS

Opponent	M	Overs	Mdns	Runs	Wkts	Avrge	5i	Best	RPO
Australian Capital Territory	1	9.0	1	32	1	32.00	–	1–32	3.56
New South Wales	10	98.0	5	386	14	27.57	–	4–46	3.94
Queensland	8	80.0	3	386	17	22.71	–	4–61	4.83
Tasmania	7	63.0	4	248	5	49.60	–	1–26	3.94
Victoria	9	85.2	12	295	12	24.58	–	3–27	3.46
Western Australia	8	76.0	8	307	9	34.11	–	2–26	4.04

BEST BOWLING

4–46 South Australia v New South Wales, Sydney, 1995–96

BATTING

Season	M	Inn	NO	Runs	HS	0s	50	100	Avrge	Stk/Rt	Ct
1995–96	2	2	1	0	0*	1	–	–	0.00	0.00	–
1996–97	1	1	–	2	2	–	–	–	2.00	50.00	1
1997–98	1	1	1	3	3*	–	–	–	–	100.00	–
1998–99	5	3	2	16	13*	–	–	–	16.00	57.14	1
1999–00	1	1	–	15	15	–	–	–	15.00	46.88	–
2000–01	5	1	–	0	0	1	–	–	0.00	0.00	–
2001–02	4	2	–	5	3	–	–	–	2.50	38.46	–
2002–03	3	3	3	6	6*	–	–	–	–	37.27	–
2003–04	1	1	–	19	19	–	–	–	19.00	57.58	–
2004–05	1	1	–	4	4	–	–	–	4.00	19.05	–
2005–06	10	7	2	97	42	–	–	–	19.40	75.78	3
2006–07	9	5	3	28	17*	–	–	–	14.00	63.64	3
Total	43	28	12	195	42	2	–	–	12.19	59.23	8

OPPONENTS

Opponent	M	Inn	NO	Runs	HS	0s	50	100	Avrge	Stk/Rt	Ct
Australian Capital Territory	1	–	–	–	–	–	–	–	–	–	–
New South Wales	10	8	3	53	19	–	–	–	10.60	60.78	3
Queensland	8	6	3	18	13*	2	–	–	6.00	72.00	1
Tasmania	7	4	2	36	19*	–	–	–	18.00	52.94	–
Victoria	9	4	4	21	17*	–	–	–	–	48.84	1
Western Australia	8	6	–	67	42	–	–	–	11.17	63.21	3

HIGHEST SCORE

42 South Australia v Western Australia, Adelaide, 2005–06